Best Sermons 5

Best Sermons 5

James W. Cox, *Editor*

Kenneth M. Cox, Associate Editor

HarperSanFrancisco
A Division of HarperCollins*Publishers*

Quotations from the Bible are from the Revised Standard Version, the King James Version, and the New International Version. In addition, some contributors have made their own translations and others have used a mixed text.

Library of Congress Catalog Card Number 88–656297
ISSN 1041–6382

92 93 94 95 96 HAD 10 9 8 7 6 5 4 3 2 1

This edition is printed on acid-free paper that meets the American National Standards Institute Z39.48 Standard.

Contents

87444

VI. DEVOTIONAL

Preface

What is a "best" sermon? That question must follow a more basic one: What is a sermon? A sermon is the expression of God's word through the preacher, an attempt to articulate the wonderful, terrible, hopeful mysteries of the Scriptures and God's presence in the world. The purpose and message in a sermon may take many forms, depending upon the preacher's style and the tenets of his or her faith. Likewise, how a sermon is received depends upon the listener's or reader's experiences and beliefs.

We believe that the best sermons included in this volume meet the following important criteria: originality, scriptural and/or Christian basis, relevance, clarity, and interest. Of course, sometimes elusive factors also come into play in the selection process. No doubt a felicitous turn of phrase, a captivating flight of imagination, or a poignant application that peculiarly touches the heart will make one sermon stand out from others essentially as good. Such are life and its subjective judgments! We hope that you find the forty sermons selected for this volume both helpful and meaningful.

What is the process by which the sermons were chosen for this volume? First, note that twenty-two of the sermons are not a part of the competition. These sermons, for the most part, have been commissioned by the editor. Next, there are eighteen sermons—three in each of six categories—that have been chosen by six judges from the group of thirty-six finalists. Before the finalist sermons are sent to the judges, authors' names and addresses are removed to make each sermon anonymous. The editor chose the finalist sermons from all sermons submitted in accordance with the rules as defined by the publisher. Every sermon so submitted has been read and evaluated.

Requests for rules for each annual competition should be made of Best Sermons Competition, Harper San Francisco, 1160 Battery Street, San Francisco, CA 94111-1213.

Judges for the competition were as follows:

James W. Cox, Editor, Victor and Louise Lester Professor of Christian Preaching, The Southern Baptist Theological Seminary.

Martin B. Copenhaver, Pastor, Church of the Beatitudes (UCC), Phoenix, Arizona.

R. Kirby Godsey, President, Mercer University.

Edwina Hunter, Joe R. Engle Professor of Preaching, Union Theological Seminary (NYC).

Krister Stendahl, Myra and Robert Kraft and Jacob Hiatt Distinguished Professor of Christian Studies, Brandeis University.

W. Sibley Towner, Professor of Biblical Interpretation, Union Theological Seminary in Richmond, Virginia.

Arthur L. Walker, Jr., Executive Director-Treasurer, Education Commission, The Southern Baptist Convention.

Once again we thank all those who submitted sermons for the competition, and we encourage those and others to send us more of your best sermons. Also, we thank Patti Rimmer and Cassie Gallion for preparing the indexes.

JAMES W. COX
KENNETH M. COX

I. EVANGELISTIC

1. On Being Wise in This Generation

Elizabeth Achtemeier

Hosea 11:1–11; Luke 16:1–13

The story that we heard for our New Testament lesson is a strange tale. It tells about the steward or manager of a rich man's estate, who is about to be fired from his job. It seems that he has been wasting his rich boss's money, and therefore he is soon going to find himself unemployed. And he wonders to himself, "How am I going to live? I'm not able to do anything else."

Despite all his ineptitude, he is a rather shrewd person, however. And so he decides that if he cannot support himself, he will persuade others to furnish him a living. And he will do so by being generous to them—but with his boss's money. He quickly calls in all of the people who owe the rich man money, reduces their debts, lets them pay them off, and closes the books. And the debtors are so grateful to him that they will, indeed, in the future be glad to help out the unemployed steward.

The amazing thing about this little story, however, is the rich man's reaction to the scheme. He doesn't get mad, as we would expect of him. Instead he actually commends the steward for his shrewdness, as much as to say, "Well, I've got to hand it to you. You

Elizabeth Achtemeier has served as adjunct professor of Bible and homiletics at Union Theological Seminary in Virginia since 1973. She is the author of several books on preaching, including *Creative Preaching, Preaching as Theology and Art, Preaching About Family Relationships,* and *Preaching from the Old Testament.* Dr. Achtemeier is coauthor with her husband Paul of *Easter,* Series B, in the *Proclamation Series.* She is a graduate of Stanford University, Union Theological Seminary, and Columbia University (Ph.D.) and pursued postgraduate studies at the universities of Heidelberg and Basel.

really know how to take care of yourself!" The shrewd steward made a deal, using the rich man's money, and the rich man's reaction is, "That's pretty clever!"

Now you and I know, of course, that such a thing would never happen—no boss is going to be happy with a dishonest employee who lets his debtors pay him half of what they owe him. And so we wonder why Jesus told such a far-fetched parable. It certainly does not seem to have a religious point, and it does not seem to have anything to do with God. The rich man in the tale commends the steward for cheating, for buying friendship, and for looking out for himself—and those are not the attitudes we normally associate with the God of the Bible. So what is this story doing in the New Testament anyway, and why did Jesus tell it?

Jesus told it because it is a very good picture of you and me. Not that we are cheaters or social parasites living off our friends, not even that we bungle jobs. But Jesus told this parable because it portrays how shrewd we are. We know how to get along in the world, don't we? We know how to turn things to our advantage, in everything from handling our money to running our homes and businesses to climbing up the social ladder. We are very efficient people. In fact, we Americans are famous for our "know-how." We know how to throw a successful party and how to chair a committee. We excel at sports, appreciate culture, and can fix almost anything. We raise healthy kids, have comfortable homes, and wear the smartest clothes on the market. We are friendly, outgoing, energetic, and have a country that is the envy of the world. And just in case we have trouble solving some problem, we can always drive out to the shopping center and buy one of those "how-to" books at the bookstore. We Americans are, indeed, those who are wise in this generation—shrewd people, able people who know how to succeed in the world.

But our Lord puts an ironic twist on the end of this little story in the New Testament. "Make friends for yourselves," he says, "by means of unrighteous mammon"—that is, make friends for yourselves with your money, or your shrewdness, or your ability to get along in the world—"so that when it fails they may receive you into the eternal habitations." Make friends by means of your "know-how," so that when everything else fails those friends can still give you eternal life. But that's a ridiculous ending to the story—isn't it?—because none of our friends can give us eternal life.

And you see, that is just the point—that none of the things that we are so good at doing, none of all our marvelous abilities to make friends and influence people put us right with God or win for us his abundant and eternal life. We are very shrewd and able people, wiser than many in this generation, but we are not shrewd enough to realize that is not all there is to human life. No, we pursue our secular round, thinking we are in charge of our affairs, believing we can manipulate our own futures and run our own lives as we please, when all along we have been created by a God who made us for fellowship with himself.

God planned each one of us, you see, to trust him, to obey his commandments in the Scriptures, to serve his purpose in the world. And such obedient trust and service, God knew, would bring us a life so full of joy and running over with blessing and vitality that it would last to all eternity. But we have ignored those facts. Fantastic as it may seem, we have forgotten them and turned our backs on them. And now we just go along, efficiently dealing with the moment. For all our shrewdness, for all our know-how, for all our wisdom in this world, you and I have often made the dumb mistake of forgetting about God and his will for our lives.

And so it is that Jesus pronounces the judgment that we heard in our New Testament lesson. You would not trust your money to someone who was dishonest, would you? he asks. Well then, when you are unfaithful to God, neither will he give you that which he planned to be yours—his life, his abundant and eternal life, so full of joy and good. You cannot forget the Lord your God and expect to receive his gifts.

And that would be a terrible judgment, wouldn't it? In fact, it would be the worst judgment that we could face in our lives, because it would mean that God is just going to abandon us. Because we have not trusted him and depended on him, God is going to withdraw from us his guidance, his love, his sustaining power—as if Jesus Christ had never lived and redeemed us by his cross and resurrection. Yes, that would be a dreadful verdict.

But let us not deceive ourselves into thinking it can never happen. Oh no, our Old Testament lesson shows it is very definitely a possibility. For there the prophet Hosea says that was what God was going to do to the unfaithful Israelites. He was going to send them back to Egypt—going to send them back to slavery in the mud pits of the Pharaoh, as if he had never redeemed them from the house of bondage and made them his beloved people—because as often as God called to the Israelites, they went away from him. And so God's judgment on them was going to be to give them over to their sin, just as our Lord says in Luke that God's judgment on our faithless folly is going to be to give us over to our sin and death and to let us try to run our world on our own, simply by our shrewdness and efficiency.

Yes, that would be an awful judgment, because we can see the results all around us of trying to live by our own wits in a world without God. We have indeed been very efficient. We have built great cities, but now we cannot eliminate the urban crime that makes us afraid to go out at night, and inner city slums and chaotic schools send us, fleeing, to the suburbs. We have unlocked the secrets of the atom and gazed at the very heart of nature, but now we have nightmares about a planet slowly dying under a cloud of radioactive dust. We overcame our Victorian prudishness and turned sex into a free and easy game, and now we spend billions fighting genital herpes and AIDS and trying to support the children born to teen-age mothers. We have lovely homes and gardens and children, but half of our marriages fall apart. We have extended our lifespan with good nutrition and health care, and now we wonder what to do with senile parents and whether or not the Social Security system will pay us anything in return.

I sometimes think the story of the novelist Arnold Bennett typifies our society. Rich and renowned, but on his deathbed in his sumptuous London apartment, he whispered to his mistress, as she bent over his dying form, "It's all gone wrong, my dear." Somehow, left to our own devices, in a world abandoned by God, everything seems to go wrong, and we leave nothing but bloody footprints and scrawled four-letter obscenities on the landscape of the earth. And that would be the worst judgment of all—that God should abandon us to that.

But there is a further picture in our Old Testament lesson from Hosea—of God determined to abandon us to our sin and yet overcome by his own heart of mercy. "My people are bent on turning away from me," God says, and so "the sword shall rage against their cities"—and we know that sword. "They shall return to the land of Egypt, because they have refused to return to me." But when this God of the Bible thinks about the consequences of such judgment, his heart recoils within him; his compassion grows warm and tender, and he cries out in the agony of love, "How can I give you up, O Ephraim? How can I hand you over, O Israel?" And so too, he cries out over us, How can I abandon you?

Certainly he has been with us a very long time, has he not? Think how many years ago he founded this church, calling together a few pious souls to be the beginning of the Body of Christ in this place. Think how many faithful elders he has raised up in this congregation, how many committed pastors he has called to this pulpit. And then think of the funerals that have taken place here, when God has been present with his comfort; or the number of babies that God has received into his welcoming arms at their baptisms; or the number of marriages that he has blessed before this congregation. God has been here from the very beginning of the life of this congregation, teaching you, comforting you, inspiring you, forgiving you—like that Father in our Old Testament lesson, tenderly raising up his young child. When you were an infant church, Hosea says, God loved you, and through all the years it is he who has taught you how to walk.

And as for you personally, is that not the story of your individual life also, that God has been on the scene since the day that you were born? Indeed, while you were still in your mother's womb, his hands fashioned and made you, planning the person that you would be, giving you your unique voice and personality and fingerprints like none other in the world. Since the day that you came forth into light, his breath has sustained your life, faithfully filling your lungs to inhale, exhale, in that regular rhythm of his love. Through your childhood, youth, adulthood, his Spirit has never been absent from you. When you have ascended into some joyous heaven, he has been there; when you have dwelt in hell, he has been with you.

But, says our Old Testament lesson, the more God has been with us and called to us, the more we have run away from him— like those errant children of our time, advertised on our televisions as "missing." Oh sure, we use the hotline once in a while to call home, to let our Father know we are still alive. But we do not return home to him, figuring that we are perfectly able to wander the streets on our own.

And so God wrestles, dear friends, wrestles with the judgment we deserve and his own heart of love. And this God who has known us all our life long is overcome by his own compassion.

"How can I give you up, O my people? How surrender you, O my child?"

The result is that God tries one last time to woo us home to himself—to get us to return to that trust and obedience toward him that will mean for us abundant and eternal life. God sends us his Son—the only child who has ever fully trusted and obeyed him. And that Son comes telling us the story that we heard from Luke—the story that warns us that God can abandon us to our own devices. But there, too, God's own compassion overcomes him, and so the Son takes all of our disobedience and distrust of the Father upon himself and bears the judging punishment that we deserve from the Father's hand.

We are forgiven, friends, forgiven by the cross and resurrection of Jesus Christ. There is nothing now in our past that bars the way home to the Father. No mean act we have ever done, no selfish or silly pride, no mistake, no weakness, no indifferent or callous deed—nothing; nothing in our lives is now held against us by God. The road is open; the way is clear; the Father peers down the path for some sight of us. We can go home again—home to life and joy and love, home to peace that the world can neither give nor ever take away, home to a fellowship that death itself cannot destroy, home to a security that cannot be shaken, though heaven and earth pass away.

And there we can be glad, good Christians. How did the poet G. M. Hopkins put it?

> In the staring darkness
> I can hear the harshness
> Of the cold wind blowing.
> I am warmly clad,
> And I'm very glad
> That I've got a home.

Well, shall we refuse such gladness? Or shall we really be the wisest people in this generation? We have a God who has never left us and who, in his love, will not leave us still. We have a God whose mercy has crowded out all his judgment on our sin. We have a God who, if we trust and obey him, will give us abundant life to all eternity. Come, let's really be wise; let's trust him; let's go home again. Amen.

2. By Hook or By Crook

R. Benjamin Garrison

Matthew 4:18–20

Among the alibis offered for *not* attending corporate worship, this particular pastor finds it easiest to excuse those of the anglers. Sometimes on Sunday morning, as I reach into my closet for a clerical shirt, my hand rests affectionately upon an old manila-colored fishing jacket. If you arrive here some Sunday but find that I have not, the reason will be that I have finally succumbed to the temptation to take the fishing jacket instead of the clerical shirt from its hanger.

If that happens, some of you will recognize the signs: The sky is slightly overcast. The wind, from just the right direction, has teased the tip of my fishing rod until the whirr of its song, soft and irresistible, seduces me into sacrilege. So, tackle box in one hand and fishing rod in the other, I have made my way to a quiet lake and have joined my pagan brothers and sisters.

Oh, I know all the counter-arguments: "I just haven't that much patience, sitting there for hours waiting for a silly little fish to bobble my bobber or grab my hook. The worms are dirty. The hooks are sharp. Then, late home and dead tired, you have to clean the pesky things. No thanks."

There's no use arguing with the person who talks that way. You can't talk people out of blindness. Verily, they shall have their reward!

Despite such blindness, fishing is relevant and applicable to the

R. Benjamin Garrison was until recently pastor of the Seward United Methodist Church in Seward, Nebraska, and is now retired. He was educated at DePauw, Drew, and Cambridge universities, and he was awarded a D.D. degree by MacMurray College. Dr. Garrison is the author of numerous articles and books, including *Creeds in Collision, Worldly Holiness, Seven Questions Jesus Asked,* and *Are You the Christ?*

gospel enterprise. "By hook or by crook" we say, forgetting the saying's Christian symbolism. Nevertheless the church lives by what that symbolism involves and implies. I will speak to you this morning about the first half of it: by hook—fishing.

> And Jesus, walking along the Lake of Galilee,
> saw . . . Simon (afterward called Peter) and
> Andrew, casting a round weighted net into the
> water (for they were fishermen). And he said to
> them, "Fall in behind me, and I will teach you how
> to fish for persons." And they dropped their nets
> at once and followed him. (Matt. 4:18–20, *author's translation*)

Notice some interesting things about this passage.

Note that Jesus took the everyday, customary skills of Peter and Andrew and gave them new direction. Peter and Andrew did not so much drop their nets as they replaced them: fishers—fishers of men. They were replaced persons—put in a new place, going after the big ones now, with old skill and new power.

This is the way the call of God usually comes: while we are doing the tasks that daily fall to our hands. Every once in a while someone is called by God from the cash register to the pulpit. Many clergypersons know that to be an ordained minister is the greatest privilege in the world and rejoice when a qualified layperson has heard that call.

But more usually it is a call to *stay* at the cash register, to witness in business to kingdom business—a call to keep on fishing. The most able business leaders in the community are, many of them, the most able church leaders. A survey indicates that of the 200 top AFL-CIO leaders, 89 percent of them had some connection with a church or synagogue. If our economic life is ever even to approximate the will of God in the ways of humans, these business, labor, and agricultural leaders must maintain those connections, must keep on fishing.

When Simon and Andrew decided to go for the big ones, note how they decided: "*At once* they followed him." In earlier days when the boys in our family were writing sermons or playing cowboys and Indians and the outrageous call to lunch was heard, we answered, "Just a minute," which sometimes meant, "Just fifteen minutes," or "As soon as I'm ready," or "When I'm finished doing what I'm doing." Not so the big fisherman and his brother: "At once they followed."

This "In a minute, Master" kind of postponement can take place within the Church, even when surrounded by all the trappings of evangelism. I had a grandfather who, despite his many virtues, had one black mark on his record: For forty-six years he owned a summer place on a lake in northern Indiana, but not once did he go fishing!

So sometimes the Church: The lake is there (the world), the boat is there (the Church), and the bait is there (the gospel), but we are satisfied with reading the fishing guides and with repainting the boat that we expect other people (the preacher, surely, the membership and evangelism committee possibly) to fish from.

But, to return to the anglers who, perhaps at this very minute, are pulling in beauties: There is a certain amount of irrationality about them. No argument will convince them that it is raining too hard and therefore they should come in off the lake or that it is too late in the day to gather their paraphernalia and shove off from shore or that, since they caught no fish yesterday, they will catch none today.

So it is with the genuine fisher for persons. There is a sweet unreasonableness about such a person. If a given cynic is hard to win, if the fisher (evangelist) is being rained upon by abuse or unbelief or indifference, no matter—the fisher stays on the lake, baits another hook, tries another lure, makes another cast. Even if the quarry has long eluded the gospel grasp until the sun is about to set upon his or her life, still no matter.

Again, anglers have an almost endless assortment of rods and reels, of spoons and plugs, of lines and leaders. Never, 'tis true, as many as needed. Certainly not as many as they want. Sporting goods stores and magazines exert an almost irresistible temptation upon their peculiar forms of angler's alcoholism. Tackle boxes always have room for one more lure. And in winter, provided they haven't cut holes in the ice somewhere and provided they aren't sitting beside them in frozen optimism, they are ready, at less than a moment's notice, to learn of another fisher's haunts or habits.

They have nothing on the gospel fishers who, too, have learned that in certain places some people can be caught, and by certain baits others can be claimed. They know that all the fish are not in the same spot, all will not respond to the same attractive bait, and—

above all—they know they're not all big ones. This time one uses the solitary pole of individual evangelism, another time the trotline of the mass approach. They know that Billy Graham is an evangelist and are willing to learn from him. Graham is a fisher. That's all they need to know. They do not assume that a person is not really caught unless he or she is caught by a particular kind of bait or pole, whether it is face to face evangelism or mass appeal.

I have seven grandchildren who would agree that among Jesus' winning qualities is his love for fishers. Little boys and girls may further our theme in another regard. Trying to fish with a couple of small children in the boat may be compared to juggling with bowling balls or running in leg irons. Merely keeping them going is a full time activity: baiting hooks, taking the fish off, ducking as a hook whizzes past your face in a child's still-clumsy effort to throw out the line, pouring lemonade with one hand, wiping a nose with the other, all the while propping your own fishing rod between your knees, hoping that the fish that has just taken your bait will not get away in the meantime and knowing that it probably will! It is a poor way to catch fish, but it's a whale of a way to catch children.

Analogies to the church's evangelistic calling: The pastor, while a fisher of persons, is also more importantly a trainer of them. Most laypersons feel that they are terribly inept at this sort of thing. Nevertheless once the indescribable thrill of catching someone is felt, it gets into the blood and stays there.

Besides, theirs is a much more effective kind of fishing. In my first parish in New Jersey, a middle-aged couple reported that they wanted to join our fellowship. I called in their home and inquired as to why, after living in the community fifteen years, they had now decided to take this important step. They told me that a few weeks previously a young couple from our parish had visited with them on behalf of the claims of Christ. (I suspect that several pastors had called on them. I know I had. But our testimony is subject to a clerical discount: People do not take it at face value because we are "pros." We're paid to say the right things.) I remember with what fear and trembling Norman and Betty had gone out to make those calls that evening. They were sure that they couldn't do it. But when they cast their line in—bam: the big strike.

Any church claiming to be a New Testament community will have more than one person fishing, or two or more paid, ministerial ones. It will be a community of fishers. It will develop and strengthen a group of devoted laypersons with the skills necessary to fish for the Lord.

One Monday evening when our sons were small, we came into shore from a late afternoon fishing excursion. Our total catch was five small fish. The boys had caught four. I had managed one.

The lesson in that is this: I had been fishing "scientifically," using the season's proper bait and a lure designed for that particular depth of water. My young sons, however, had been using just plain little old bluegill hooks, baited rather jaggedly and jerked around far too much. But, dropping their lines in right where they were, they had caught fish.

This is not to suggest that gospel fishing—evangelism—is to be undertaken without carefulness and thoughtfulness.

It is to suggest, however, that in the church's fishing for persons there is a danger in over-multiplication of equipment. We are to drop our lines in right where we are, not worrying overmuch about the size of the catch, not being concerned at all about reporting it afterward. (Sometimes, when I have filled out the reports we are required to file with the denomination, I have almost had the feeling that United Methodism would prefer to go to hell if she had to go to heaven without reporting it!) If we have even the tiniest supply of the bait that the New Testament calls trust, and if with it we bait the hooks of our lives, howsoever small they may be, the catch will come.

In one important respect comparing evangelism with modern anglers fails to do justice to the Peter and Andrew story. They were full-time fishers. Fishing was their livelihood, not their leisure. When Jesus announced that if they would fall in behind him he would make them fishers of persons, it was not an entirely pleasant promise. They knew what fishing meant: long, cold nights on the lake, at the end of which empty nets for their efforts meant empty stomachs for their children; rain beating down until they were soaked clean through; hands rubbed raw from pulling in the heavy nets; gathering the catch and salting it down before their fiercely tired bodies could drop into bed. And then doing it all over again the next day and the next.

The promise of the Lordly Fisher was no romantic thing, no quaint collection of the sportsman's regalia, no mounting of the prize catch against the wall to gaze at and reminisce about on sleepy winter evenings.

The reverse in fact: Before the long winter of their disciple-lives was over, it was they—some of them—who were nailed up, as the Master Fisher had been. This was no Passover picnic. It was a costly, sober affair, this net-casting for souls. The more remarkable, then, their readiness to follow at once and to keep on following—until the end.

Nor is this, for their time or for ours, a merely individual enterprise of fishing to be done in your own private lake. The Sea of Galilee, stretching menacingly toward the horizon, was their beckon and the Lord's call was their beacon. The word *idiot,* in the Greek, refers to a person who has possessions used only for him- or herself, not for the common good. The early church members were not idiotic enough to assume that the gospel they possessed was theirs alone. Rather they were possessed by a holy obsession to gossip the gospel everywhere, far and wide, by hook or by crook.

They were not under the illusion, as were those in the Middle Ages, that this trembling truth in their hands was to be hied off to a monastery and protected and prayed over.

They were not under the greater illusion, as are many members of modern Protestantism, that "saints can be made in a social vacuum."[1] They knew that "to be good means to be good for something."[2] They knew, too, that this would be controversial because trying to transform persons and structures is always controversial. But they did not shrink from the task. They up and followed—into all the world.

We are only pretending to follow if we do otherwise. We say that we cannot mix religion and politics. My friends, they *are* mixed: Some kind of religion (pagan and half true or vital and striving to be faithful to the truth) is already mixed with politics. The only question is, what kind of mixture will it be? Will it be made up mostly of brotherhood or of bigotry? Will it be a religion that enjoins the Ten Commandments upon individuals but winks at the social flauntings of them: the polluted radioactive air that reputable scientists warn may murder our grandchildren; the devastation of Panama and Kuwait and Ethiopia; the idolatry that worships success at any human cost?

Until we learn to take the religious fervor engendered within these walls and make it live outside these walls—in our schools, in our halls of government (whether across the street or across the state), in our real estate restrictions, in our public welfare policies, in our government fiscal measures—until we have Christian citizens who are willing to act like Christians as they fulfill their duties as citizens, our evangelism is only half-baked, half-true, and half-hearted.

The call to Christians to be fishers is as boundless as the Christian life itself; it is, in fact, the basis of that life. If people believe that Christ has something to say to life and something to do for life, if they see that Christ *is* life, they will be eager to share him—in personal faith and lasting allegiance; in the sanctuary, but also on the farm and in the mart—that others may live too, until, at his guiding, all life beats with the throbbings of his life. He will be evident in the children we bear, the ideas we share, the money we earn and spend; in the church we love and serve, the nation we build and protect; in souls that kneel before him and lands that now adore him: each of us, all of us, caught in the living net of the gospel.

"Fall in behind me," he said, "and I will make you fishers of men. And at once . . . they followed."

NOTES

1. John Hutchison, ed. *Christian Faith and Social Action* (New York: Scribner, 1953), 245.
2. Ibid., 15.

3. Acknowledgment

Richard Lischer

John 9:1–41

Jesus is adhering to an ancient and mysterious standard of care when he mixes dust and spit into a sticky paste, places it on a man's eyelids, and kneads the man's eyes. He "anointed" them, the text says. We don't know if he prayed or uttered an incantation as he did so: "Light of the world, Light of the world." He sends the man to a pool called Sent; Siloam, thus named because its waters are figuratively sent by aqueduct from the mountains above to the pool below. The man goes to the pool and begins bathing dead tissue that has never seen a sunset or the olive-colored eyes of a woman, *eyes* that have never *recognized:* dead from birth. And something happens.

He first saw light. Then he saw his own reflection in the pool of Siloam. Then what a fantastic tapestry of colors he must have seen in the narrow, crowded streets of a Middle Eastern marketplace. He saw the geometrical shapes of buildings, the green and brown of olive trees, the purple and yellow of exotic fabrics being sold in the stalls, the blue sky and puffy white clouds. Only later did he see the face of the one who healed him. Only later did he see the light.

In that instant he probably forgot how he had been a lifelong object of theological speculation. I'm sure Jesus' disciples were not the first to toss a nickel into his cup, thinking that action entitled

Richard Alan Lischer has taught homiletics at Duke University Divinity School since 1979. He received his B.A. degree from Concordia Sr. College, his M.A. in English from Washington University, St. Louis, his B.D. from Concordia Seminary, and his Ph.D. in Theology from the University of London. He was ordained to the ministry of the Lutheran Church in America in 1972, and before beginning his teaching career, he was pastor of Lutheran churches. He is the author of *A Theology of Preaching* and of *Speaking of Jesus.*

them to speculate out loud concerning the cause of his misfortune. "Rabbi, who sinned?" This man has been afflicted from birth. If we assume that all afflictions are caused by sin, it follows that either this man sinned *in utero* or his parents sinned before his birth.

What the poor man didn't realize was that now, as a sighted person, he would continue to be an object of intense speculation. The cause of blindness—that's theologically interesting. But the cure of blindness! That is a matter of life and death because, depending on the explanation, you are making a decision about Jesus, about the one who only days earlier had stood in the Temple courtyard as they lit the great torches and had cried out like a lunatic or a demented god, "I am the Light of the World!" "We'd better get to the bottom of this," the authorities said.

In the Evangelist's story, the cure itself takes exactly two verses; the controversy surrounding the cure takes thirty-nine verses, and that, as Paul Harvey would say, is the rest of the story.

The rest of the story is that the organized church has always been pretty good at sniffing out sin but not so good at acknowledging the power of God that can be contained by no religious premises. When this man returned to his community healed and praising God, why didn't the religious leaders rejoice with him? I would have expected the neighbors to fall on his neck with kisses, as they would if he had just won a big basketball game. Why not indeed?

In the last church I served, one of the pillars of the congregation stopped by my office one morning to tell me he'd been "born again." "What?" I said. "Yes, last week I visited my brother-in-law's church, the Running River of Life Tabernacle, and I don't know what it was, but something happened, and I'm born again." "You can't be born again," I said, "You're a Lutheran. You're the Chairman of the Board of Trustees." He was brimming with joy, but I was sulking. Why? Spiritual renewal is OK so long as it occurs in acceptable channels, so long as it occurs within a Lutheran or Methodist or Presbyterian framework, and, most of all, so long as it doesn't threaten my understanding of God.

You may know the acclaimed first novel by Peggy Payne entitled *Revelation*. It's the story of a Presbyterian minister who has a revelation in Chapel Hill, North Carolina. One afternoon while grilling steaks in the backyard of the manse, he hears the voice of God speaking to him. It's a revelation. It's the kind of revelation that will change his life; he will never be the same. The rest of the story is the price he pays for revelation. Does his congregation rejoice with him? Not exactly. They do provide free psychiatric care and paid administrative leave.

You can imagine how we would react if our chaplains were to stand up here and announce that they had been the recipients of a direct revelation. The church could not contain such a thing. After appropriate counseling, they would both be transferred to Development or some other department in the university. We would do deep background investigations on both of them, recheck their transcripts, reread their references, but eventually they would have to go, because they were claiming to see things to which we are blind. After all, the university is a place in which we must guard against fanaticism and against any power we cannot explain or rationally confine.

As much as I am taken with the chutzpah of the man blind from birth, as a university person I also sympathize with the Pharisees. They are only trying to do what we have been trained to do: to observe, describe, and explain the phenomena. To that end they conduct three ill-fated field interviews. The neighbors aren't much help. Some say it is indeed the man who was blind; others remark that he didn't have that moustache. . . . The fact is, they don't recognize him because he was never more than a piece of community furniture to them. The interview with the man's parents is an even greater disaster. They have long since learned not to stick their necks out for their child. So beyond the basic data, they only say, "Ask him, he is of age." The authorities' attempt to do a stress interview on the blind man is also disaster for them because he takes control and winds up interviewing them, toying with them like a cat with a mouse. "Would you too like to be his disciples? Would you like a tract or a marked New Testament?"

But I sympathize with the Pharisees. And you should too. Have you ever listened to the testimony of someone who has just returned from Lourdes or Tulsa "healed" of arthritis, who has thrown the crutches away, and wanted to do a background check or a follow-up study? Or have you felt even a twinge of doubt when glamourous but corrupt celebrities—call girls and congressmen— whose sins are so much more interesting than ours, manage to find Jesus just as their scandals are cresting in the media? Wouldn't you like to check out those conversions?

One of the themes of John's Gospel is the discrepancy between the truth of God, which God reveals in Jesus, and the religious explanations of those who claim to know the truth. This discrepancy produces a lot of strange conversations in this Gospel in which people are talking right by one another, the way George Burns and Gracie Allen used to do. Jesus is always speaking from the perspective of the Father in heaven while his dialogue partners are speaking from their own dimwitted perspectives. For example, earlier on Jesus met the great Pharisee Nicodemus at night in the shadows of the temple where the teacher said to Jesus, "Rabbi, I gather you come from God because you are doing great things." Jesus replied, "Nicodemus, you must be born again." To which Nicodemus said, "Let me get this straight: You mean I have to go back into my mother's womb? . . ." Jesus answered, "You are a teacher in Israel?"

Now in our story we have the ancient version of not "Who's on first?" but "Where's he from?" The authorities, desperate now, sink to the oldest of all debate tactics. Assail the source of your opponent's argument. Poison the well. Where's this guy Jesus from? What rabbinical school did he attend? Where did he learn to break God's law by doing cures on the Sabbath? We would like to see this professor's C.V. The formerly blind man replies, "Where's he from? Why, this man restored my sight. Never since the world began has a man blind from birth received his sight, and you want to know where he's from? He's from the North—way North, from the Father in Heaven!"

Things have gotten out of hand by this time because the blind man is experiencing the freedom and joy of one who sees not from a human perspective but from God's perspective.

Does the story mean you have to have special knowledge to be a Christian? Must you see the way God sees? No, not knowledge but *acknowledgment*. The formerly blind man did not know all the correct religious phrases with which to interpret his salvation. He was not even pious in a religious sense or even respectful of his elders. What he knew for sure was that once upon a time he sat in the darkness and the dust waiting to die, and now the whole world was drenched in sunlight. And he acknowledged that.

"One thing I know . . ." he might have said, "I don't have all the churchy jargon about Jesus down pat like some of these preachers have it. I may never speak in well-rounded certitude about God and the meaning of life, and I may be a little rough around the edges when it comes to relating to my elders, but one thing I *do* know . . ."

And as he makes his witness to us, we realize that the man blind from birth has a multitude of sons and daughters, each with their own story to tell:

"One thing I know," one of you might say, "is that back in September, when I was a thousand miles from home and drowning in loneliness and more work than I'd imagined, somehow I got through that, and I think that *somehow* was God."

Or another of you might say, "One thing I know is that when I was going through my divorce, I hurt so much I couldn't sleep or eat, and was so filled with hate I couldn't think, but somehow I passed through that, and I've come to recognize that *somehow* was God."

Another of you might say, "One thing I know was that I was getting *blind* every weekend and my weekends began on Tuesday. Such a big man I was. But one day I looked in the mirror and really saw myself for what I was. But only now have I come to recognize that that loser in the mirror was really Jesus calling me to something better."

"One thing I know. . . ." Isn't that a marvelous understatement? As if the *only* teensy little thing you happen to know is—who saved your life. No, you don't start with special knowledge but with acknowledgment. You may not start with a public profession of faith (the way the blind man did) but with prayer. You say, "God I am not sure how to name you, but I am sure that I need you." Or "I can't talk about you as others do, but I acknowledge my dependence upon you."

Oh sure, you've got to be careful, keep your bases covered, check everything out, but in the end God will break through. God's going to get you with a power and a grace that will burst your prudence and give you real vision.

Such seeing has two consequences (and they are related). The one is suffering; the other is joy. In the story the man pays a terrible price for his vision. He is cast out of the synagogue, cut off from religion, Torah, family, the sweet-smelling incense of the Sabbath, the certitude of the Law—all because he has looked deeply and directly into the Light. We really are the sons and daughters of this man. His story marks the rupture in the family of Jews and

Christians, of synagogue and church, that tragically endures to this day. We live with that separation every day and must never stop praying for God to work yet another miracle.

The second consequence is joy—not pride, but the kind of joy that is born of freedom. We are free from having to be religious experts or models of piety, free from having to calculate the cost-benefit ratio of every decision we make; there is freedom to stand up in a university where so many know so much and to say, "One thing I know. . . . And it is no small thing!" May God bless you in this Lenten season with the joy and the gravity of seeing.

Let us pray: Light of the world, Light of the world, we acknowledge you. Amen.

4. Backyard Religion:
THE STORY OF THE MAN WHO BUILT A CHURCH JUST TO SUIT HIMSELF

Craig Skinner

Judges 17, 18

Good inventors occasionally discover useful ideas just working in their own backyards. But homemade articles are not always the best. I heard of one wise pastry cook who advertised "Pies just like your mother made—$5.00 each. Pies just like your mother used to *think* she made—$7.50 each." Which reminds us that the quality of everything homemade may not be perfect or in any way better than regular store-bought goods. Some backyard discoveries may be valuable, but many are just mediocre. Backyard religion is the same. The faith that an individual forges on his own, mostly turns out to be a poor, low-quality substitute for the real thing.

The Book of Judges tells of one man who built a church in his own backyard. Micah lived in the hill country around Mount Ephraim. The scribe who recorded the history of the years when great judges, such as Gideon and Sampson, led Israel seems to have felt that readers needed to understand the nature of the times about which he wrote so he added Micah's story as a kind of appendix in chapters 17 and 18. He tells us why in chapter 17:6: "In those days there was no King in Israel; every man did what was right in his own eyes." Without a central government, no one ruled to see that things were done right and done well. So Micah's story illustrates what happens when every one does just as he or she pleases about religion.

Craig Skinner is Professor of Preaching at Golden Gate Baptist Theological Seminary in Mill Valley, California. His graduate degrees include doctorates in Education and Social Psychology and in Theology. Dr. Skinner has published many books and articles and often has presented a one-man stage dramatization, *C. H. Spurgeon Tonight* (Gateway Films, 1991).

Every person holds to some religion. Each of us possesses some working philosophy of life. We all live according to some stack pole of beliefs or principles, some basic ideas of right and wrong that govern our behavior, and Micah's family was no exception. Micah built a chapel right at his own house. He wanted his church to be very convenient and very close at hand. He chose to create a little backyard religion that could be tailored to fit his needs and be easily available just where it suited him. But he found that when he put together what he *thought* was right all by himself he made some unfortunate mistakes and experienced some frustrating consequences.

"Now there was a man of the hill country of Ephraim whose name was Micah. And he said to his mother, 'The eleven hundred pieces of silver which were taken from you, about which you uttered a curse in my hearing, behold the silver is with me; I took it' " (Judg. 17:1–2). Here we have a very superstitious family. Mother missed some money from the housekeeping and immediately pronounced a curse on the thief. This apparently frightened Micah so much that he immediately confessed his guilt to avoid the bad luck he felt was liable to fall upon him because of his mother's curse. But that confession created a further set of problems. After Micah returned the eleven hundred pieces of silver to his mother she said, " 'I had wholly dedicated the silver from my hand to the Lord for my son to make a graven image and a molten image; now therefore I will return them to you' " (Judg. 17:3).

Now that sounds like a truly religious family, doesn't it? But the Israelites were forbidden by God to make any idols or images! Furthermore, when the suggestion was adopted verse 4 says that the mother kept back 900 of the 1,100 silver pieces for herself. She returned only 200 of them for her son's little backyard religion. Then Micah made his silver image, chose one of his own sons to be a priest, and built a shrine at his own house (v. 5). Now he possessed his own private little religion, with all that he needed conveniently lodged in the spare bedroom or maybe just outside in the backyard.

The image he created is described as both molten and graven. This means it was silver melted down, cast into a rough shape, and then other details were carved and engraved into its surface. Perhaps this image was a copy of the Ark of the Covenant? The only major religious object of which Micah would be aware would be the ark—a gold-covered box holding the two stone tablets on which the Ten Commandments were recorded as originally given to Moses. This real ark was installed in the temple at Shiloh, which was just down the road from where he lived in Mount Ephraim. Two angels carved to face each other stood on its lid. The Jews called the space between them "the mercy-seat" for there God promised to dwell among his people (see Exod. 25:10–22). Before the ark in the sanctuary of the real temple, the high priest wore a special garment called an *ephod*. So, when Micah ordained his own son to be his priest (although the Law commanded that only members of the tribe of Levi should have that honor), he made him a similar priestly robe.

So Micah's own chapel and religion appeared therefore to be somewhat after the fashion of the real thing. But he also included objects that the story in the original describes as *teraphim* or "household gods." These were little figurines that families kept as tribal reminders of their ancestors. Possibly such carved objects began life as the original clay tablets that were the property deeds to the family lands, describing them with such words as ". . . all the bottom land down by the river, beneath the mountain, and one day's journey east. . . ." Then one day someone thought it might be nice to carve a particular title deed in a way that represented grandfather's bald head and thick beard so as to have a kind of memento of him. Then, over time, all these title deeds became shaped after the likenesses of former family members, and thus they became "household gods" and the basis for a kind of ancestor worship. All the heathen nations around them prized their own *teraphim* as relics of their family history and objects to be greatly honored. So we find Micah making sure he covered all the bases by taking his family deeds, now venerated as vehicles for ancestor worship, to include in his little chapel alongside the other components of his backyard religion.

He ended then with an unusual mixture of elements, some of which imitated Hebrew worship, and others that reflected heathen superstition. Like most homemade religions, his contained some ingredients that reflected features found in the regular worship of God as well as some components that were quite strange. Micah's private little religion was just that which he thought was "right in his own eyes." Everything there seemed fine, especially because of its location, so handy and so convenient. But that little backyard religion, in reality, turned out only to be a poor imitation of other materials copied from here, there, and everywhere. Micah designed his own faith to be just as he wanted it to be, handy, convenient, and broad. But he manufactured it out of second-hand elements and ideas. So you see, like all self-created beliefs, this backyard religion was a superficial religion.

I. A Superficial Religion

Did you ever furnish your home from a Goodwill store? In our early married lives much of the home decor that my wife and I could afford might best be described as "Early Salvation Army" or "Vintage St. Vincent de Paul"! We managed with it, but it certainly was less than desirable. Second-hand goods are usually just that. They don't compare in quality to original materials. Occasionally you may find a bargain, but usually you get no more than exactly what you pay for. This is true with furniture—and it's also true with religion. Micah built his own faith by borrowing ideas from others, and it turned out to be pretty worthless. Very little in the way of religion that you pick up from others is authentically first class. What you secure when you create your own religion may be comfortable and convenient. But when you put together your own beliefs you always have to borrow from somewhere else, and you mostly end up with a very strange mixture of good, bad, and terrible.

Micah's little chapel looked fine on the surface. At first glance it seemed to be fairly genuine, but the more you study it the less integrity it appears to possess. Behind that authentic-looking facade all you discover is a bunch of second-hand, second-rate copies of other ideas. His faith featured an appointed priest who wore the right garments, it boasted a miniature ark just like the big one down at the Shiloh temple, but these apparently respectable elements were mixed with other very unusual ones. Even the priest was a counterfeit, with an unauthorized ordination. That's so like many of the homemade religions some folks hold today—systems of belief that easily reveal themselves to be just as unreal.

"Well, I hunt, and fish, and I go to the beach on Sundays. I believe a person can worship God much better in his great outdoors than you can in some stuffy church!" I'm sure you've heard someone offer that kind of backyard religion. But do you know people who actually take time to worship when they go fishing or hunting or visit the beach?

"Well, so long as a man provides for his family, doesn't kill or steal, gives to charity and helps others it's OK. As long as you do the best that you can everything will work out all right in the end!" But how many persons do you know who could ever honestly assert that they have *always* done the best that they can? None of us is perfect, and if we could be from now on no amount of good works could ever remove the guilt of our wrongdoing or release us from the conviction that we must be judged for our past sins. Like all backyard, homemade religions, Micah's faith turned out to be shallow and superficial. But it also revealed itself to be a self-righteous religion.

II. A Self-Righteous Religion

Micah set up a system of *doing* things for God in order to deserve his blessing. Micah believed that if only he could get all the right things together in his religion it would ensure that he was blessed by God. His idea of a real religion was one that centered on how he behaved and what he did to earn acceptance. Yet Micah, despite all that he had done, still felt uneasy about his religion. His backyard chapel held many good things, but underneath it all he knew how superficial it truly was. The things that seemed wrong really bothered him. His strange mixture of homemade and half-baked ideas, borrowed from here and there, did nothing to make Micah feel his was worship acceptable to God.

A major stress that deeply concerned him was the fact that he knew the priest he appointed was his own son. His son had not been born from the priestly tribe of Levi. He was never therefore properly authorized to act as a servant of God. Micah knew his priest to be false, and he felt guilty about that lack of authenticity, just as all men and women who build homemade religions that mix imitations of the real with other elements that are strange, know they are not right with God. That deep-down sense of discomfort and uneasiness always persists in every religion that is built upon "doing" things for God.

Yet just then Micah received a totally unexpected stroke of amazing good fortune. Judges 17:7–13 tells of a *real* priest, a Levite, traveling through the countryside who came past Micah's house. Micah grabbed him quickly and offered him the pastorate! He promised ten pieces of silver a year, a suit of clothes, his accommodation, and all his food (vv. 7–10). It so happened that the young man was seeking just such a position so he gladly accepted, and Micah cried: "Now I *know* that the Lord will prosper me, seeing I have a Levite as a priest" (v. 13). This seemed to be just the final touch of authenticity for Micah's homemade religion. For him this unexpected development appeared to authenticate his focus on doing what seemed right in his own eyes.

But real religion is not centered on what we do for God but on what he does for us. Micah thought that he had to do everything that was absolutely right in order to be good enough to earn God's blessings. But the whole of the Bible teaches us that because we cannot be sinless and perfect, the Lord is a God of love and grace who takes our faith and trust in him and counts *that* as if it were righteousness. You can never be good enough for God to accept and bless you. You can only trust that he will accept you because of his great mercy and forgiveness.

Just down the road at Shiloh was the temple with a God-given system of sacrifices that pointed toward the time when God would give his only Son on a cross for the sins of all the world. To be accepted by God, all Micah had to do was to offer those sacrifices saying that he believed he could be forgiven through God's grace. But instead Micah tried to earn acceptance from God by continually improving his behavior, by upgrading his chapel worship, by improving the quality of all that he did for God. And that was also the reason why, like all homemade, backyard beliefs, Micah's religion turned out to be an unstable religion.

III. An Unstable Religion

Judges chapter 18 tells us of a wandering tribe of Danites that passed by Micah's house. They heard the voice of the priest saying prayers, turned aside, saw Micah's chapel with all its trimmings, and then came back later to steal it for themselves. When the priest saw them taking the images and the ephod and the household gods, he asked them what they were doing. So they invited him to go with them and be a priest to their whole tribe. Now the priest was a real opportunist who saw more money and more prestige in that offer so he, and Micah's little backyard religion with all its artifacts and worship aids, went marching off down the road! (vv. 14–21). Poor heartbroken Micah gathered his neighbors and ran after them, but the Danite warriors frightened him with warlike threats so he returned home after watching his religion being stolen out from under his nose, taken away from him by a changing situation (vv. 22–26). Homemade religions do not possess power enough to stop themselves from being stolen! Backyard, homemade faiths do become lost in the changing circumstances of life.

In many of my early pastorates I made a habit of making special friends of the local undertaker. From such association I could volunteer ministry to persons who were related to no church and needed help in their crisis hours of sudden bereavement. I still recall the sadness of those funerals. I saw much grief, many tears, and often deep bitterness. Yet every person I met possessed some religion, some value system, some ideas about right and wrong and about living life as it should be lived. Yet those beliefs all dissolved when the crises came. Secondhand, second-rate, superficial, and self-righteous ideas sound so fine in the sunshine, but they always let you down in the dark! Religion has to be real to last when the crisis comes.

Before my first *Christian* funeral, as a very young pastor in a country church, I went to comfort a bereaved church member, an unremarkable lady, but one who was always faithful and supportive. She had no great gifts, but her husband, so suddenly taken from her, used his many talents in the service of Christ and the church.

I trembled as I walked up the front pathway to her little home for I just knew she'd be really upset. As a very inexperienced pastor I really did not know how to comfort her, nor what I could say. Sure enough, when she met me at the door, her eyes were red with weeping as she sobbed out the great tragedy of her loss and its pain. Then she said, "Pastor, I must ask you a very important question. I must know the truth!" My heart sank to my boots for I just knew she was going to ask me to explain why God had taken her husband, and I had no answer.

But then, surprisingly, she said, "I have many tears on the outside but there's a great calm inside—just as if God's big hand has a firm hold around my heart. I know I'm going to get through this with God's help—but I need to understand it. Pastor, tell me, why do I feel like I do, with this wonderful peace within?" What a joy it was for me to be able to take her to the story Jesus told in Matthew chapter 7! Do you remember that one about the two men who erected their houses, but one built on the rock and the other built on the sand? "Both houses looked the same," I said, "but no one knew what the foundations were like until the floods came and the winds blew. All those years you've been in Sunday School, all those prayer meetings in which you have participated, all those humble hours of worship you have spent in the Lord's house—all these have been strengthening the foundation beneath your spiritual life. And you never discover the strength of your faith's foundation until the storm breaks. You feel as you do because you are standing in the storm and right here is where you best feel the power of the reality of your faith!"

Backyard religions do let you down in a crisis. But genuine faith in God builds a deep foundation, the strength of which you seldom discover until the winds blow and you find yourself standing against the storm. Of course the greatest tragedy about Micah's self-constructed religion was that the real thing was just down the road all the time! (Judg. 18:31). You see his little home-manufactured faith turned out to be nothing but an unnecessary religion after all.

IV. An Unnecessary Religion

Verse 30 in chapter 18 of Judges names Micah's priest as Jonathan (since corrected to Moses in most modern translations), the grandson of Manasseh. The scribes who copied early manuscripts manufactured this name by adding one letter to the real word for Jonathan's grandfather, which is actually the name *Moses*. They changed this because they could not bear to accept the tragedy of Moses' grandson going so badly astray. So Micah's priest turns out to be a heretic! He was traveling through the country in search of a place because he had deserted Moses' faith. He was so far away from real religion that he was willing to serve in a chapel with images and heathen idols and to run off with the first tribe who offered him a promotion.

Everything Micah did when he manufactured his backyard religion was so unnecessary; the real thing was just around the corner and down the road all the time! Sometimes folks can adopt a pretty fair imitation of the right thing. They can include elements in their self-manufactured faiths that display some fine-looking values. But it is not what is *good* that we should evaluate about homemade religions—*at issue is so much else, which is always included with them and which destroys their quality, that we need to understand.*

Many years ago my friend Rev. Keith Langford-Smith, a pioneer Episcopalian missionary in the outback of the Australian Northern Territory, told me about a sheep ranch that he was always delighted to visit. The farmer owned an old horse they had nicknamed Hungry Harry. That old horse possessed such a voracious appetite that he would eat anything in sight. Harry jumped the gates and broke the fences to get at the crops growing in the fields. Harry ate the wheat out of the haulage trucks. Harry begged kitchen scraps. Harry munched the household vegetables in the garden, and stole the food out of dog's dishes. Harry was a first-rate pest! And so my friend was always delighted to visit that ranch and hear the latest version of one of Hungry Harry's constant searches to satisfy his never-ending appetite.

The final "Harry" story the farm hands told my friend was about the time they locked Harry in an old barn as they went to work elsewhere on the property. They knew that hungry old horse could not get into any trouble in a completely empty barn, for it contained absolutely nothing to eat. Yet, at the end of the day when they returned, they found Harry lying on his side looking very ill with his stomach bloated up to almost twice its size. When they stood him up he seemed top heavy and just fell down again. They then discovered that someone had spilled a few oats over a pile of sand in the corner, and that Harry had been so determined to eat those oats he had swallowed pounds and pounds of sand along with them! The sand that Hungry Harry ingested became so heavy that he could no longer stand upright. Finally all that he swallowed, along with the few oats he really wanted, killed him. You see the real trouble with backyard beliefs, with every homemade religion, with every self-manufactured system of faith, with every false cult, is not how much good it includes *but what else you swallow along with it!* That can wreck your balance and kill anything that is at all real about your faith!

Jesus said, "I am the way, and the truth, and the life, no one comes to the Father but by me" (John 14:6). The one way of acceptance before God is to rest in his grace and forgiveness by claiming Christ to be the Savior who took your sins and settled them once and for all through his cross. "For God so loved the world that he gave his only begotten Son, that whoever believes in him should not perish, but have eternal life" (John 3:16). Anything more—anything less—anything else—is always useless. The only religion worth possessing is the everlasting gospel of God's Grace, which reveals the depths of his love for sinners, displays the wonder of his free forgiveness, builds a secure foundation beneath your feet to help you weather the storm, and satisfies all your spiritual needs. Are you resting by faith in God's revelation of the acceptance that can be yours in Jesus Christ today or still going about trying to establish your own righteousness? Are you building a backyard religion of your own that is superficial, self-righteous, unstable, and unnecessary?

5. Peter: A Disciple Restored
Michael Duduit

Acts 2:1–41

He was the grandson of a duke, born into the nobility of the world's mightiest power. From the moment of his birth, Winston Churchill was given remarkable access to the corridors of British power.

Churchill was a man of great gifts. He distinguished himself as a journalist and as a soldier, then was elected to Parliament as a young man. His early career in Parliament was exceptional—by the age of thirty-three he was a cabinet minister and one of the nation's most popular speakers. Within a few years he was at the very pinnacle of power, heir apparent to the prime minister's post.

Yet in a series of setbacks, Churchill became a political pariah. Despite his remarkable gifts, by the early 1930s he was ostracized by former allies and excluded from the seats of power. As Hitler moved into power in Germany, Churchill's prophetic warnings were ignored by a hostile British public that wanted to hear only words of peace.

Yet when Britain was plunged into World War II, the nation turned again to Winston Churchill—then sixty-five years old, already eligible to draw his government pension. At last, he became prime minister, prepared to lead his nation through a war in which its very existence was threatened. So on June 18, 1940, the new prime minister went on the BBC radio network to encourage the

Dr. Michael Duduit is Director of Development and Church Relations at Samford University in Birmingham, Alabama. Duduit is also editor and publisher of *Preaching* magazine and is director of the National Conference on Preaching, an annual event sponsored by the magazine. "Peter: A Disciple Restored" is one of a series of biographical sermons based on characters in the Book of Acts.

nation, saying, "Let us therefore brace ourselves to our duties, and so bear ourselves that if the British Empire and its Commonwealth last for a thousand years, men will still say, 'This was their finest hour.' "

From outcast to hero; from failure to victory. There is something in us that longs to know that such restoration is possible, if only because we have known the need for such restoration ourselves. We know what it means to fail at something and wonder if it will ever be the same again.

Peter knew that feeling. He was one of the twelve, the inner circle of disciples with whom Jesus had surrounded himself. He had been Simon, son of John, but Jesus had given him a new name—*Kephas* in Aramaic, *Petros* in Greek. Both meant "rock."

And at times he seemed like a rock—strong, determined. We visualize him as the biggest of the twelve, a rugged fisherman—a rock of a man. And in Matthew 16, after he was the first to declare Jesus as the Messiah, the Lord said, "You are Peter—you are a rock—and on this rock I will build my church."

Yet moments later, the "rock" of verse 18 became the "stone of stumbling" of verse 23. As Jesus explained what would be happening to him when they went to Jerusalem—how he would be arrested, tried, and executed—Peter objected. And we read: "Jesus turned and said to Peter, 'Out of my sight, Satan! You are a stumbling block to me.' "

As F. F. Bruce has observed, "Peter had it in him to be a stone of stumbling or to be a foundation stone." Perhaps that's why so many Christians point to Peter as the New Testament character with whom they most readily identify. Because we also know what it's like to have within us potential for good or for evil, for victory or for failure.

For Peter, the worst was the night Jesus was arrested. Outside the place where Jesus was being tried by the Sanhedrin, Peter sat by the fire, waiting. Three times he was recognized as one of Jesus' disciples, and three times he denied he even knew the One with whom he had spent the last three years.

Peter knew what it was like to hit rock bottom. That is why the story of his rehabilitation, his restoration, is so thrilling. Despite the tragedy of his sin and denial, the Lord reached out to Peter and drew him back to discipleship and even to leadership within his church. In the second chapter of Acts, we witness the culmination of that restoration process as Peter becomes the church's first great proclaimer of the gospel.

Jesus Christ can take our lives—even at our deepest point of failure—and he can restore us to wholeness. Peter is a marvelous example of that truth, and Acts 2 shows us what results from such a restoration.

I. We Receive a New Power

Pentecost was a Jewish harvest festival that came seven weeks after Passover. Jerusalem was crowded with Jewish visitors from throughout the ancient world who had traveled back to Palestine to worship in the temple.

The followers of Jesus were gathered together in one place that day when at about 9:00 in the morning they were startled by the sound of a tremendous wind as the Holy Spirit filled the room and then filled the believers.

What a remarkable image! The Spirit of God breaking into their presence as the wind—the Greek *pneuma* was the word used for both wind and for the Spirit. When the prophet Ezekiel stood in the Valley of Dry Bones and prophesied to the wind, it was the breath of God—the *pneuma*—that entered into them and brought new life.

The coming of the Holy Spirit brought new power to Peter and his fellow disciples—power to offer new life through Christ.

If you have given your life to Jesus Christ as Lord, then you have received the same Holy Spirit—and access to the same power Peter experienced at Pentecost. It is not power given for its own sake; rather, it is power for service, power for witness.

Throughout the Book of Acts, we will see the filling of the Spirit accompanied by new power to boldly proclaim the gospel. As William Willimon points out, "In Genesis 2:7 the Spirit of God breathed life into dust and created a human being. In Acts 2:1–4 the Spirit has breathed life into a once cowardly disciple and created a new man who now has the gift of bold speech."

Jesus had promised them (in Acts 1:8), "But you will receive power when the Holy Spirit comes on you; and you will be my witnesses." The power so absent in Peter's life as he had sat by the fire just seven weeks earlier is now clearly evident—power made available through the filling of the Holy Spirit.

God wants to bring that same power into your life and mine. Like Peter, we may feel that we are inadequate—that the Lord deserves someone more worthy, someone less tainted. Yet the message of Peter and Pentecost is clear: No matter who you are, no matter what you have done or failed to do, God is ready to bring new life and new power to you right now.

This church has already experienced new life, and today we stand in need of great power. There are tremendous challenges that lie ahead of us in the coming weeks: to continue to seek God's direction for this family of believers, to reach out and share God's love and grace with new folks.

Like Joshua and the children of Israel, we stand at the edge of a land of promise. Today as never before, we must claim that power as we seek the filling of God's Holy Spirit by yielding ourselves to him completely. As we give ourselves fully unto him, we will know for ourselves the power he gives.

As the Holy Spirit fills our lives, we not only receive new power, we also proclaim a new message.

II. We Proclaim a New Message

The same Peter who swore he did not know Jesus now steps forward to announce his allegiance to Christ. The night of Jesus' arrest, "We left him weeping in the courtyard, a disciple tested and found wanting. . . . Yet here, before the half inquiring, half mocking crowd, Peter is the first, the very first to lift up his voice and proclaim openly the word that only a few weeks before he could not speak, even to a serving woman at midnight" (William Willimon).

What was the difference? Peter had a new power because of the filling of the Holy Spirit, and he had a new message to proclaim. What was that message?

1. Jesus Christ Is Risen

Peter announces: "God has raised this Jesus to life, and we are all witnesses of the fact" (Acts 2:32). The Resurrection was at the heart of the early church's message, and it ought to be at the center of our proclamation as well.

R. W. Dale was a busy preacher and pastor, and the preceding months had taken a heavy toll on him. Easter Sunday had arrived but he felt weary, lethargic about even getting into the pulpit. He was pacing the floor of his study that morning, wishing he didn't even have to step into the pulpit at all, when suddenly a thought burst into his mind with great force: "Christ is alive! Christ is alive!"

Suddenly, the weariness vanished and was replaced with an explosion of energy and enthusiasm. He was eager for the moment to arrive when he could step into the pulpit and tell people the difference Christ's resurrection could make in their lives.

The reality of Christ's resurrection can animate and empower every area of our lives and service. Nothing in life need be mundane and ordinary, for we serve a living Lord who has overcome death and the grave and promises us the same victory!

Peter had a new message: Christ is risen. Even more, Christ is Lord.

2. Christ Is Lord

Peter boldly proclaimed: "God has made this Jesus, whom you crucified, both Lord and Christ" (Acts 2:36).

No wonder Peter had a new boldness. Not only was Jesus risen from the grave; he is even now sitting at the right hand of God (v. 33), Lord of Lords and King of Kings. We not only proclaim what Jesus did in the past, but what he does today.

There was yet another element to this new message that Peter proclaimed: We must respond.

3. We Must Respond

As Peter declared the death and resurrection of Jesus, the people were "pierced to the heart" and they asked, "What shall we do?" To that question Peter responded: "Repent and be baptized, every one of you, in the name of Jesus Christ so that your sins may be forgiven. And you will receive the gift of the Holy Spirit" (Acts 2:38).

Before Peter's sermon, the people had seen the believers' unusual activity and asked, "What does this mean?" Now, as the Holy

Spirit has convicted them of their own guilt while Peter spoke, the question becomes far more personal and more pressing: "What shall *we* do?"

And Peter—who has so recently experienced God's love and forgiveness in his own life—shares with his listeners how they can also experience Christ's forgiveness.

First, he tells them they must repent. *Repentance* literally refers to a change of direction; you are going one way, and you turn and start going in the opposite direction. Repentance is a change of mind—a change in our attitude toward Jesus Christ—that results in a changed life.

A driver stopped his car to ask a farmer how much farther before he reached his destination. The farmer answered: "Well, if you keep going the direction you're headed now, about twenty-five thousand miles; but if you turn around and go the other direction, about three miles."

Millions of people are hurtling through life, desperately seeking satisfaction, happiness, purpose in life. The message of the gospel is that without Christ, we're headed in the wrong direction and we'll never find what we're looking for. Only through repentance—turning around and going a new direction—will we find life's best in Christ.

In addition to repentance, Peter calls on them to be baptized in the name of Jesus Christ. Baptism was the way people publicly identified and announced their faith in Christ.

So they were to repent and receive Christ as Lord in their own lives. What Peter is talking about is not something you add onto your life, like choosing an option on a new car; rather, it is a life-transforming experience. Once you come to Christ in repentance and faith, life will never be the same.

A man bought an expensive picture of Jesus. When he brought it home, he couldn't seem to find the right place to hang it, so he called in a decorator, then an architect. They agreed that there was simply no good place to hang the picture in that house. What was needed was a brand-new house.

When Jesus Christ comes into your life, he's not interested in finding a wall to hang on. He will build you into an entirely new house, in which he will be at the center.

As a disciple who had been restored, Peter experienced a new power through the filling of the Holy Spirit—and so will we. He proclaimed a new message—and so will we. There is yet a third result of Christ's restoring power in our lives.

III. We Make a New Impact

We read in verse 41: "Those who accepted his message were baptized, and about three thousand were added to their number that day."

What an amazing turnabout! A weak, discouraged disciple has become a powerful, effective messenger of the Kingdom of God— one whom God could use to reach three thousand persons in a single day. That's quite a revival!

But the revival had to begin in Peter. First, he had to experience God's forgiving, restoring love; first Peter had to receive the Spirit's presence and power. Then he was capable of being used in such a remarkable way.

God wants to use you and me to accomplish some powerful things in the life of this church and in the lives of others. Like Peter, we may be a stone of stumbling or a foundation rock on which Christ can build his church. The choice is ours.

You see, the title of Thomas Wolfe's novel had it all wrong. You *can* go home again. The risen Lord stands ready, waiting for us to take that step toward him. He'll take care of the rest.

6. Repent, *Metanoeite*
Susan Auchincloss

Last week I spoke about new life: how advent is a death of sorts that prepares us for God's coming into the world as new life, symbolized by the baby Jesus—and not just into the world, but into our very lives. Today we shall explore what that new life is.

I remember once when my grandparents were visiting us—they always did over the Christmas holidays, since my mother was an only child. It was a Sunday morning and we were going to church. My grandmother couldn't bear to be on time for church; she had to be early. If she couldn't sit in the front near the center, she scarcely cared if she went to church or not. So she would corral us children and make sure we were ready and waiting in the car with her. We, at least, wouldn't cause any delay. That Sunday I followed her out of the house, down the flagstone steps through the garden, almost to the car, and then I said, trying to hide my glee—for even children enjoy it when the mighty are fallen—"Mimi, you forgot your skirt!" She peered with difficulty over the elegant, hand-knitted suit jacket, which covered an ample bosom, but sure enough, there she stood in her slip. Needless to say, she turned on the spot and went to set herself right.

I tell that story, because I want to talk about repentance. Repentance translates the Greek word, *metanoia,* which means literally, a mental turnaround. But it is much more than a change of mind or even a change of mind and heart. The whole being makes a 180 degree turn in *metanoia*—heart, mind, will, body, spirit, soul—and all together like a pond turning over in the spring.

This is what John the Baptist preached, and this was Jesus' message too; but what a difference! John was "preaching a baptism

---

Susan Auchincloss is helping to form a "full-service" Anglican Church in Prague, Czechoslovakia. An Episcopalian, Auchincloss is a graduate of Stanford University and the Church Divinity School of the Pacific. She is the former assistant chaplain at the National Cathedral School for Girls in Washington, DC.

of *metanoia* for the forgiveness of sins." Jesus was "preaching the gospel of God, saying the time is fulfilled, and the Kingdom of God is at hand; *metanoiete* and believe in [the new life]." One a negative, one a positive, and the first necessary to the second. Yet to go from John's *metanoia* to Jesus' is not a progression, it is a transformation, a metamorphosis. It is as if John said *turn* (180 degrees) and Jesus said *turn* (inside out).

John's job was easy, compared to Jesus'. He was dealing in familiar terms with a familiar struggle. He was talking about what everyone knew, God's Law, the commandments. The struggle was to make one's life comply with the commandments. Not easy, but at least you knew what was required.

Jesus, on the other hand, was introducing a whole new reality. There were no words for it. He spoke about it indirectly, in parables, and most essentially he taught it without words at all in the way he lived. He didn't so much announce the Good News, as he *is* the Good News. His message was so radical that even after 2,000 years we still do not grasp it, and in spite of these 2,000 years we still do not have the words to talk about it. Let me put it this way. John the Baptist came to call the people back to their religion. Jesus came and ended religion.

Religion, as many of you know, comes from the Latin, *religio*. It means to rebind, retie. Religion is what binds together two incommensurate entities: God—omniscient, eternal, omnipotent; and humankind—fallible, mortal, inconstant. Religion, then, consists of the things we do and say—either corporately or individually—that link us to God.

No wonder St. Paul was blinded and tossed from his horse onto his head when Jesus' message finally came through to him. It is a matter of becoming blind to our normal way of seeing and of turning upside down our former way of being in the world. God is not "up there" or even "out there," God has made his dwelling in us, in his creation. Immanuel: God is with us. Rebinding, *religio,* is no longer needed. It is easy to say this, but almost impossible to grasp it. It's like telling people to lift themselves up by their bootstraps. How do you get outside yourself to do it? The Kingdom of God is like that; "you can't get there from here," as the old Maine saying has it.

Can you imagine Jesus' frustration? There are no steps for getting there, no formula or recipe to follow. All he could do was tell stories about how it is to be there. All he could do was live out how it feels to live there. And if Jesus was frustrated, how must the disciples have felt! There he was with that unquenchable well-spring of joy, with the peace that only comes when all fear is gone, with that love that seemingly embraced all creation, and there they were, like poor children on a cold, dark street, their runny noses pressed to the glass, watching a party unfold in a splendor of color, music, and feasting. They wanted in, but they didn't know how to get there.

You would think that with 2,000 years of working on the problem there would have been more progress. Yet we can't change how we see things—change our reality—just by changing our glasses. We see ourselves as individuals; Jesus saw himself and the whole of creation as part of one indivisibly woven whole, held together by love. This is God-with-us; this is the new life Jesus came to describe through stories and through living. Some of us may have a dim, intellectual appreciation of this as reality, but Jesus felt it, lived it. It takes an unimaginable, unquantifiable capacity for love, to actually feel and experience our kinship to all creation. It means experiencing oneself as if part of an intricate and delicate spider web, on a cosmic scale, where there cannot be a rend in one corner without the whole network being weakened. We can see Jesus living out this way of seeing things in his treatment of the tax collectors and the prostitutes.

These outcasts of his society—tax collectors, prostitutes, lepers—have multiplied in ours. We have in addition, not only the homeless, the people with AIDS, the drug culture; we also have the environment. A gospel of Jesus if he lived in our time would tell of a man who wept—as Jesus did in the Gospel of John—to see the degradation of the air and water, the soil and growing things. We trash so much of God's treasured creation—not only people, but nature. The truth is, we are incapable and unwilling when it comes to recognizing how tied together we all are in the great web of creation.

Incapable and unwilling. We are unwilling, because even the little we do feel tied to causes us worry enough. Believe me, I feel my linkage with the drug addicts and dealers. I don't walk out on the streets without wondering about my safety. I don't want to feel my linkage to all of creation; I simply cannot stand that much worry. The less a part of it I feel, the better. But wait; why then are we so attracted to what we see in Jesus? If it is so painful to feel our connectedness to all creation, why is Jesus so full of joy and hope, love and peace? The problem is that we are failing to make a distinction here. There is all the difference in the world between worrying about the environment and loving it. That is not to say that, loving it, we do not feel its pain. But worrying has to do with outcomes, and how things turn out—that is in God's hands. Loving has to do with caring and cherishing, one day at a time. It is part of our faith that, as St. Paul says, we and the whole creation "await the redemption of our bodies; for in this hope we were saved." So worry has no part in the Kingdom of God. But love! Our capacity to love measures our capacity to live! We cannot love too widely or too deeply.

I said before that we are incapable and unwilling to recognize how tied in we all are to the great web of creation. We can overcome our unwillingness, especially after we make the distinction between worrying about creation and loving it. But incapable is another matter. We are back on the cold street with our noses pressed to the window. How can we get where we so desperately want to be? The key seems to lie in that word, *metanoia*. John's *metanoia* was a 180-degree turning. So our first step is a turning away from, as Jesus called it, "this world"; that is, a letting go of those things we cling to that pull us away from life in Christ. What we turn toward, metaphorically speaking, is an underground time—time alone, time spent out of sight and hearing of the busy world of "getting and spending," time in prayer, time in silence. Seed time.

Then the second *metanoia*, the turning inside out. The first turning we could initiate. The second only God can accomplish. We can only put ourselves in position and wait, expectant and hopeful, virgin souls, seeds warm in the soil of God's love. We are still moist with the water of the baptism of John; we await our baptism in the Holy Spirit—our metamorphosis. What is it to be a seed at that moment of metamorphosis? That moment when one is transformed from a hard and individual kernel to a seedling, taping with its root deep into the body of aeons of lives that went before, shooting leaves into ether breathed through lungs beyond number? What does a seed experience? We cannot really say, but we can want it. Oh, how we can want it!

Remember Mimi, my grandmother? I never dreamed I'd be taking her as a guide, but think about her turn. She didn't stop and think: should I or shouldn't I. She didn't think: I'll do it in a minute. She didn't weigh alternatives. She turned. And so, changing Jesus' words slightly, what I say to you I say to all: Repent. *Metanoiete.*

7. "Relax—He Is Risen"
Lavonn D. Brown

Luke 24:36–43; John 20:19–23

Robert L. Lindsey served as a missionary in Jerusalem for more than forty years. He developed a close friendship with Professor David Flusser of the prestigious Hebrew University of Jerusalem. In his recent book, *Jesus Rabbi and Lord,* Dr. Lindsey tells of an interesting experience Professor Flusser shared with him.

The occasion was a return trip from the United States to Israel. Custom counters always made him nervous. He obviously showed his nervousness to the customs officials. Finally, one of the officials said, "Mister, don't be worried, just relax!"

Evidently Flusser had never heard this American phrase. He meditated on its meaning. Later he said to Lindsey, "That is exactly what Jesus is all about. Jesus says to people, 'Relax'!" Lindsey concluded, "And if you think about it a bit that is indeed the tone of the events and words of Jesus at the first Easter."[1]

Jesus' appearances to different people and groups after the Resurrection seem to be relaxed and relaxing. His first recorded words after the Resurrection reflect this same attitude. To the women at the tomb he said, "Do not be afraid" (Matt. 28:10). Mark records him saying, "Do not be amazed" (16:6). He gently, almost playfully, teased the two men on the road to Emmaus (Luke 24:13 ff.). When he appeared in the midst of the ten in Jerusalem, he said, "Peace be with you" (John 20:21). So, the central message of Easter is "Relax—he is risen."

Lavonn D. Brown is Senior Minister at First Baptist Church in Norman, Oklahoma. Brown is a graduate of Oklahoma Baptist University and Southwestern Baptist Theological Seminary. He has served as President of the Baptist General Convention of Oklahoma as well as on the boards of a number of religious institutions.

I. We May Relax Because Our Greatest Problem
Now Has a Solution

From the beginning mankind's greatest concern has been the problem of sin. In the process of creation God made man and woman in his own image (Gen. 1:27). What that means, above all else, is that God gave us freedom of will or choice. That's where the problem started. We are free to love or not love, follow or not follow, obey or not obey.

God must have had high expectations. But we blew it. We exercised our freedom of will and chose against God (read Gen. 3:1–7). We fell short of what God intended.

The result was sin—mankind's greatest problem. Sin is expressing our freedom by pushing God away. Sin is going my way and not God's way. Sin also pushes other people away, widening the gap between us and others. The ultimate goal is that we may be God to ourselves.

One of the favorite New Testament words for sin is a word that means to miss the mark. You draw the bow. The arrow speeds through the air, falling to the ground before reaching the intended target. That is sin. Paul concluded that "all have sinned and fall short of the glory of God" (Rom. 3:23, rsv). Frederick Buechner has said that original sin means "we all originate out of a sinful world which taints us from the word go."[2]

What happens when we sin? How serious is the sin problem? Paul described those who are "alienated from the life of God" (Eph. 4:18, rsv). Sin results in separation from God, estrangement, broken relationships. The situation, however, is more serious than that. Paul also said that "the wages of sin is death" (Rom. 6:23). Initially this is spiritual death. Ultimately physical death is included. Sin means death for the total person. The results of sin are eternal unless something happens to change the situation.

What is the solution? How can sinful people be brought back into right relationship to God? That is the message of Easter: You may relax—he is risen! "In Christ God was reconciling the world to himself," said Paul (2 Cor. 5:19, rsv).

How has he taken care of our sin problem? "Yes, although you were dead through your shortcomings," Paul wrote, "God made you live again through fellowship with Christ. He graciously forgave us all our shortcomings, canceled the note that stood against

us, with its requirements, and has put it out of our way by nailing
it to the cross" (Col. 2:13–14, Williams).

The wonder of it all is expressed in John Masefield's poem,
"The Everlasting Mercy":

> O glory of the lighted mind,
> How dead I'd been, how dumb, how blind.
> The station brook, to my new eyes,
> Was babbling out of Paradise;
> The waters rushing from the rain
> Were singing Christ has risen again.
> I thought all earthly creatures knelt
> from rapture of the joy I felt.

II. We May Relax Because Our Greatest Enemy Now Has Been Destroyed

Paul spoke of death as "the last enemy to be destroyed" (1 Cor.
15:26). We fear death as we fear anything unknown. The Bible is
realistic about death. It takes death seriously, understands our
fears, and shares our natural anxieties. In Bildad's second speech
to Job he referred to death as "the king of terrors" (Job 18:14).

Our universal fear of death may explain our interest in people's last words, epitaphs, and requiems. "Dying is a very dull,
dreary affair," said Somerset Maugham, "and my advice to you is
to have nothing whatsoever to do with it." Woody Allen admitted,
"It's not that I'm afraid of death. It's just that I don't want to be
there when it happens."

In southwestern Oklahoma, just out of Lone Wolf, is an old
graveyard. So old that some of the grave markers date back prior
to statehood. Nearby, on a dirt farm-to-market road a sign reads,
"This road ends in the cemetery." It is difficult for us to believe
that all roads end there.

Jane Walmsley, in her book *Brit-Think, Ameri-Think*, gives a
tongue-in-cheek guide to the difference in the thought patterns of
the two countries. While the British live their lives with a certain
detachment, she concludes that "Americans think that death is op-
tional."[3] There is a nagging suspicion, she proceeds, that you can
delay death, or avoid it altogether, if you really try. In the final
analysis death becomes your fault.

What would it be like if we could be freed from the fear of death? What if death could be viewed as a normal stage of life— like birth? We struggle against birth. We are brought into the world kicking and screaming. We struggle against death. But what if death is merely birth into a new life of unlimited possibilities? That is the message of Easter: You may relax—he is risen!

After all, Paul did say that death, the last great enemy, had been destroyed. Jesus Christ took the full weight of the blow of what sin and death can do and, by the power of God, broke the chains of death and rose triumphant. In so doing he put death to death. Paul insisted that God can make dead things live again (see Rom. 4:17).

How has Jesus taken care of our fears concerning death? In his classic statement on resurrection Paul answered the question:

> then shall come to pass the saying that is written:
> "Death is swallowed up in victory." "O death,
> where is thy victory? O death, where is thy
> sting?" . . . But thanks be to God, who gives us the
> victory through our Lord Jesus Christ. Therefore,
> my beloved brethren, be steadfast, immovable,
> always abounding in the work of the Lord,
> knowing that in the Lord your labor is not in vain.
> (1 Cor. 15:54–58)

By his resurrection Jesus has shifted the focus of our concern from trying not to die to learning how to live.

III. We May Relax Because Our Deepest Need Now Has Been Fully Met

Our deepest need is for power for daily living. The dailiness of the Christian life presents problems for us all. Jesus warned, "Every day has trouble enough of its own" (Matt. 6:34, TCNT). The Old Testament promised "as your days, so shall your strength be" (Deut. 33:25). But can we count on it?

Between Good Friday and Easter Sunday the followers of Jesus were fearful, defeated, doubting, and despairing. They spent most of their time behind closed doors. After the Resurrection they became courageous, daring, bold, triumphant witnesses. How are we to explain the difference? The fearful became fearless, the cowardly became courageous, the timid became triumphant, the inept did the impossible; now what might we expect?

Our deepest need is for the power to cope. We often wonder how we can keep going. From whence will our strength and help come? Is power available for today? That is the message of Easter: You may relax—he is risen!

The same power that brought Jesus forth from his grave is available to each of us. The resurrected Christ said, "All power is given unto me in heaven and in earth. Go ye therefore, . . ." (Matt. 28:18–19, KJV). By his death and resurrection Jesus released a new power into the world.

Now we understand Paul's keen desire, "that I may know him, and the power of his resurrection" (Phil. 3:10). The great aim of Paul's life was a personal, intimate acquaintance with Christ. Specifically, he wanted to know the power overflowing from his resurrection. That same living, dynamic power is available in the life of each individual Christian.

Bill and Gloria Gaither are among the best-known gospel songwriters of our time. In 1971 they were greatly concerned about the condition of the world into which their new son had been born. Yet, the Resurrection of Christ was a living reality for them. They felt they could face the unknown future without fear, because he lives. They wrote a hymn for their newborn baby:

> God sent his Son, they call him Jesus;
> He came to love, heal, and forgive;
> He lived and died to buy my pardon,
> An empty grave is there to prove my Savior lives.
> Because He lives I can face tomorrow;
> Because He lives all fear is gone;
> Because I know He holds the future,
> And life is worth the living just because He lives.[4]

IV. We May Relax Because Our Greatest Hope Now Has Been Fully Realized

The March 1984 issue of *National Geographic* had an unusual cover picture. It was a laser-sculpted image of an eagle with wings spread. It reveals what is called the magic of the hologram, which is like seeing a three-dimensional scene through a window. As you move the image from side to side or up and down, you see the same image from new perspectives, angles, and colors. In fact, the eagle is seen in all the colors of the spectrum.

Life itself has many dimensions. It is a mysterious blend or harmony of body, mind, and spirit. Life is physical but more than physical. It is mental but more than mental. It is spiritual but more than spiritual. There is something about every person that cannot be told in human categories. Life is more than mere physical existence where all colors fade into a sickly gray.

Life is an eternal reality. Mankind needs the conviction that life has meaning, purpose, and goal. Many are asking, "Is this all there is?" or "Could there be more?" Is life going somewhere and not nowhere? After physical life is there still something more to come? That is the message of Easter: You may relax—he is risen!

We may relax because our greatest hope—eternal life—has been realized. Peter wrote,

> Blessed be the God and Father of our Lord Jesus
> Christ! By his great mercy we have been *born anew*
> *to a living hope* through the resurrection of Jesus
> Christ from the dead, and to an inheritance which
> is imperishable, undefiled, and unfading, kept in
> heaven for you, who by God's power are guarded
> through faith for a salvation ready to be revealed
> in the last time. (1 Pet. 1:3–5, RSV)

In an extensive battle during World War II, eleven young soldiers were killed. Later their buddies gathered behind the lines for a committal service. It was a gloomy, dreary, rainy day. A chaplain intoned lifeless words from a prayer book. There was not a spark of life or hope, until a young, red-faced boy from Arkansas in a beautiful, clear tenor voice began to sing. "There's a land that is fairer than day and by faith we can see it afar."

On this Easter Sunday it is good for us again to remember Paul's words, "What no eye has seen, nor ear heard, nor the heart of man conceived, what God has prepared for those who love him" (1 Cor. 2:9), and, "If for this life only we have hoped in Christ, we are of all men most to be pitied" (1 Cor. 15:19). Also, it is good to remember the promise of Jesus, "because I live, you will live also" (John 14:19).

So, relax—he is risen.

NOTES

1. Robert L. Lindsey, *Jesus Rabbi and Lord* (Oak Creek, Wis.: Cornerstone Press, 1990), 172.

2. Frederick Buechner, *Wishful Thinking* (New York: Harper & Row, 1973), 89.

3. Jane Walmsley, *Brit-Think, Ameri-Think* (London: Penguin Books, 1986), 2.

4. William J. Reynolds, *Songs of Glory* (Grand Rapids, MI: Zondervan Books, 1990), 93.

II. EXPOSITORY

8. Spirits and the Spirit
Bill J. Leonard

John 2:1–11

Something always goes wrong at weddings. Well, almost always. Indeed, I think weddings are among the most stress-laden occasions in the world. All those impossible details, all those deep emotions, all those relatives together in the same place create a perfect environment for unlimited logistical complications. Consider the possibilities for mishap: the florist runs late, the tuxedos don't fit, the in-laws get angry, your best friends don't show up, and your crazy uncle George does. I once conducted a wedding in Texas where the bride's uncle sat on the second row and watched the entire ceremony with a cowboy hat on his head and a big, unlighted cigar clenched securely between his teeth. We preachers sometimes compound the confusion. I know one couple who, near the celebration of their first anniversary, found out that their minister had forgotten to send in their marriage license and they were appalled to think they had been living in sin for almost a year!

All kinds of things can go wrong at weddings—and that is nothing new. The Bible says so too. There was this wedding, you recall, at a place called Cana in Galilee. It was apparently quite a party and a good time was had by all, so much so that they ran out of wine before everybody was through celebrating. And every first-century Miss Manners knew that such a mistake was a major *faux*

Bill J. Leonard has until recently served as William Walker Brookes Professor of American Christianity at the Southern Baptist Theological Seminary in Louisville, Kentucky. He is now professor of Religion at Samford University in Birmingham, Alabama. Leonard received his Ph.D. in American Church History from Boston University, has published many articles, and has been author or editor of several books. His newest book is titled *God's Last and Only Hope.* He writes frequently in *The Christian Century,* reporting and interpreting denominational events.

pas—quite embarrassing for the host. Jesus was there, Scripture says, along with his mother and his disciples. And when the wine ran out, Jesus and his mother have words, shall we say. "They have no wine," Mary said. The text implies: and you can do something about it, Jesus. Save them from humiliation; do not let them lose face; help out a little, son. "O woman," Jesus says sternly, "what have you to do with me? My hour has not yet come." How did Mary know he could help? Why did she lay this on him? Had she nagged him before? Is this what the Messiah was about, providing refreshments at parties?

But Mother Mary refuses to take no for an answer. Next thing we know she is giving orders to the servants: "Do whatever he tells you." And apparently Jesus acquiesces. Six stone water jars—big rascals with a capacity of twenty to thirty gallons—are filled (to the brim) with water. And then, somehow, in a twinkling water becomes wine, and not just any old wine. Indeed, the caterer takes one taste and says to the bridegroom: "Usually we serve the good stuff first but you have saved the best until last." One hundred eighty gallons of excellent wine. And scripture comments, this was the first of his signs.

Now I know what you are thinking. He'd better be careful here—talking to a bunch of Southern Baptists, in Kentucky, of all places, about Jesus making 180 gallons of vintage wine. After all, we are the total abstinence people who live by the well-known Bible verse—"lips that touch wine will never touch mine." In all seriousness, we all know of the problems of alcohol and substance abuse in our modern world, so events at Cana aren't such a good subject, particularly the Sunday before Southern Baptist Convention; we've got troubles enough. If you're going to preach about Jesus, Cana, and chardonnay or Chablis, do it with the Episcopalians, the Roman Catholics, or the Lutherans, not here in Calvary Baptist Church.

Yet here this text, staring out at us from Holy Scripture on this Pentecost Sunday, reminds even temperance folks like ourselves of the nature of gospel life. You see, this story isn't just about Cana, it's about the Kingdom of God. It isn't just about spirits, it's about the Spirit, the Holy Spirit. On this day when with Christians around the world we celebrate Pentecost and the coming of the Holy Spirit, what better way to prepare for the Spirit than with a story about a wedding, an embarrassed host, a sensitive woman, an obedient son, and a surprising gift. When the Spirit comes, it's like water turning into wine. Perhaps the spirits in this story are a kind of first century symbol for the Spirit itself.

When the Spirit comes, you see, we celebrate, like at a wedding, at the birth of a baby, at a graduation, even at worship. There are times when you get a little high, a bit intoxicated, not from man-made spirits but from just being with people you love, people who love you, accept you, care for you, and encourage you. People who are fun and bring out the best in you. We've all known those kinds of occasions, haven't we? You went to a party, or a family reunion, a wedding or a church service, mostly out of duty, habit, or boredom, and you did not expect for a moment to enjoy yourself. But something unexpected happened and you started talking to someone, or telling stories, or you just relaxed and listened, and when it was over you were surprised at how good you felt, and you celebrated that moment.

Jesus did too. Jesus loved celebrations, loved having people around him at weddings, on fishing trips, at meals, even an occasional dinner on the ground where he said the blessing and everybody was fed. He carried the spirit of celebration with him wherever he went. Everybody shared in it, except the humorless folk who were worried God would punish them if they had a good time. Even the people who were not used to having much to celebrate. The crippled people, blind people, street people—who had not had occasion for celebrating for a long time—those people felt the Spirit. And, as you might expect, all that celebration got him in trouble with the really religious folks. The disciples of that old anorexic, John the Baptizer, inquired, "Why don't your disciples fast the way we do?" By the way, Jesus, we haven't seen *you* at Wednesday night prayer meeting for quite a while. "Certainly," Jesus replies, "the time for fasting will come, *but*"—and here again is the wedding analogy—"while the bridegroom is nearby, enjoy." And enjoy he did, apparently, so much so that the Pharisees denounced him for "hanging out" with gluttons, winelubbers, tax collectors, and other public sinners and party animals.

No matter when the Spirit comes, when that holy guest is at hand, when you get even a fleeting glimpse of the kingdom, you celebrate. In his book, *The Fire Next Time*, writer James Baldwin writes of life in the black urban ghettos of the 1950s and his efforts to escape that world:

> In spite of everything, there was in the life I fled
> a zest and a joy and a capacity for facing and
> surviving disaster that was very moving and very
> rare. Perhaps we were, all of us, bound together
> by the nature of our oppressions, the specific and
> peculiar complex of risks we had to run; if so,
> within these limits we sometimes achieved with
> each other a freedom that was close to love. I
> remember, anyway, church suppers and outings . . .
> where rage and sorrow sat in the darkness and did
> not stir, and we ate and drank and talked and
> laughed and danced and forgot about "the man."
> (pp. 59–60)

A despairing people sometimes found their way to celebration, together. When Spirit comes, even in oppression, something powerful happens.

In a wonderful movie called *Babette's Feast,* a small Scandinavian religious sect takes in Babette, a French refugee down on her luck. They are a strict and pious, gentle and joyless people, rejecting any hint of worldliness. Babette works for them, cooking and sharing in their somber meals. When Babette receives a financial legacy, however, she shows her gratitude to her Christian friends by preparing a wonderful feast—it turns out she was one of Paris's renowned chefs. And in that feast prepared in love, those austere believers discover the Spirit and a sense of celebration they had never known before: They share warmth, generosity, community, and love. When the Spirit comes, celebration slips in among the predictable, joyless, even painful, moments of our lives.

The Spirit also brings unexpected energy and strength to live out God's good news. Jesus often spoke about the energy of the kingdom, often through the metaphor of fermentation. The kingdom, he said, is like leaven-yeast, a source of fermentation that, when tucked away into an unsuspecting hunk of dough, makes it explode and changes everything inside. Or, he warned, the kingdom is like new wine, just beginning to ferment. Best to put it in new bottles that can endure the stress. They can hold more energy than the old, worn out bottles can contain. Some vessels can't handle the explosion.

That kind of energy descended on the church at Pentecost and impelled that rag-tag band of disciples out in the world, unashamedly proclaiming the story of the resurrected Christ. Pentecost burst out of the old wineskins with new word of God's grace and forgiveness in the new community of the Church. But the Spirit was no flash in the pan, no temporary high. The Spirit brought the energy of endurance. It was energy for the long haul. In every age, the people of God need the energy of the Spirit to help them endure. The world forever seems a dangerous place—the Church itself is torn by conflict and schism. The early Christians, like ourselves, needed energy to endure the hard times, the misunderstanding, the persecution, the bone-tired moments of Christian discipleship. Paul, so energized by the Spirit on Damascus road, learned to endure by the Spirit's power. Thus he wrote, "Hardpressed on every side, we are never hemmed in; bewildered, we are never at our wit's end; struck down, we are not left to die" (2 Cor. 4:8–9). "As God's Servants, we try to recommend ourselves in all circumstances by our steadfast endurance: in hardships and 'dire straits' " (2 Cor. 6:4–5). Sometimes churches and denominations confront dire straits when they require not just the energy of enthusiasm, but the energy of endurance as well—the energy to keep on keeping on, to work through crisis, difficulty, and struggle. When the road to the kingdom takes an unexpected detour and things don't work out as we had planned, even in the Church of Jesus Christ, we need the enduring presence of the Spirit.

Sometimes we cannot celebrate, we can only endure—a spouse dies, a marriage breaks apart, a church or denomination faces crisis, a person experiences fear or depression. In such moments we may endure by remembering the wedding feast, the celebrations, the moments when water turned to wine. Sometimes the Spirit sustains us through memory. I've been to funerals—perhaps you have too—when grief was deep and all too real, and then someone told a story of better times and stronger moments—and that bittersweet moment helped us endure.

Which brings me to a final observation on this Pentecost Sunday. The Spirit brings courage: It has been like that from the first. John's Gospel says that following the Crucifixion, "Late that Sunday evening, when the disciples were together behind locked doors," for fear of the authorities, "Jesus came and stood among them"—the resurrected Christ showed up in their midst bringing courage with him. "Fear not," he said, and the best had again been saved until last. Forty days later, they were gathered again, still scared no doubt, but determined, and the Spirit struck like tongues of fire "dispersed among them and resting on each one." And they were all filled with the Holy Spirit and they went out, fearlessly and sometimes not so fearlessly declaring the good news, in the tongues of people from around the world. That first Pentecost was so amazing that some observers said contemptuously: They are drunk! (Acts 2:1–13). And I guess they were—not drunk with the kind of courage you get from a bottle, but the courage God gives—courage to speak out, speak up, speak dangerously about faith, hope, and love, when people receive you with celebration and when they throw your gospel back in your face. The Spirit doesn't come over us just to make us feel good—it comes to give us courage to face the terrible moments of life:

> like Stephen's courage in the face of his murderers;
> like Paul's courage in shipwreck and prison;
> like Franciscan courage caring for medieval plague
>   victims;
> like Baptist courage in the face of persecution by the
>   state;
> like Rosa Parks's courage on a segregated bus in
>   Montgomery, Alabama.
> Courage to get married and stay married;
> courage to be a single parent;
> courage to stay and courage to go;
> courage to believe in God;
> courage to remain in the Church;
> courage to wait on the kingdom in a world where life,
>   marriages, churches, schools, and families don't turn
>   out the way we'd hoped.

The Spirit does not simply give us courage. Rather, it takes courage to follow the Spirit—for who knows where it will take us? Scripture says that that day in Cana was the first of Jesus' signs. Great fun, turning water into wine; the disciples must have been pleased that they had decided to follow such a hospitable Messiah. Neither they, nor Mother Mary, for that matter, realized for one moment where it would take them, that things would get complicated and controversial, that one day they would drink wine together one last time and Jesus would talk not of water and weddings, but of body and blood, life and death. The Spirit moves where it will—carries us into circumstances not of our choosing, demands more than we expected. No one of us when we start the journey can be certain what faith will require of us down the road. So we need courage, not simply to accept Christ, but to profess Christ on the way, when the wine is new and heady, and when we drink it to the dregs.

So here we sit on another Sunday morning. Some of us are celebrating; some of us are enduring; some of us are desperate for courage.

Whatever our sober condition, we can remember a day when the water turned to wine; a day when the Spirit fell like fire; a day when the Church seemed drunk with the Divine explosion.

And, in times of light and darkness, we can hold on to the God who saves the best until last and who saves the last one best. Good news!

9. Do You Believe in Angels?
Roger Lovette

Psalm 23:6

Do you believe in angels? What kind of a twentieth-century question is that? Angels? Of course we don't. Who here has seen an angel? We smile at such a thought. They are part of that prehistoric time when the world had four corners and the earth was flat. We who live at the end of the twentieth century know better.

In the Bible angels were everywhere. These messengers of God were spiritual beings who served as his command. An angel stood at the gate of the garden to block Adam and Eve's entrance ever again. Isaac would have died in child sacrifice if an angel had not held back the hand of his father, Abraham. Jacob had his ladder of angels that went up and down. And do you remember Elijah's experience? He had run away from Jezebel, the mad queen. And after a long flight for safety he was depressed and felt terribly low. The Scriptures say that an angel came and gave him food to eat. The Psalms may summarize this promise for divine messengers best when it says: "He shall give his angels charge over thee, to keep thee in all thy ways." In the New Testament angels seem to be everywhere. They spoke to Mary and to Joseph. They whispered "Do not be afraid" to shepherds and wise men and it seemed, to everyone. That first Christmas the heavens were filled with angels singing glory and praises to God. Later, at the edge of Jesus' ministry, Luke says that "angels came and ministered to him" in the wilderness. This encounter becomes a prelude to the whole story.

Roger Lovette has served as a pastor in South Carolina, Kentucky, and Tennessee. He is a native of Columbus, Georgia, and a graduate of Samford University (B.A.), The Southern Baptist Theological Seminary (B.D.), and Lexington Theological Seminary (D.Min.). He is the author of *For the Dispossessed, A Faith of Our Own, Questions Jesus Raised,* and *Come to Worship.*

Underneath the surface of life angels really do come and touch God's children in their hour of need.

Embedded in Psalm 23 I have discovered a word about angels that speaks to every age. "Even though I walk through the valley of the shadow of death, I fear no evil; for thou art with me; thy rod and thy staff they comfort me. Thou preparest a table before me in the presence of my enemies; thou anointest my head with oil, my cup overflows. Surely goodness and mercy shall follow me all the days of my life; and I shall dwell in the house of the Lord forever."

Psalm 23 views the world as a difficult place. Notice the psalmist's words. *Valleys. Shadows. Death. Enemies.* His world was filled with pain and evil and injustice and unfairness. Genesis began the story by saying that at the heart of life there is a snake. Most of us encountered him early. I saw his presence scribbled in those ugly words written on that basement bathroom wall in the first grade, but I was too young to understand what they meant. I only knew there was something wrong. Later, on a bus when that old black maid sat down tired and the white man screamed, "Nigger, get up and move to the back," I knew something was wrong. Then, in college when the church I finally joined split right down the middle over the pastor—and I watched him leave, broken and devastated—I knew something was wrong. In my first parish I stood on the porch late one night while an eighteen-year-old mother held a new baby in her arms. She cried and cried. "He won't come home," she sobbed through the tears. "He's drunk and he won't come home." And I knew something was wrong. I faced it again last summer in Germany. Our tour bus passed a road sign that said "Dachau—10 miles" and I remembered the thousands and thousands that did not get out alive. All our lives we have all known that something was wrong. We have seen the power of evil in rape and cancer and child abuse and AIDS and divorce and hurricanes and depression and heartbreak and suicide and death.

The psalmist addressed a difficult world when he wrote about sheep and all their vulnerabilities. They were at the mercy of the elements and their own stupidity, eating poisonous plants and encountering wild animals everywhere. The psalmist says, right in the middle of all this pain and heartbreak there is prepared a table. And on that table, set amid the candlelight and the linen cloth and the best silver, we find a feast for all of life. "Surely goodness and mercy shall follow me all the days of my life. . . ."

Last summer I stood at the Heidelberg Castle in Germany. The castle was high, high on a hill. I pointed to another tourist and said: "Look over the door. Do you see it?" Over the archway of a little entrance there were two tiny angels carved in stone. As people walked back and forth and in and out, overarching all they did were these twin angels. Most people never looked up. But the tiny angels were there. And here, nestled between the pages of a book so large and so filled it is easy to ignore these same angels: goodness and mercy.

A little girl heard this text read one day and said: "No, there are not two angels here—there are three." "Three?" someone asked. "Where?" And she said: "Surely, goodness and mercy." But surely is not the name of an angel, surely is a promise. The promise says: "Only goodness and mercy shall follow me all the days of my life." In the middle of a world shot through with evil—loaded like a land mine—there is a way. We are given these twin angels, goodness and mercy. The biblical scholar Samuel Terrien says they pursue us all the days of our lives. Dr. Terrien says the word *follow* is too weak. The Hebrew text says that goodness and mercy stay close by us. We are overtaken and captured by the goodness and mercy of God.

These messengers come in a hundred different ways. Last Christmas I came home tired one evening and sat down. My wife said: "How do you like it? I found it at an antique store today. It's hand-carved and very old and from Malaysia. Isn't it something." And I asked: "What is it?" "It's an angel," she said. And hanging over the television in the kitchen, next to the table where we take most of our meals, there was suspended this angel. She looked a little like Wonder Woman. And I didn't know that day if I liked that peculiar looking creature or not. But I have gotten used to her. I have even grown to love our angel. She is a reminder that over my life there hangs a providence. And over us all. We are all watched and kept by these twin angels. Wherever we reluctant believers go, we are not alone.

So I am beginning to understand this word *pursued*. My angel is there in the morning when I gobble down my cereal before work. And the angel is there when I read the headlines in the morning paper. And the angel does not move when the phone rings and someone tells me about a bad lab report. And even at night, in the darkness, when I wake from a bad dream and shuffle out of bed and make my way to the faucet, I see her presence glimmering there in the moonlight. Isn't this what the psalmist had in mind? Always with us. Always there, not one angel but two. Never letting us go. Pursuing us always. Goodness and mercy. Let us look at what they mean.

I

We are pursued by the goodness of God. This goodness means many things, but first it especially signifies grace, stubborn steadfastness, faithfulness. This goodness will not let us go, ever. The psalmist reminds the sheep that this shepherd will provide the strength and firmness that they will need. But the promise involves an ethical dimension. The shepherd will always "do the right." And from here there flows that wonderful biblical word *righteousness.* It is what God does: that which is right. "The statutes of the Lord are right. . . ." (Ps. 19:8).

Do you hear it? In the middle of all this mess we call life—there is a center. This grace isn't worked for or earned. But we are pursued by the goodness of God.

The fourth Gospel understood this goodness when the book opened with Jesus' first miracle. A wedding was in progress. And the wine ran out. And they did not know what in the world they would do. It was embarrassing and the hostess was standing there in the kitchen crying, hoping her daughter, the bride, wouldn't find out and spoil the greatest week of her life. The mother did not know what to do. The story said that Jesus was there—enjoying himself enormously. And someone whispered to him: "They have no wine." Jesus did the strangest thing. He took the water pots. There were six of them. And Jesus turned the water into wine. Each water pot held twenty to thirty gallons of water. And Jesus created 120 to 180 gallons of wine. And they tasted it—and said this is the best wine of them all.

Why would anyone begin a gospel or a first miracle with such a story? John was saying that what God brings, in his son Jesus, is not just provisions like drink. But God offers something very, very good. At the table of the Lord we find the best that there is—and nobody need go away thirsty or empty. John's word is abundance.

Is this not what Paul had in mind when he wrote with a flourish to his friends at Ephesus: "Now to him who by the power at work within us is able to do far more abundantly than all that we ask or think, to him be glory in the church and in Christ Jesus to all generations, for ever and ever. Amen" (Eph. 3:20–21).

In a world where babies die and parents disappoint us and someone we love is always dying, we remember this wonderful word *abundantly*. There is a table prepared and over the table there is an angel. And her name is *Goodness*. Pursuing you and me and us and this church and the whole wide world. At the heart of life we are abundantly graced, over and over again, by the goodness of God.

II

But there is another angel in this story. Her name is *Mercy*. This word is used 148 times in the Old Testament alone. Mercy has many meanings. Kindness. Loving-kindness. One translation calls it unfailing love. But the most accurate definition of mercy in our language may be compassion. It is God's kindly and generous disposition, which flows out to any of us in our weakness or misery or helplessness.

Mercy comes from the root word *womb*. So mercy reflects that motherly feeling that is linked to the child she carried in her very body. And no wonder we talk today of the motherhood of God. For mercy is that gathering together as a hen doth gather her brood. We are connected and we are tied with cords that go even beyond the grave. And those of us who have lost our mothers know this in our heart of hearts. They may have slipped into the mystery. But we who have been given this mercied grace of delight and love and kindness carry these gifts like a mantle all our lives. That angel's name is *Mercy*.

In 1970 the strangest thing happened in the Crescent Hill Baptist Church in Louisville, Kentucky. In January of that year the church came together one cold afternoon to attend the funeral service of little Laura Claypool, the pastor's daughter. After a long struggle with leukemia this little nine-year-old girl died. Her father, Dr. John Claypool, has traced his own pilgrimage with grief in a little book called *Tracks of a Fellow Struggler*. But what is not quite as well known is that in that same year there was another little nine-year-old girl in the church. Her name, too, was Laura. She was the daughter of another church staff member, Temp Sparkman. And in that summer when the church was just beginning to recover from its grief the second little Laura died quite suddenly. And the devastation to the family was so hard. And the church wondered how much they could take.

Dr. Sparkman now teaches at a seminary in Kansas City. In 1985, fifteen years after his own great loss, he told his own story in a little volume called *To Live with Hope*. In that book, he looks back over his shoulder at those painful, painful days and this is what he writes:

Was the grass really ever green, the sounds of birds really clearly heard? And did we picnic in the park six short months ago? Here in the cold winter they seem so far away. The naked trees, the leaden skies seem always to have been, and out ahead for endless time, so that we ask if earth were ever green, and if the spring come back again.

Oh yes, the spring will make return. The gray, dull days of cold will pass. The routines now holding us will break. Despair will pass; a reassuring word will come. Presumption that all is lost will be replaced by a shining, fresh expectancy. The future will become a possibility again. The crushing claims on our lives will not forever dominate. In liberation we will learn to choose, and in our choices to be secure.

The sadness weighing down upon us will lift, as Joy sounds her call to us. The cause of sadness will not disappear, but joy will come in spite of it. Then we will laugh again, will dance and sing, will celebrate the life, God's gift to us.

Our draining conflicts will not dissipate. No wind will sweep them fast away. We will go through them and we will withstand. Redemption will accrue from our transactions. Relationships will be rescued and restored. Where breaks are too severe for reconciliation, a healing will in time, be known.

Was the earth really once green, and will
spring come back again? Oh yes, as sure as ever it
were here, as sure as winter is now here, as sure
as God exists, the spring, it will return, the earth
be green again.[1]

Isn't this the heart of our faith? Over our lives, as over that door at Heidelberg, are these two angels. Though there be valleys and shadows and death and enemies we shall not fear for these twin angels follow us all the days of our lives. Wherever we go and whatever we do goodness and mercy are with us always.

NOTE

1. G. Temp Sparkman, *To Live with Hope* (Valley Forge, PA: Judson Press, 1985), 68.

10. Remarks on Rosh Hashanah

Richard Marius

Psalm 98 KJV

> O sing unto the Lord a new song; for he hath done marvelous things; his right hand and his holy arm hath gotten him the victory.
> The Lord hath made known his salvation; his righteousness hath he openly shewed in the sight of the heathen.
> He hath remembered his mercy and his truth toward the house of Israel: all the ends of the earth have seen the salvation of our God.

This is Rosh Hashanah, the Jewish new year. Christians finally adopted the Roman custom of beginning the new year in January. I think we missed a great opportunity by not taking up the Jewish custom of beginning it now. I for one can tell little difference between December and January, at least here in Massachusetts. They are both cold and miserable, and although January is named for Janus, the Roman god of beginnings, it is a month when much of life seems almost to cease or to slow to a dead crawl.

But in September or early October when Rosh Hashanah comes, there seems to be a quickening in the earth. Here in our university the mood of renewal is strong. I never get over my simple joy at seeing the Yard fill up with students after its August emptiness and at greeting my colleagues back from their summer

Richard Curry Marius was born in Martel, Tennessee, and educated at the University of Tennessee, The Southern Baptist Theological Seminary, and Yale University. He is director of expository writing and senior lecturer in English at Harvard University. One of Dr. Marius's books, the biography *Thomas More*, was a finalist in the 1984 American Book Award nonfiction competition. He has also written three novels.

dispersions, ready to take up again our rituals and routines of teaching and learning and simply being together in this community. There always comes a morning—it has come early this year—when I push my bicycle out into the street and realize that the maple tree in front of my house is already turning red, that there is a sharpness in the air portending autumn, and that I have to go back into the house and put on a windbreaker before I pedal to my office. On that morning I am ready to begin a new year.

Our faith, in both its Jewish and Christian manifestations, takes pleasure in new beginnings. They are taken to be a sign that God is still with his people. The rejoicing at a new start is all the greater because of an earlier fear that perhaps we were alone and that God had forsaken us. So it is with the familiar Psalm that I have read to you this morning. "O sing unto the Lord a new song; for he hath done marvelous things: his right hand, and his holy arm, hath gotten him the victory."

Why sing a new song? Because God has led his people back to Jerusalem after captivity and exile in Babylon. The old songs were of distance, of unsatisfied yearning: "O Lord: keep not silence: O Lord, be not far from me." The new song is of victory, return, a new beginning in the land of promise, and in the new beginning is the hand of God.

The Bible abounds with such new beginnings. Abraham goes out from Ur to a new covenant in a new land; the oppressed Israelites make their exodus from Egypt, the land of bondage, and make a new start in the land of promise. And the New Testament is yet another new beginning. "Therefore if any man be in Christ," Paul wrote to the Corinthians, "he is a new creature: old things are passed away; behold, all things are become new."

And yet for both Christians and Jews, there is a paradox here. The new in the Bible is always seen not as something *utterly* new but as a step on the way back to the pristine and original state of the old. The covenant with Abraham and the testament of Christ both look back to Eden and the conviction of Jews and Christians alike that God created this world neither by accident not aberration but for some good purpose. The new song that our psalmist sings in the text of the morning is of return to the old holy city of David, Jerusalem the golden—a new start in an old place sanctified by an ancient promise. God is in the new start because he was also in the older beginning that provided the materials from which the new start might be made and shaped. He is in the new year because he was also in the old.

Every new academic year represents a new start. Here a new class comes gingerly into Harvard Yard, many of its members sure that they got here by accident, because some fool on the admissions committee nodded. But in fact they are here for this new beginning because of a past life that has added up to something. Their faculty members will teach them traditions from the past seen in the light of new books, new theories, new discoveries. A university exists, it seems to me, to preserve, to revere, and to pass on the old through the continual transformations of new beginnings. Education is a living process of eternal return.

Yes, there *is* something perverse in human nature or perhaps in the nature of things that makes our products fall short of our plans and at times fatigues us so that like the world-weary writer of the Book of Ecclesiastes we may lament, "The thing that hath been, it is that which shall be; and that which is done is that which shall be done; and there is no new thing under the sun."

Yet our faith that creation is fundamentally good means that we can labor within it in the trust that something good from our work will endure to provide the material for a new start someday. Our hope at new beginnings is a reaffirmation of the faith that we have inherited something worth transforming. And so I wish for you all a happy new year and new songs to sing in its new days.

11. What Shall I Cry?
H. G. M. Williamson

Isaiah 40:1–11

We have an expression in English (I don't know whether it comes across in American!). Imagine two students in discussion about someone they know, and one is running him down by saying "Oh, he's not a very good student, he doesn't know what he's talking about." The other might remark "Well, you've got nothing to shout about." It is a way of saying, "Who are you to talk? You're no better yourself."

In the passage we have before us, the first eleven verses of Isaiah, chapter 40, we find that there is somebody who has a great deal to shout about, and indeed the keynote of this passage in the older translations are the words *to cry,* which simply mean "to shout." It comes in verse 2, "Cry unto her that her warfare is accomplished." It also comes in verse 3, in verse 6, and in verse 9. There is a lot of shouting going on in this passage. The question is, what does this person, or indeed in some cases, what do these people or maybe these angelic beings have to shout about? I want to suggest that they have three things to shout about.

First, in verses 1 and 2, they shout to *encourage* the people. "Comfort ye, comfort ye my people, saith your God. Speak ye comfortably to Jerusalem, and cry unto her that her warfare is accomplished, that her iniquity is pardoned, that she hath received of the Lord's hand double for all her sins." These words are addressed to

H. G. M. Williamson is Regius Professor of Hebrew in the University of Oxford. He was graduated from the University of Cambridge with the Ph.D. degree and taught there from 1975 until taking up his appointment at Oxford. For several seasons he participated in the archaeological excavations at Lachish and at Jezreel. He has written commentaries on the books of Chronicles and on Ezra and Nehemiah, and numerous articles in a wide variety of journals, Festschriften, encyclopedias, and so on. This sermon was preached on the Tuesday after Easter Sunday.

a people who are in the depths of despair. If you just glance down a little further in the chapter to verse 27, you will see what characterizes their attitude. They say, "My way is hidden from the Lord, and my judgment"—that is to say, my appeal, my case—"is passed away from my God." This is a people, as I am sure you are aware, who are in exile 900 miles away from Jerusalem and from the Promised Land. They have been there for several decades, and most of them feel that away from the temple and the holy city, away from the land of Israel, there is no way in which they can communicate with God. They feel as foreigners, strangers, alienated not only from home but more poignantly alienated from their God, and most of them are in despair. "Our way is hidden from God. We have prayed, we have lamented, we have cried to God, but it seems that the heaven is closed and that God no longer cares."

Of course, a few of them took a more pragmatic attitude. They said, "Here we are, we are away from home and so we are away from God. Let's make the best of a bad job. Let's see if we cannot advance ourselves and improve our position. Let's eat, drink, and be merry, for tomorrow we die." And so, some of them began to rise to quite senior positions in the foreign land, whether in Babylon or later under the empire of the Persians. We know, for instance, of a character like Nehemiah (later than this, of course), who rose to a very important position of trust in the Persian court.

Now, it seems to me that these two responses to a sense of exile characterize much of our society today. Certainly in England, and from what I can see also here in America, I guess that there are many people who feel either that God doesn't exist, or if he does exist he doesn't care, he doesn't really know what is going on. He is some far removed and distant being. People are what they make of themselves. And so they respond by saying, "Let's make the best of this life, it is all we've got. Let's try to advance ourselves and promote our own interests. If we trample on a few others in the process, no matter. If we destroy the environment for future generations, what does it matter? All that matters is today and now—advancing myself and perhaps my family." That seems to characterize so many people today.

And yet at the same time, we need to have eyes that are open to the other type of person, to those who are plunged into despair, to those who are hurting because they are the ones who are made poor by others' wealth; because, like the psalmists of old, they cry to God, but they feel that their words are not getting through. It is to people in such a situation that these words are addressed, "Comfort ye, comfort ye my people."

For years, particularly as a child, these words were familiar to me from Handel's *Messiah*. As I am sure you know, they are the opening words to that oratorio. You will remember how the tenor soloist sings "Comfort ye, comfort ye," and goes on singing "comfort ye" for a very long time. At the end, he tacks on "my people, says your God," almost as an afterthought. And, because I was familiar with it in that form, I thought that this was addressed to the people: "Comfort ye, O my people; cheer up, my people." I thought the words "my people" were what we technically call a vocative.

But actually, that is not the case, and the newer translations make that clear. It is a command in the plural to a group of people, perhaps to God's messengers, to go and bring comfort to his people. And please notice that these are not empty words. This isn't just "cheer up, put on a happy face." I remember very vividly when my father died. I was only fifteen at the time, and I was away at boarding school. Of course, I came home to be with my mother and my sister. And in those few difficult days before the funeral a very well meaning lady rang up to express her sympathy. The best she could say was, "Well, never mind." "Never mind?!!" The bottom had just fallen out of my world. I didn't know what the future held for me. "Never mind?" Those words sounded so hollow and so empty, and yet aren't they typical of the way that we often speak to people whose hurts may be much deeper than what we can see from their faces? We say, "Cheer up." We try to be kind, but our words are an empty mockery.

But when God speaks to encourage his people, he doesn't speak like that. When he says, "Comfort my people," there is reason for comfort, there is substance to what he says. I scarcely need to remind you that these words, "Comfort *my people,* says *your God,*" resonate with hundreds of years of Israelite history and religion. They are the reaffirmation of that great covenant statement, "You shall be *my people,* and I shall be *your God.*" These words begin to affirm again that there is a relationship being reestablished between the people who felt so far off and the God who, in reality, was so near.

My people, your God! There is substance to God's word, and that continues in verse 2: "Cry to her that her warfare is accomplished. Her iniquity is pardoned. She has received double for all her sins"—a difficult phrase, that; it is probably legal language saying that full restitution has been made. These words mark a wholly new beginning in God's dealings with his people. And it seems to me that they are words that we can take with very little difficulty and apply to ourselves today in the latter part of the twentieth century. For the God who says "Remember not the former things, . . . behold, I do a new thing" is the God who is active in our Lord Jesus Christ to do a wholly new thing.

Two days ago was Easter Sunday. When Christ burst the bonds of death, he inaugurated a whole new way of life in which you and I share. The work of Christ is something that enables God to proclaim, "Behold, I make all things new." And because of that, we don't have to be shackled by the past. So often we feel bound by past failings and mistakes. In your academic work (those of you who are still studying) I am quite sure that there have been occasions when you have been despondent because of some paper you turned in on which you got a lower grade, a lower mark, than you had hoped. And you feel, "Should I go on; is it worth it?" But God is a God of new beginnings. More widely and more generally, people are sometimes crippled by guilt. Even in the Christian Church they feel that they have done something that means they can never advance in the work of Christ. For others it may be a difficult time in a relationship when we feel that things have gone irrevocably wrong. We need to hear again these words of encouragement. "Comfort my people," those messengers were told; "cry that their time of hard service is over." What a wonderful time, Easter, to remind ourselves of the new things that God can do.

But the shouting is not only to encourage the people, for second, in verses 3 through 8, we are told that they cry in order to *empower* the people as they face the future.

These verses split into two equal parts. You will notice that each part begins the same: "The voice of one who cries" in verse 3, and "The voice of one saying 'Cry' " in verse 6. And each little bit ends the same: The end of verse 5 says "the mouth of the Lord has spoken it," and verse 8, "but the word of our God shall stand for ever." Parallel beginnings and endings; it makes a neat little package.

In the first half of the paragraph, verses 3 to 5, we read, "The voice of one who cries, 'Prepare in the wilderness the way of the Lord, make straight in the desert a high way for our God. Every valley shall be exalted, and every mountain and hill shall be made low; the crooked shall be made straight, and the rough places plain. And the glory of the Lord shall be revealed, and all flesh shall see it together, for the mouth of the Lord has spoken it.' "

These people are shortly to be summoned to go on a journey back from their captivity in Babylon to Jerusalem. It is a long, hard, dangerous journey through desert country, through mountainous terrain. Tremendous problems confront them before they can get back to the holy city. And they are given words here that should empower them before they set out on their journey. Although the difficulties seem to pile up like mountains, although the problems go deeper than any valley, there is a way through. (These may be literal mountains, but not long afterward we are reminded in Zechariah chapter 4 that mountains can speak of difficulties. Zerubbabel, as he was rebuilding the temple, was told, "What is this great mountain? Before Zerubbabel it will become like a level plain.")

How is it that these physical difficulties that they face will be made surmountable? Well, the secret is that it is not just their journey, it is not just their own passage through the desert: "Prepare in the wilderness the way *of the Lord.*" So far as I am aware, this was the first time in recorded history that an exiled people returned to their homeland, and people then, as in the centuries since, have seen in that remarkable reversal evidence that this was the work of God—the way of the Lord. And so, if it was God's journey, if God was in their midst, then the glory of the Lord was in it. That glory may not have been revealed in bright lights and flashing neon signs, but it was nevertheless equally truly revealed in more mundane forms of humble service.

Similarly, as you confront difficulties in looking to the future, you may feel that they rise up before you like great mountains. The prophet says, "Prepare in the wilderness the way of the Lord." If it is God's way, my experience has been, and I trust it will be yours as well, that as we step out in faith and in obedience to God's call it is as though the great chasm floor rises up to meet our feet. And though we approach mountains that seem insurmountable, God has his way through. Some of you, for instance, may face difficulties as you continue your study in the seminary. The debts you are running up at the bank may seem like a pretty big mountain sometimes. But if it is God's call, then I can testify from my own experience that God has a way through that for you. Or maybe it is simply in living out our Christian faith. That produces difficulty enough sometimes, doesn't it? How can we go forward, living the Christian life of humility, of love, of kindness, of self-control—the fruits of the Spirit? How can I live as a Christian in today's world? There are external difficulties that may face us, but if it be God's way, then we have the assurance that he will accompany us on the journey to drive a way through for the sake of his glory.

So the first part of the paragraph deals with external difficulties, but the second half deals with internal problems. You may be saying right now, "That's all very well, Mr. Preacher, that's all very fine, but I know my own heart, I know how weak I am." That, at any rate, is how the prophet seems to have responded. "What shall I cry? All flesh is grass, and all the goodliness thereof is as the flower of the field. The grass withers, the flower fades, because the breath of the Lord blows upon it." And to that sense of weakness that we all share the response comes, "Yes, that's quite correct; that's absolutely right: 'Surely flesh *is* grass. The grass *does* wither, the flower *does* fade—BUT the word of our God shall stand for ever.' "

You may say, "What has that got to do with it? The word of our God? I thought that was the Bible. That may stand for ever, but how does that help me inside with all of my doubts and upsets and turmoils?" Well, Peter has the answer for us, because, of course, this is not speaking of the word of God in the sense of the Bible; Peter tells us very plainly what it is. At the end of chapter 1 of his first epistle, he quotes these verses. He introduces the quotation by saying "Having been regenerated, not of corruptible seed, but of incorruptible, through the word of God, which liveth and abideth," and then after the quotation he adds, "And this is the word of good tidings which was preached unto you." I keep to the translation "regenerated" advisedly. Many translations here use "born again," and of course that is what it means. I have no objection to that, but the trouble is that those words, *born again,* have become so debased and devalued in our modern Christian parlance that they have lost the impact and the meaning that both Peter and the other New Testament writers would have brought to them. We glibly talk about someone being a "born-again Christian," which means that they talk our kind of language or something like that. And we fail to realize what it means to be born again, to be born of the Spirit of God, to be given new life that comes into our feeble and tormented mortal bodies and that, by his Spirit, works inwardly to begin to produce new fruit. This is the Word of God by which the heavens and the earth were made. When God said, "Let there be light," there was light! And that light has shone into our hearts, we are told, to bring the knowledge of the glory of Jesus Christ. This is the most powerful word that there could possibly be, and we must not devalue it; we must not just use it as a glib slogan. We need to use it bearing in mind that this is the mighty creative Word of God that transforms and renews, so that even though the external problems are there, and even though inwardly we feel weak, the prophet is given a message to empower his listeners and, I believe, *us* also today as *we* confront God's call to the future.

And finally, in verses 9 through 11, having spoken to encourage them as regards the problems of the past and to empower them for the future, he speaks to *evangelize* them in the present. "O thou that tellest good tidings to Zion, get thee up into the high mountain; O thou that tellest good tidings to Jerusalem, lift up thy voice with strength; lift it up, be not afraid; say unto the cities of Judah, Behold, your God!"

I wonder when was the last time in common language that you said "Behold!" It is one of those words that carries enormous overtones for us, but any of you who have spent some time in Israel and know how it is used in modern Hebrew will realize that it is just about one of the most common words in the language. Maybe you are sitting at a table, and you're eating your hamburger and fries or whatever it is, and you want a little salt, but it is across the table. So you say, "Will you please pass the salt?" And the other person, who may not be feeling very sociable, pushes it across and grunts "Here y'are." Well, in Hebrew they say, "Behold the salt." And so, if I may say it reverently, when the prophet says, "Behold your God," he simply means, "Here's God." Right here, as close as that, as normal and as common as that. It is not particularly church language. It is not great ecclesiastical phraseology; it is something close and intimate and real. And those who tell good tidings to Zion are encouraged to say as they see these people returning from Babylon, "Here is God." And what a God we have here! He comes as a conqueror with his captives: "Behold, the Lord God will come as a mighty one, and his arm shall rule for him." He comes as a workman with his wages: "Behold, his reward is with him, and his recompense before him." He comes as a shepherd with his sheep: "He shall feed his flock like a shepherd, he shall gather the lambs in his arm, and carry them in his bosom, and shall gently lead those that give suck."

Let me conclude with that lovely picture of the shepherd and his sheep. You are all thinking of John, chapter 10, aren't you—the Good Shepherd? Fair enough, but let me give you an alternative of the shepherd that I think is very illuminating—the shepherd in the Near East leading his flock through sometimes very desolate and hot country. In Genesis 33 we have a good picture of that shepherd. You remember Jacob returning home and meeting Esau? He was frightened at first, but Esau had met him and said, "Come on, I have a great party waiting for you back home. Let's rush on and get to it." But Jacob says (vv. 13–14), "My lord knoweth that the children are tender, and that the flocks and herds with me give suck; and if they overdrive them one day, all the flocks will die. Let my lord, I pray thee, pass over before his servant; and I will lead on softly, according to the pace of the cattle that is before me and according to the pace of the children, until I come unto my lord unto Seir."

That is a good shepherd. Some of the sheep have recently had lambs, and if they go too fast the sheep's milk will dry up and the lambs will die. If you are taking a flock through difficult country, you have to go at the pace of the slowest. You have to drive gently, for if you overdrive them in your haste, it will be to your and their cost. And our God comes to us as a good shepherd. "He shall feed his flock. . . . He shall gather the lambs in his arm, he will carry them . . . and gently lead those that give suck." It is in that character that God comes with his people on their journey.

Sometimes people come and say, "We must go out there and do great things for God." Up near Boston the other day I heard a sermon that I was most impressed with. The preacher said that we hear too much of doing great things for God today. We should concentrate on doing little things for God. We hear too much of power and changing the world and the Church; we hear too little of service, of self-abasing, of following in the footsteps of our Lord Jesus Christ who took the form of a servant, "becoming obedient unto death, even the death of the cross." And it is the Good Shepherd who leads us; one who isn't necessarily asking you to go out and change the world and then get hung up with all kinds of guilt complexes when you don't succeed. We are dealing with a shepherd who knows each one of his sheep intimately, who knows your strengths and weaknesses, who understands exactly what is going on in your heart—those things that you don't even share with your spiritual mentors or your professors. He says, "I will take you at your pace, in order that you may fulfill that ministry for which I have called you." Don't be dissuaded by people who try to turn you from that path. "Behold your God." He is close; he is at hand; he wants to deal with you like that.

So, as you will appreciate, this is a favorite passage of mine in Scripture. To encourage us, yes; and to empower us for what God would call us to do; but also to evangelize us, Christians though we be, in the best sense of the word—to point us again to the gracious character of the God with whom we have to do.

12. Rhythms

Richard F. Wilson

Ecclesiastes 3:1–15; Romans 12:1–2

Georgia author Ferrol Sams captured the moment with uncanny accuracy and feeling, a moment that has been repeated countless times over decades—including the 1990s—and will be repeated a few more times this weekend, even on our own campus. Hear the words and live again the scene:

> He approached his mother with an impersonal kiss
> and conflicting feelings. Over the summer she had
> become the focus of his eagerness to leave home.
> She had found innumerable tasks for him to do
> around the house and yard, "before," she said,
> "you leave for good." He began to feel that her
> sole function that summer was to annoy and
> irritate him. He felt so nagged and nattered, so
> constantly suppressed and directed, so badgered
> and harassed that he often wanted to scream,
> "Leave me alone!" Such rebelliousness, of course,
> would have produced upheaval in the secure order
> of things and was unthinkable. Instead Porter had
> responded with exasperated sighs, patient and
> formal answers through gritted teeth, unwitnessed
> rolling of eyes, *and extreme feelings of guilt.*[1]

Porter Osborne, Jr., was leaving for his first year of college; he and his mother had been and were responding to the rhythms of life that set the beat for such times. All summer Porter had known

---

Richard F. Wilson is Associate Professor and Dean of the Chapel at Mercer University in Macon, Georgia. He received his Master of Divinity and Doctor of Philosophy degrees at the Southern Baptist Theological Seminary. Wilson was a contributor to the *Mercer Dictionary of the Bible.*

it was a "time to keep silence" as well as his mother had known it was a "time to keep." But now he was leaving. Leaving was a different time, a "time for casting away" for his mother, Vera, and for the self-conscious teenage boy it was a "time for speaking"—although in measured tones.

With eyes brimming the mother prepared to let her son go. "Oh, my son," she said. "I'm going to miss you! Walk with God and grow in grace."[2] What happens next is a double-exposure only possible in good writing—Porter gives his mother a tight hug and sincere kiss and offers a casual "good-bye." The reader, however, hears the thoughts, the quiet speaking, in Porter's heart:

> What moved him of a sudden was a feeling of remorse that he could have ever been ashamed of this lovely person who had done him nothing but good all his life. . . . [But h]e could not bear to let anyone see how very precious this woman was to him. Big boys had to outgrow their mothers.[3]

Life does have its rhythms. Rites of passage—like leaving home for the first time and arriving at a new place for the first time—measure the beats that set the rhythm that establish the tone of our lives. We knew that long before we heard it expressed in the beautiful poetry of Ecclesiastes; the poetry of Ecclesiastes merely reminds us once more of the universal truth of life: There is a rhythm to our existence.

Through the ages philosophers and sages have attempted to extrapolate the meaning of life by focusing on the rhythm; the results have run the gamut from the Stoics of ancient Greece who insisted that everything in life was precisely determined, to the twentieth century nihilists who deny the possibility of any enduring meaning in existence. The Stoics claimed that the meaning of life *was* its rhythm and, therefore, they encouraged one another to "go with the flow" and experience the harmonies of life. In quite the other direction, the nihilists of our century have flatly refused that life and time have any meaning whatsoever. For them life is to be endured, little more. Any attempt to find meaning in life is futile.

William Faulkner's Quentin Compson echoes the despair of those who decide life is a meaningless rhythm and an empty tune. In *The Sound and the Fury* Quentin awakens in his Harvard dormitory and hears the steady ticking of his watch.

When the shadow of the sash appeared on the
curtains it was between seven and eight o'clock and
then I was in time again, hearing the watch. It was
Grandfather's and when Father gave it to me he
said, Quentin, I give you the mausoleum of all
hope and desire; it's rather excruciatingly apt that
you will use it to gain the *reducto absurdum* of all
human experience which can fit your individual
needs no better than it fitted his or his father's. I
give it to you not that you may remember time,
but that you may forget it now and then for a
moment and not spend all your breath trying to
conquer it. Because no battle is ever won he said.
They are not even fought. The field only reveals
to man his own folly and despair, and victory is an
illusion of philosophers and fools.[4]

Stoic determinism and the pessimism of Faulkner's Quentin
Compson provide the "tick" and "tock" of the available approaches
to the rhythms of life. They provide something of the extremes of
expression folks like you and I adopt when we face the undeniable
ebb and flow of life and life's experiences. "Tick-tock"; "tick-tock";
"tick-tock"; beneath life's rhythm comes the call: "Get with the program! Listen to the beat! Go with the flow!" Or, again, the "tick-
tock"; "tick-tock"; "tick-tock" issues the subtle invitation to become
numb to life and life's rhythms, or the subtle invitation to be lulled
into hopeless complacency or inactivity.

The good news this morning is that neither the Stoics of old
nor Faulkner of late has said all that can be said about life and its
rhythms. The good news this morning is that there is another way
to understand our rhythmic existence. The good news this morning can be found in the poetry of Ecclesiastes that we heard read
some moments ago:

For everything there is a season, and a time for every matter under
   heaven:
a time to be born, and a time to die;
a time to plant, and a time to pluck up what is planted;
a time to kill, and a time to heal;
a time to break down, and a time to build up;
a time to weep, and a time to laugh;
a time to mourn, and a time to dance;
a time to cast away stones, and a time to gather stones together;

a time to embrace, and a time to refrain from embracing;
a time to seek, and a time to lose;
a time to keep, and a time to cast away;
a time to rend, and a time to sew;
a time to keep silence, and a time to speak;
a time to love, and a time to hate;
a time for war, and a time for peace. (Eccles. 3:1–8)

The "tick-tock"; "tick-tock"; "tick-tock" of life is clear in the poet's words. Yes, the poet does speak of a regularity of life: Time does give way to time. What separates the writer of Ecclesiastes from the cynical Stoic or the pessimistic Quentin Compson is that the poet refuses to listen to the "tick" apart from the "tock"—refuses to listen to the "tock" without first hearing the "tick."

The rhythms of life may indeed form a beat, of sorts. But for the poet of Ecclesiastes the ebb and flow of life is nothing more than the rhythm of God's grace. Life in its fullness, its ups and downs, its brightnesses and darknesses, is the rhythm of grace. Life itself is a *gift* from God, as the poet says: "it is God's gift . . . that every one should . . . take pleasure in all his toil" (Eccles. 3:13). Said another way, the poet of Ecclesiastes understands that God sets the rhythm of all life so we might establish the tone of our lives!

At least that is how *I* understand the provocative words, "He has made everything beautiful in its time; also he *has put eternity into [the hu]man mind,* yet so that [we] cannot find out what God has done from beginning to the end" (Eccles. 3:11). Imagine! God putting all of eternity in our minds, giving us the ability to grasp the enormity of all that is and, at the same time, liberating us from the need to understand all that is!

Thomas Kelly, an American Quaker now fifty years in the grave, left behind a powerful influence when he died prematurely at age forty-seven. His words ring with the rhythm of grace, capturing the tone of a life fully lived. Listen!

> Deep within us all there is an amazing inner
> sanctuary of the soul, a holy place, a Divine
> Center, a speaking Voice, to which we may
> continually return. *Eternity is at our hearts, pressing
> upon our time-worn lives, warming us with intimations
> of an astounding destiny, calling us home unto Itself.*
> Yielding to these persuasions, gladly committing

ourselves in body and soul, utterly and completely
to the Light Within, is the beginning of true life.[5]

I do not know if Thomas Kelly built the sentiment just expressed around the thoughts of Ecclesiastes 3. I do know, however,
that Kelly and the Old Testament poet are kin of heart and mind
and soul. And I am convinced of the truth that rings through the
words of the Quaker seeker and the Hebrew poet: *God has placed
eternity in our minds and hearts and souls.* God in us—in heart and
mind and soul—is nothing more and nothing less than grace, it is
"a gift from God." God in us—in heart and mind and soul—is "a
Divine Center" around which our "time-worn lives" may find "the
beginning of true life." God in us—in heart and mind and soul—
provides the harmony of our lives as we respond to the rhythms
of grace.

Each of us here this morning has been brought to this place
through myriad turns along life's journey. Collectively, I am sure,
we have plumbed life's depths and scaled the heights as well. Collectively we know and have known times of birth and death, times
of laughing and weeping, times of holding tight and times of letting go. Collectively we stand at the very edge of eternity, strangely
shaped and moved by the mystery of God's grace as it has been
made known to us through the rhythms of life's ebb and flow.

And so it seems to me that our task of the day—and those days
that loom ahead in our immediate future—is to pursue once again
the rhythms of grace as we plunge headlong together into the future that awaits us.

But how? How is it possible to plunge headlong into the future?
Is not the future filled with snares and traps that threaten to crush
all of our past? The Stoic of old would counsel us with the confidence that "things will work out" because, after all, they always do.
The pessimist of the day would caution us not to expect too much
because, after all, the future is always uncertain. But what would be
the counsel of one attuned to the rhythms of God and God's grace?

Perhaps the New Testament lesson we heard earlier can instruct us. Hear again those familiar words of Paul:

> I appeal to you therefore, brethren, by the mercies
> of God, to present your bodies as a living sacrifice,
> holy and acceptable to God, which is your spiritual

worship. Do not be conformed to this world *but be
transformed by the renewal of your mind,* that you may
prove what is the will of God, what is good and
acceptable and perfect. (Rom. 12:1–2)

The apostle reminds us that grace is always a present reality!
By the mercy of God the living of life day by day is the arena where
we meet and are met by God. When Paul encouraged his friends
in Rome to "present your bodies as a living sacrifice" he was also
encouraging every generation—including this one—to pursue God
in the present so that God will be known in the future. For Paul it
is living *now* according to the rhythms of grace that allows us to
recognize God and his "will" in all tomorrows.

The "will of God," as Paul calls it, is an elusive and mysterious
concept. There are those in our world who would have us believe
that the "will of God" is a fact that is discovered and *then* acted
upon—some kind of blueprint for life bestowed from above that
directs the path of people like you and me through the mazes and
struggles of life. For these same people the will of God seems to be
little more than a memory that still exerts some influence.

How different from the idea of Paul! For Paul the "will of God"
is the result of a constant, daily *renewal of the mind* that breaks free
from the expected and accepted patterns of life. "Do not be conformed," the apostle says, "but be transformed by *the renewal of your
mind,* that you may prove what is the will of God."

I do not know if Paul built his sentiments around the thoughts
of Ecclesiastes 3, the poet's conviction that God "has put eternity
into [the human] mind." But I do know that both Paul and the poet
challenge us to see more in life than the patterns left in the wake
of our changing world, and I know that both Paul and the poet
challenge us to hear more than the tick-tock, tick-tock, tick-tock,
that marks the turns we take each time we come to a fork in life's
road.

Seeing *only* the patterns we leave behind and hearing *only* the
clatter of our past choices robs us of the genuine power of the
gospel—the good news that there is another rhythm at work in our
world, another rhythm at work in our lives, and that is the rhythm
of the grace of God.

These are dangerous words falling from Paul's pen (but of
course the gospel is always "dangerous")! "Do not be conformed,"

he says. Do not get locked in to the expectations others have for you or even the expectations you have for yourself. "Do not be conformed," he says, "but be transformed by *the renewal of your mind,* that you may prove the will of God."

There is that elusive, mysterious concept, again, "the will of God." For Paul, it seems, the will of God is not something we can find and *then* act upon. No. The will of God is the transforming power of grace that we experience day by day in seeking to respond to the rhythms of our life. The will of God is not something I find and act upon; the will of God is what I experience in the transforming presence of grace.

I do not know if Paul was thinking about the poetry of Ecclesiastes when he suggested that an experience of the will of God comes about through the renewal of the mind. But I do know that Paul and the Old Testament poet are kin of heart and mind and soul. And I am convinced of the truth that rings through the words of the apostle and the Hebrew poet: *God has placed eternity in our minds and hearts and souls.* God in us—in heart and mind and soul—is nothing more and nothing less than grace, it is "a gift from God." God in us is nothing less than the source of the rhythm of grace, that transforming power of heart and mind and soul that sets us free so we might "prove what is the will of God, what is good and acceptable and perfect."

We began twenty minutes ago with a glimpse of Vera Osborne bidding her son, Porter, farewell as he left for college. She gave him good advice, you will recall. Her advice is also good for us today. "Walk with God and grow in grace," she said.

Walk with God and grow in grace.

Amen.

NOTES

1. Ferrol Sams, *The Whisper of the River* (Atlanta: Peachtree Publications Limited, 1984), 13, emphasis added.

2. Ibid.

3. Ibid., 14.

4. William Faulkner, *The Sound and the Fury* (New York: Random House, 1929), 93.

5. Thomas R. Kelly, *A Testament of Devotion* (New York: Harper & Row, 1941), 29, emphasis added.

13. For Those Who Trust in God

Michael Hough

Matthew 14:22–33

For a proper understanding of our Gospel story, we need to go back to the beginning of the Bible, to the opening verses of Genesis. There we find the author presenting a clear theological understanding of our human existence. Without God there is an empty void, chaos, and darkness. With God's powerful presence, there is creative life and light:

> In the beginning the earth was a formless void. A
> raging ocean covered everything and darkness
> engulfed the waters. Over the deep hovered the
> Spirit of God.

The sea, especially a storm at sea, conjured up for the Hebrew people visions of this original state of terror and chaos. They were just not a seafaring nation, and the savage storms that rushed down upon the Sea of Galilee and the Mediterranean seemed to attack the very order of nature itself. They felt powerless. Tossed around by forces that they could neither predict nor control. This was the state of things before the intervention of God. Into this primeval chaos came the creating and ordering hand of Yahweh. But central to an understanding of this action is an appreciation of the fact that the darkness was not destroyed by God. Nor was the deep dried up. Even though it was potentially destructive for his creatures,

---

Michael Hough is Dean of the Anglican Cathedral, Thursday Island, Australia. Hough has served as a missionary priest in Papua, New Guinea, and was the general secretary of the YMCA in Wellington, England. Hough received his STL at Gregorian University in Rome.

God did not destroy it. He controlled it, just as he controlled the darkness, setting limits to its powers and even enabling good to come from it—nighttime and rest from the darkness, and life supporting food from the sea. In God there is peace, not because the terrors are destroyed, but because in the midst of the terrors God's creative powers are at work limiting them and transforming them into agents of peace and light.

Matthew, the most Jewish of the Gospel writers, would have been well aware of this background to the storm at sea, and the way he has written his account of this incident from the life of Jesus highlights some exciting insights into our human existence.

In our story we have both of these elements—water and darkness—and both of them are raging around the disciples. They know where they want to be: at a rendezvous with Jesus on the far side of the lake, but despite their efforts, they are just not making any progress. They have been working hard all night, shifting sail, pulling on oars, bailing out the water from the bottom of their small boat and all the time getting nowhere. There were men among them who were skilled fishermen, used to this sort of work, and they would have been applying their many skills and natural strengths to make landfall. There would have been others who were anxious, perhaps frightened, and more than likely one or two who were quite ill. For all their efforts they could make no headway against the combined forces of the elements. The water, the wind, and the darkness were too much for them and nothing they could do could bring them any closer to their meeting with the Lord.

And so, in the fourth watch of the night, between three and six in the morning, just as the night was ending, Jesus came to them. Over the top of the water. Walking on the water that was proving to be such a threat to the men in the boat. Here we have the wonderful picture of the Son of God coming to the disciples over the water. And the extraordinary thing is that they did not recognize him. Even worse, they thought that he was a ghost! These are the men who had traveled with him, sat at his feet, heard him preach and teach, and generally shared their intimate lives with him—and yet they failed to recognize him. Why? At this stage, apart from noting that Matthew makes it clear that it is possible for disciples to fail to recognize the Lord, an answer to this question will have to wait until a little later in our reflection.

It is the response of Jesus that is significant at this stage. He does not calm the storm. He does not still the waves. He does nothing to take away the forces that are working against the disciples. Instead, he addresses the disciples in the bottom of the boat: "Take courage! It's me! Don't be afraid!"

And here Matthew goes straight to the heart of biblical spirituality. There is no need to fear the wind and the waves if "I am here." Jesus is demanding courage from the disciples. Courage in the midst of the waves and wind. His first action is not to calm the storm but to remind them that if they were to focus their attention on his presence, then they would not be so concerned about the storm. They would be relieved that their Lord was with them, coming to them over the top of the water, unharmed and undeterred by the wind and the waves. While the storm with all of its fury is hindering their progress, it is unable to stop Jesus from coming. It is this very clear picture that Matthew wants etched into the hearts and minds of the believers to whom he is writing.

And then we see Peter speaking out first, and his response is almost as amazing as the appearance of the Lord. He says: "Lord? If it is truly you, tell me to come to you over the top of the water."

Peter wants to be able to come to Jesus over the water, or on top of the water. Not in the water, or through the water, but over the water. He wanted to find his way to Jesus without getting his feet wet, without having to worry about the storm, the wind, and the waves. He wanted to be raised up to a new level where the furies could not reach him and where he could be free of fear and anxiety. It is significant for our story that he did not ask Jesus to save them or ask him to calm the wind and the waves. That kind of rescue has little to do with the real meaning of the story. Peter is shown as seeking to come to Jesus free from the buffeting of the waters that were tossing his fellow disciples around and filling them with fear. He wanted a way through the storm—and this is just what Jesus offered him. We do not know from the text just how Jesus answered this demand, but I suspect that there was something of a chuckle in his voice when he told Peter to come on.

Everything went ahead smoothly. At least for the start. Peter, heading toward Jesus, was walking on water. He could do it! While he was focused in on the Lord he could walk over the turbulent seas. But then something happened. As Matthew pointedly puts it—Peter suddenly noticed the wind. He looked around and saw the huge waves rolling round the lake and felt the wind whipping at his face. He turned from Jesus and began to see what was happening to him. How absurd it must have seemed! There he was, a mere man, walking over the top of a stormy sea. What he was doing was impossible! The wind and the waves must defeat him. Common sense says so. Experience says so. It is only Jesus himself who disagrees when he says, "Yes, come on." But Peter had taken his eyes from Jesus, and the consequences were felt at once. He did not immediately sink to the bottom, but rather, more significantly, "began to sink." It is as if the more he turned from Jesus, the more he began to go down. The more he focused his thoughts on the storm and the waves, the further and further he sank beneath the waves. Till in the end, all but overcome, he once more calls out to Jesus, "Lord. Save me." At once, Jesus stretched out his hand and took hold of him. He saved him. He pulled him into the boat with the admonishment: "Why did you doubt?" Jesus did not tell Peter that he could not walk on water. He did not say that he was a fool for trying. He seems to be saying that the only thing that stopped Peter from being able to come to him across the top of the water was his inability to believe that it was possible for him to break through his old barriers.

Once in the boat the wind ceased, and they made it to the far side of the lake, their destination. Once more we find that Jesus did not command the wind and the sea to be calm as he does in the accounts of the calming of the storm. Here, in the midst of his disciples, there is no wind. No storm. They are comfortable and safe and able to proceed to their goal without any further problems.

Matthew's Gospel presents us with many images that tease out for us the way of life of the disciple. He is well aware of the problems facing the infant Christian community and in his accounts of the life and teachings of Jesus, it is the coming of the kingdom of heaven that emerges as the main focus of his attention. At the moment of his conception Jesus was revealed as "God-with-us" (Immanuel), and his ministry made the implications of this quite clear to the disciples. That is why he could say to his disciples, "Courage! It's me!" When God is with us, then there is no need to fear. What could storms and seas possibly do? Of course, the storms and the wind and the seas are all meant to bring to the reader's mind the trials and struggles of life itself, as well as those that face the would-be disciple of Jesus. Life and discipleship have their own difficulties. There are always things that rage around us and seek to drag us down. It is a part of our weak humanity and a part of the consequences of our believing in the midst of a world that does not always believe. But because Immanuel has come, there is no reason to lose heart and be afraid. He is the one that will come to us while we are in the midst of the raging wind and sea. The turmoils of life do not present an impenetrable barrier to the Lord. He wants to come and he will come, and his coming brings change and peace.

Of course it is possible to miss his coming. It is possible to be expecting God to act in a particular way, to demand that he take a certain course of action, only to miss him when he moves in other ways. Presumably the disciples would have expected Jesus to calm the wind and the sea when he came to them, and if he had done so then they may well have recognized him. But he didn't. He did the unexpected. He came and stood with them—in the midst of the storm. That was his message and they could not see it. They could see no point in having a God who would not remove the storm from around them. They knew what they wanted him to do, what they expected him to do, but forgot to allow God to move as he wants. Because they were not prepared to allow God to be God, they did not recognize him. Because they were demanding that God be God as they, the disciples, felt they needed him to be God, they thought that he was a ghost and they panicked. Matthew here is highlighting the necessary starting point of any discipleship. The ones who want to follow Jesus have to be prepared to let go of their lives and allow God to move and act as he pleases. He spells it out later in terms of taking up the cross and following him to Jerusalem and death. Without this willingness it is quite likely that the actions of God will be missed and misunderstood.

Peter was the one exception. He sensed the presence of Immanuel, though his actions show how it is also possible to misunderstand the call to discipleship. He wanted to come to Jesus, but he wanted to do so over the top of the water. He was looking for an easy way, assuming that being called and responding meant that life would somehow be much easier, that storms would not touch his life, that the wind and raging seas of life would not trouble him. When Jesus tells him to "come on," he is acknowledging that Peter's insight is right though misunderstood. At the invitation of Jesus, Peter can walk over the water. He can come to God undisturbed by all that is crashing down around him—but only as long as he has his eyes firmly on the Lord. Peter manages to cross the sea without getting wet until he "notices the wind." Once he takes his eyes from Jesus and begins to notice and worry about what is going on around him and wonder how he is going to cope, he begins to sink. Once he becomes aware of his own weaknesses and limitations and shows fear, the things that are threatening him drag him down. He goes beneath the waves. The only thing that kept him above all of this was Jesus. When Jesus told Peter to come to him, he did not calm the sea around his friend so that it would be an effortless passage. Peter had to cross stormy seas to arrive at his goal. There was no guarantee that the crossing would be easy. The only guarantee was that it was possible. But only under certain conditions. Only in the presence of Jesus would the seas not overwhelm him. With Jesus present, the wind and the waves would not be enough to stop Peter. Life and discipleship need the divine presence to keep them in the proper perspective. Without it, doubts, fears, and uncertainties take over, and the storms begin to win.

This is why the final picture with which we are left is so important. In the end, Jesus raises Peter up from the water (still without having calmed the storm) and climbs into the boat with the other disciples. It is only now that the wind drops and the sea is calm. In the boat, gathered around Jesus, there is calm and peace. Peter and the others have been saved from the storm, not through their own efforts and abilities or their skills as fishermen, but by the presence of the Son of God in their boat. Gathering around that presence in humble acknowledgment of who he is transforms their world. They now have a new perspective, a new understanding and are now able to complete their journey to the other side of the lake. They know that storms are as much a part of life on the lake as they are a part of life and discipleship. Now they have been shown in a most dramatic way that it does not matter how severe the storm; for the one who believes there is always peace and calm. Jesus is not presented here as the one who calms the sea and quietens the wind. He is the one who comes to the disciples in the midst of the storm, unhindered by what is raging around them, and who brings peace and comfort—who enables them to continue with their journey in safety. He is the one who is able to do what they, with all their strengths and talents, could not achieve. He comes to them not as the transformer of the world but as the transformer of human lives. The disciples are the ones who are changed in this story, and once they are changed the storms die down. Whether or not it continued to rage is irrelevant, because they now approach it differently, with a new perspective. In their boat, regardless of the sea around them, they have courageous hearts and peaceful minds.

14. Love Made Perfect
Russell Seabright

Leviticus 19:1–2, 15–18; Matthew 22:34–40

When I was a boy studying the catechism in a Lutheran church in West Virginia, I was taught something about the "church year," that calendar of seasons and celebrations that is followed among us. As I recall, there were two major categories: the life and work of Christ, which became the focus of Advent through Pentecost, roughly December through May; and the life of the Christian, the focus through the post-Pentecost season, roughly June through November. All of that was brought to my mind as I looked at this Sunday's lessons and realized that they represent the last, and perhaps culminating piece, in the church year's attention to what we called the life of the believer. Next Sunday (the twenty-fourth Sunday after Pentecost) there is a shift that represents a transition to the Advent Season, and those lessons deal with the "last things," a day of judgment, the return of Christ.

So in this last Sunday, before the focus adjusts itself to another theme, there is attention to what might well be the summation of all that can really be said about the Christian life—beyond all of the partial and fragmented attempts to say what a Christian is and does—one classic statement, beautiful in its simplicity, comprehensive in its profundity: "You shall love the Lord your God . . . ; you shall love your neighbor as yourself" (Matt. 22:37–39). Among

---

Russell F. Seabright is Associate Professor for Ministry and Field Education and Director of Field Education at Union Theological Seminary in New York City. Seabright was awarded the Master of Divinity from Lutheran Theological Seminary and a Doctor of Ministry from United Theological Seminary in Dayton, Ohio. In addition to serving as a parish pastor in Maryland and Ohio, Seabright spent six years as an institutional chaplain for the mentally ill and the elderly.

those early Christian believers, seeking to understand themselves and their identity, it must have been seen as just that—profound, simple, comprehensive, summing up all that could be said about "being a Christian."

It certainly became a part of Paul's teaching and appears more than once in what he wrote to the early Christian communities: "Owe no one anything, except to love one another; for one who loves the neighbor has fulfilled the law. The commandments, 'you shall not commit adultery, you shall not kill, you shall not steal, you shall not covet' and any other commandments are summed up in this sentence: 'You shall love your neighbor as yourself.' Love does no wrong to a neighbor, therefore love is the fulfilling of the law" (Rom. 13:8–10).

The statement was not new with Jesus. It had roots in the Hebrew tradition in which he was trained as a boy; he learned it through the school that he attended. We heard it read in the first lesson of the day. In contrast to hating, taking vengeance, and bearing a grudge, "you shall love your neighbor as yourself" (Lev. 19:18). The teaching is firmly rooted in the religious tradition that nourished Christianity's beginnings, as well as the tradition that teaches and sustains us.

It may seem at this point in our lives that we have heard enough about loving the neighbor and the importance of that in the Christian life. We have come to know something of the limits of that in a predatory society where one must often protect oneself from exploitation and manipulation, where love, as usually understood, leaves one vulnerable to being taken advantage of and defenseless against those who know all too well how to capitalize on another's religious commitments. I am not forgetting that while Jesus said that we should be as gentle as doves, he also said that we should be as wise as serpents! Love as patience, kindness, longsuffering is right on target as long as one also knows how not to be victimized by the exploitation of others.

That observation begins to lead us to a more finely nuanced reflection. When I read of "loving the neighbor" in these passages, I see something more than kindness and patience; I see love being understood as justice. Love is not a charity that I extend but a response to the rights that others have—because God is God and since I am through baptism in a covenant with God I am bound to see things in a different perspective. Hear again some of the details of that passage from Leviticus. "You shall not harvest your field to its very border" (which means that you shall leave some in the corners for the poor to gather); "you shall not strip your vineyard bare" (same principle); "the wages of a hired servant shall not remain with you overnight" (the employee should have them for immediate use); "you shall not curse the deaf or put a stumbling block before the blind" (dealing with the handicapped), and the list goes on: protection from sexual exploitation, of children from abuse, of the rights of aliens. Each verse ends with the words: "I am the Lord your God." There has to be some muscle in these directives for they are addressed to those who have power as they deal with those who have less power! God's self backs up what is being said. It is not a matter of love as charity—it is a matter of love as justice, protecting the rights of other persons. Leaving unharvested grain in the field was not a matter of charity. It was respecting the right of the other to a living.

One of my mentors in seeing the difference between justice and charity has been Sr. Marie Augusta Neal. She has taught and lectured in many places but never received the recognition that her insight, that the needs of the disadvantaged are claims for justice, not opportunities for charity, deserves. Her voice is joined by that of Victor Furnish, New Testament scholar and commentator:

> To love an oppressed neighbor surely means not
> to take advantage of his voiceless, powerless
> condition. But it means far more than that. And it
> even means more than acting in kindness. It
> means raising up those who have been put down
> and including those who have been left out. It
> means making sure that the unseen become visible,
> that the voiceless find speech, that the powerless
> are given power. There is no doubt that this is a
> radical love. It attacks the well-kept notion that
> only the competent and successful are worthy of
> inclusion and authority. (Proc. 2, Pentecost 3,
> Series A, pp. 31f)

"You shall love the Lord your God . . . and your neighbor as yourself." There is something about us there, as lovers of the neighbor. I am to love the neighbor as I love myself. Some have found a much needed basis there for self-valuing. But if love is, at least partially, the doing of justice, it indicates that I cannot claim

justice for others—if I cannot claim it for myself. That is a new
dimension to "loving myself." To the extent that I have bought into
my own victimization, I can see only victimization for other people.
That may add something of an additional dimension to loving one's
neighbor as oneself. Loving myself I claim justice for myself, in my
relationships, in my work. Justice is not just fair and impartial
treatment. It is the creation of an environment in which people
have access to resources to sustain themselves. That is what I want
for myself and that is what others should have. That is more than
a garbage sack for the homeless. It is more than a shoulder to cry
on for the abused. It is more than an impartial observer during
times of personal reversal.

We may not often think of people searching the Church out as
they yearn for justice. We have more often played the tune of
"Come ye disconsolate—where so'er ye wander. Come to the mercy
seat. There lay your burdens down. Earth has no sorrows that
heaven cannot heal." I don't know that we have ever tried to dis-
cern how many are disconsolate and burdened because of the injustice they experience in their work life, home life, neighborhood
life. How much of the domestic abuse, the vocational frustration,
the victimization that bruises spirits that seek healing, cries out for
vindication? We come to the Church and may be taught only how
to bear with injustice. Then the Church threatens to become the
home of the victimized and not the changers, characterized by pas-
sivity rather than risk-taking. We cannot claim justice for others
when we cannot claim it for ourselves. We can identify injustice for
others only when we can identify it for ourselves.

John in his first epistle joins Paul and Jesus and Leviticus in
raising the theme of love: "So we know and believe the love God
has for us. [Remember, I am the Lord your God.] God is love and
she who abides in love abides in God, and God in her. In this is love
perfected . . ." (1 John 4:16). "He who does not love his brother
whom he has seen cannot love God whom he has not seen. And
this commandment we have from God, that he who loves God
should love his brother also" (4:20–21). The point of that being: If
that love of the seen neighbor is not present then one may probably become as exploitive of God as he is of the brother or neighbor. Disciplined by the reality of face-to-face relationships, formed
by the challenges of the experienced, we will be more ready to

enter into that relationship with God, which while it offers greater depth, also offers opportunity for greater distortion.

Love means justice—loving means yielding to justice, even when that involves pain. It can be done though only after one has claimed justice for oneself. That makes love "perfect." The English-language Scriptures have adopted that word *perfect* in its older meaning of "complete." When love has so healed me that I not only claim justice for others but also for myself, when I begin to consider myself of enough value to have rights, then love is complete. Love will mean justice in all relationships, to ourselves, to our fellow human beings, to God.

III. DOCTRINAL/
   THEOLOGICAL

15. The Kingdom of God
Frederick Buechner

Mark 1:1–15

The beginning of the Gospel of Jesus Christ, the Son of God.
As it is written in Isaiah the prophet,
"Behold, I send my messenger before thy face, who shall
prepare thy way; the voice of one crying in the wilderness:
Prepare the way of the Lord, make his paths straight—"
John the Baptizer appeared in the wilderness preaching a
baptism of repentance for the forgiveness of sins. And there went
out to him all the country of Judea, and they all were baptized by
him in the river Jordan, confessing their sins. Now John was
clothed with camel's hair, and had a leather girdle around his
waist, and ate locusts and wild honey. And he preached, saying,
"After me comes he who is mightier than I, the thong of whose
sandals I am not worthy to stoop down and untie. I have baptized
you with water; but he will baptize you with the Holy Spirit." In
those days Jesus came from Nazareth of Galilee and was baptized
by John in the Jordan. And when he came up out of the water,
immediately he saw the heavens opened and the Spirit descending
upon him like a dove; and a voice came from heaven, "Thou art
my beloved Son; with thee I am well pleased." The Spirit
immediately drove him out into the wilderness. And he was in the
wilderness forty days, tempted by Satan; and he was with the wild
beasts; and the angels ministered to him. Now after John was
arrested, Jesus came into Galilee, preaching the gospel of God, and

---

Frederick Buechner was born in New York City. He was educated
at Lawrenceville School, Princeton University, and Union
Theological Seminary in New York. He is a Presbyterian. Buechner
taught English at Lawrenceville School and creative writing at New
York University. At Phillips Exeter Academy he was chairman of the
department of religion and school minister. He is the author of
novels, books of sermons, autobiography, and books on religious
themes. Buechner delivered the Lyman Beecher Lectures at Yale
University, published as *Telling the Truth: The Gospel as Tragedy,
Comedy, and Fairy Tale*. This sermon is from his book *The Clown in
the Belfry*.

saying, "The time is fulfilled, and the kingdom of God is at hand; repent, and believe in the gospel."

I always get the feeling as I read the opening verses of the Gospel of Mark that he is in a terrible rush, that he can't wait to reach the place where he feels the Gospel really begins. He says absolutely nothing about how Jesus was born. He gets through the baptism in no time flat. He barely mentions the temptation in the wilderness. And only then, after racing through those first fourteen verses, does he get where he seems to have been racing to—the real beginning as he sees it—and that is the opening words of Jesus himself. Up to that point it has all gone so fast that hardly anybody except John the Baptist knows who Jesus really is yet, just as it might be said that most of the time hardly any of us knows who Jesus really is yet either.

He is destined to have a greater impact on the next two thousand years of human history than anybody else in history—we know that now—but here at the beginning of Mark nobody knows it yet. Not a single syllable has escaped his lips yet, as Mark tells it. The ant lays down her crumb to listen. The very stars in the sky hold their breath. Nobody in the world knows what Jesus is going to say yet, and maybe it's worthwhile pretending we don't know either—pretending we've never heard him yet ourselves which may be closer to the truth than we think.

"The time is fulfilled," he says. "And the Kingdom of God is at hand. Repent and believe in the gospel." That is how he launches the Gospel—his first recorded words. There is a kind of breathlessness in those three short, urgent sentences. The question is, what do they urgently mean to us who know them so well that we hardly hear them any more. If they mean anything to us at all, urgent or otherwise, what in God's name is it?

At least there is no great mystery about what "the time is fulfilled" means, I think. "The time is fulfilled" means the time is up. That is the dark side of it anyway, saving the bright side of it till later. It means that it is possible we are living in the last days. There was a time when you could laugh that kind of message off if you saw some bearded crazy parading through the city streets with it painted on a sandwich board, but you have to be crazy yourself to laugh at it in our nuclear age. What with *glasnost* and *perestroika* and what seems to be the gradual break-up of world communism, things look more hopeful than they have for a long time, but the world is still a powder keg. The missiles are still in their silos, the vast armies are still under arms. And there are other dangers potentially more dangerous now than even nuclear war. There is AIDS. There is terrorism. There are drugs and more to the point the darkness of our time that makes people seek escape in drugs. There is the slow poisoning of what we call "the environment" of all things, as if with that absurdly antiseptic phrase we can conceal from ourselves that what we are really poisoning is home, is here, is us.

It is no wonder that the books and newspapers we read, the movies and TV we watch, are obsessed with the dark and demonic, are full of death and violence. It is as if the reason we wallow in them is that they help us keep our minds off the real death, the real violence. And God knows the Church of Christ has its darkness and demons too. On television and in cults it is so discredited by religious crooks and phonies and vaudevillians, and in thousands of respectable pulpits it is so bland and banal and without passion, that you wonder sometimes not only if it will survive but if it even deserves to survive. As a character in Woody Allen's *Hannah and Her Sisters* puts it, "If Jesus came back and saw what was going on in his name, he'd never stop throwing up."

In other words, a lot of the kinds of things that happen at the ends of civilizations are happening today in our civilization, and there are moments when it is hard to avoid feeling not only that our time is up but that it is high time for our time to be up. That we're ready to fall from the branch like overripe fruit under the weight of our own decay. Something like that, I think, is the shadow side of what Jesus means when he says that the time is fulfilled.

If he meant that the world was literally coming to an end back there in the first century A.D., then insofar as he was a human, he was humanly wrong. But if he meant that the world is always coming to an end, if he meant that we carry within us the seeds of our own destruction no less than the Roman and Jewish worlds of his day carried it within them, if he meant that in the long run we are always in danger of one way or another destroying ourselves utterly, then of course he was absolutely right.

But Jesus says something else too. Thank God for that. He says our time is up, but he also says that the Kingdom of God is at hand. The Kingdom of God is so close we can almost reach out our hands and touch it. It is so close that sometimes it almost reaches out and takes us by the hand. The Kingdom of God, that is. Not man's kingdom. Not Deng Xiaoping's kingdom, not Bush's kingdom, not Gorbachev's kingdom. Not any of the kingdoms that still have nuclear missiles aimed at each other's heads, that worry like us about counting calories while hundreds of thousands starve to death. But God's kingdom. Jesus says it is the Kingdom of God that is at hand. If anybody else said it, we would hoot him off the stage. But it is Jesus who says it. Even people who don't believe in him can't quite hoot him off the stage. Even people who have long since written him off can't help listening to him.

The Kingdom of God? Time after time Jesus tries to drum into our heads what he means by it. He heaps parable upon parable like a madman. He tries shouting it. He tries whispering it. The Kingdom of God is like a treasure, like a pearl, like a seed buried in the ground. It is like a great feast that everybody is invited to and nobody wants to attend.

What he seems to be saying is that the Kingdom of God is the time, or a time beyond time, when it will no longer be humans in their lunacy who are in charge of the world but God in his mercy who will be in charge of the world. It's the time above all else for wild rejoicing—like getting out of jail, like being cured of cancer, like finally, at long last, coming home. And it is at hand, Jesus says.

Can we take such a message seriously, knowing all that we know and having seen all that we've seen? Can we take it any more seriously than the Land of Oz? It's not so hard to believe in a day of wrath and a last judgment—just read the newspapers—but is the Kingdom of God any more than a good dream? Has anybody ever seen it—if not the full glory of it then at least a glimpse of it off in the shimmering distance somewhere?

It was a couple of springs ago. I was driving into New York City from New Jersey on one of those crowded, fast-moving turnpikes you enter it by. It was very warm. There was brilliant sunshine, and the cars glittered in it as they went tearing by. The sky was cloudless and blue. Around Newark a huge silver plane traveling in the same direction as I was made its descent in a slow diagonal and touched down soft as a bird on the airstrip just a few hundred yards away from me as I went driving by. I had music on the radio, but I didn't need it. The day made its own music—the hot spring sun and the hum of the road, the roar of the great trucks passing and of my own engine, the hum of my own thoughts. When I came out of the Lincoln Tunnel, the city was snarled and seething with traffic as usual; but at the same time there was something about it that was not usual.

It was gorgeous traffic, it was beautiful traffic—that's what was not usual. It was a beauty to see, to hear, to smell, even to be part of. It was so dazzlingly alive it all but took my breath away. It rattled and honked and chattered with life—the people, the colors of their clothes, the marvelous hodgepodge of their faces, all of it; the taxis, the shops, the blinding sidewalks. The spring day made everybody a celebrity—blacks, whites, Hispanics, every last one of them. It made even the litter and clamor and turmoil of it a kind of miracle.

There was construction going on as I inched my way east along 54th Street, and some wino, some bum, was stretched out on his back in the sun on a pile of lumber as if it was an alpine meadow he was stretched out on and he was made of money. From the garage where I left the car, I continued my way on foot. In the high-ceilinged public atrium on the ground floor of a large office building there were people on benches eating their sandwiches. Some of them were dressed to kill. Some of them were in jeans and sneakers. There were young ones and old ones. Daylight was flooding in on them, and there were green plants growing and a sense of deep peace as they ate their lunches mostly in silence. A big man in a clown costume and whiteface took out a tubular yellow balloon big round as a noodle, blew it up and twisted it squeakily into a dove of peace which he handed to the bug-eyed child watching him. I am not making this up. It all happened.

In some ways it was like a dream and in other ways as if I had woken up from a dream. I had the feeling that I had never seen the city so *real* before in all my life. I was walking along Central Park South near Columbus Circle at the foot of the park when a middle-aged black woman came toward me going the other way. Just as she passed me, she spoke. What she said was, "Jesus loves you." That is what she said: "Jesus loves you," just like that. She said it in as everyday a voice as if she had been saying good morning, and I was so caught off guard that it wasn't till she was lost in the crowd that I realized what she had said and wondered if I could possibly ever find her again and thank her, if I could ever catch up with her and say, "Yes. If I believe anything worth believing in this whole world, I believe that. He loves me. He loves you. He loves the whole doomed, damned pack of us."

For the rest of the way I was going, the streets I walked on were paved with gold. Nothing was different. Everything was different. The city was transfigured. I was transfigured. It was a new New York coming down out of heaven adorned like a bride prepared for her husband. "The dwelling of God is with men. He will dwell with them, and they shall be his people . . . he will wipe away every tear from their eyes, and death shall be no more, neither shall there be any mourning, nor crying, nor pain any more, for the former things have passed away." That is the city that for a moment I saw.

For a moment it was not the world as it *is* that I saw but the world as it *might be,* as something deep within the world wants to be and is preparing to be, the way in darkness a seed prepares for growth, the way leaven works in bread.

Buried beneath the surface of all the dirt and noise and crime and poverty and pollution of that terrifying city, I glimpsed the treasure that waits to make it a holy city—a city where human beings dwell in love and peace with each other and with God and where the only tears there are are tears of joy and reunion. Jesus said that as soon as the fig tree "becomes tender and puts forth its leaves, you know summer is near. So also, when you see these things taking place, you know that [the Son of man] is near, at the very gates." For a few very brief and enormously moving minutes that day, the city itself became tender, put out leaves, and I knew beyond all doubt that more than summer was near, that something extraordinary was at the gates, something extraordinary was at least at the gates inside me. "The Kingdom of God is within you (or among you)," Jesus said, and for a little while it was so.

All over the world you can hear it stirring if you stop to listen, I think. Good things are happening in and through all sorts of people. They don't speak with a single voice, these people. No one person has emerged yet as their leader. They are divided into many groups pulling in many different directions. Some are pressing for an end to the nuclear arms race. Some are pressing for women's rights, some for civil rights, or gay rights, or human rights. Some are concerned primarily with world hunger or with the way we are little by little destroying the oceans, the rain forests, the air we breathe. There are lots of different people saying lots of different things and some of them put us off with their craziness and there are lots of points to argue with them about, but at their best they seem to be acting out of a single profound impulse, which is best described with words like: Tolerance. Compassion. Sanity. Hope. Justice. It is an impulse that has always been part of the human heart, but it seems to be welling up into the world with new power in our age now even as the forces of darkness are welling up with new power in our age now too. That is the bright side, I think, the glad and hopeful side, of what Jesus means by "The time is fulfilled." He means the time is ripe.

Humanly speaking, if we have any chance to survive, I suspect that it is men and women who act out of that deep impulse who are our chance. By no means will they themselves bring about the Kingdom of God. It is God alone who brings about his Kingdom. Even with the best will in the world and out of our noblest impulses, we can't do that. But there is something that we can do and must do, Jesus says, and that is *repent*. Biblically speaking, to repent doesn't mean to feel sorry about, to regret. It means to turn, to turn around 180 degrees. It means to undergo a complete change of mind, heart, direction. To individuals and to nations both, Jesus says the same thing. Turn *away from* madness, cruelty, shallowness, blindness. Turn *toward* that tolerance, compassion, sanity, hope, justice which we all have in us at our best.

We cannot make the Kingdom of God happen, but we can put out leaves as it draws near. We can be kind to each other. We can be kind to ourselves. We can drive back the darkness a little. We can make green places within ourselves and among ourselves where God can make his Kingdom happen. That transfigured city. Those people of every color, class, condition, eating their sandwiches together in that quiet place. The clown and the child. The sunlight that made everybody in those teeming streets a superstar. The bum napping like a millionaire on his pile of two-by-fours. The beautiful traffic surging all around me and the beautiful things that I could feel surging inside myself, in that holy place which is inside all of us. Turn *that* way. Everybody. While there is still time. Pray for it. Watch for signs of it. Live as though it is here already because there are moments when it almost is, such as those moments in Tiananmen Square before the massacre started when the students were gentle and the soldiers were gentle and something so holy and human was trying to happen there that it was hard to see pictures of it without having tears come to your eyes.

And "Believe in the gospel." That's the last of those first words that Jesus speaks. Believe in the good news. Believe in what that black woman said. Hurrying along Central Park South, she didn't even stop as she said it. It was as if she didn't have time to stop. She said it on the run the way Mark's Gospel says it. "Jesus loves you," she said. It was a corny thing for her to say, of course. Embarrassing. A screwball thing to blurt out to a total stranger on a crowded sidewalk. But, "Jesus loves you." She said it anyway. And that *is* the good news of the gospel, exactly that.

The power which is in Jesus, and before which all other powers on earth and in heaven give way, the power that holds all things in existence from the sparrow's eye to the farthest star, is above all else a loving power. That means we are loved even in our lostness. That means we are precious, every one of us, even as we pass on the street without so much as noticing each other's faces. Every city is precious. The world is precious. Someday the precious time will be up for each of us. But the Kingdom of God is at hand. Nothing is different and everything is different. It reaches out to each of our precious hands while there's still time.

Repent and believe in the gospel, Jesus says. Turn around and believe that the good news that we are loved is gooder than we ever dared hope, and that to believe in that good news, to live out of it and toward it, to be in love with that good news, is of all glad things in this world the gladdest thing of all.

Amen, and come, Lord Jesus.

16. Taking God's Name in Earnest
Russell H. Dilday

Exodus 20:7

I was nine years old in Mrs. Taylor's fifth grade class at DeQueen Elementary School in Port Arthur, Texas, when we presented the operetta *Rumpelstiltskin* for the whole school. It was about a little man who could spin gold. The smallest person in the class who could appropriately play the part of the little man was a little girl, Mary Ann Sizemore. Besides her size, she could pronounce the name better than anybody, so she became the star.

In the story, the queen had foolishly promised to give the little man her son unless she could guess his name. She tried everything but couldn't come up with the unusual name. Fortunately, the day before she was to forfeit her son, someone overheard the little man dancing about his campfire singing: "Tonight I'll brew, and tomorrow I'll bake, and then the little child I'll take. For little knows that royal dame that Rumpelstiltskin is my name."

So with the help of the eavesdropper, the queen guessed Rumpelstiltskin's name, saved her son, and they lived happily ever after.

While this story from German folklore is fictitious, it contains the ancient idea that the name of something—a person, a demon, a god—has a life of its own. According to the ancients, knowing the

Russell Hooper Dilday was born in Amarillo, Texas, and was educated at Baylor University and Southwestern Baptist Theological Seminary, from which he received the B.A. and Ph.D. degrees. Since 1978 he has served as president of Southwestern Seminary. He has also recently served as president of the Association of Theological Schools. Before assuming his seminary presidency Dilday was pastor of the Second Ponce de Leon Baptist Church in Atlanta, Georgia. His writings include two books: *You Can Overcome Discouragement* and *Personal Computer: A New Tool for Ministers.*

name of a person, especially a deity, would give a mysterious control or power over that person.

In some cultures, even today, people believe there is power in a name. A group of aborigines in the Australian outback, for example, hold such a belief. When one of them violates a tribal law and runs away to the big city to escape punishment, the people back in his village employ a strange ceremony. They symbolically "kill" the name of the fugitive. According to their mythology, when the name is killed, the fugitive will develop a fever and die.

Today, in crowded populations of anonymity, names have become relatively unimportant. Because of duplication in nomenclature, our names are seldom our exclusive personal property. They become little more than convenient mechanisms for classifying people. But for ancient cultures, personal names had great significance, far more important than a mere listing in a telephone book.

This idea may have begun centuries ago when someone noticed that when he called his friend's name, his friend would stop, turn, and respond to him. So he began to believe there must be some power in knowing and calling that name.

With a suit bag over my shoulder and briefcase in hand, I was rushing to Gate C-25 at the Atlanta airport the other day. The terminal was crowded. Passengers were elbow to elbow, rushing to their planes. I was paying little attention to the noisy conversations around me, when suddenly I heard, "Russell!" It stopped me in my tracks, causing a chain reaction that stacked people up behind me all the way to gate C-1. A former church member, an airline pilot, had spotted me, and called my name. Penetrating all that dull conversational babble in the airport was the magical sound of "Russell." Using it, my friend had the power to capture my attention and alter my course.

According to the Old Testament, the people of Israel understood the importance of names. To them, a name summed up the essence of a person's character. *Jacob* means "deceiver." *Samuel* means "asked of God." *Korah* means "bold." They also knew their God had a proper name. *God* is a generic word used for any deity, but the God of Israel had a unique name by which his people knew him. That name was "Yahweh." So highly respected and revered was that name that the Israelites never pronounced it. Only once a year, in the Holy of Holies the high priest would say it, but at other times they would substitute the word *Adonai* meaning "Lord."

Today, we can only guess how they pronounced God's name, but it was probably "Yahweh." It means "underived," "eternally independent," "uncreated." It was a name given to them by God himself, and they surrounded it with reverence and mystery. In their case, knowing the name "Yahweh" gave them not some superstitious power, but the freedom to call upon him, to approach him, to reach out for him in need. And experience taught them that when they called his name, he would stop in his tracks, so to speak, and help them.

Since there is always a risk in putting our names at the public's disposal, we have learned not to give away our names nonchalantly. Carelessly publish your name like Rumpelstiltskin did and you'll be bombarded by unwanted mail, phone calls, and maybe worse.

But the Bible tells us that God freely gives us his name. It's an awesome truth of remarkable proportions that the Lord God, the Creator of all the universe, with gracious solemnity gives us his name. Moses said,

> "If I come to the people of Israel and say to them,
> 'The God of your fathers has sent me to you,' and
> they ask me, 'What is his name?' what shall I say
> to them?" God said to Moses . . . "Say this to the
> people of Israel, 'I AM has sent me to you.' "
> (Exod. 3:13)

God said, "I am *Yahweh* your God who brought you out of the land of Egypt" (Exod. 20:2). Again and again in the Old Testament, God stepped forth from his nameless unapproachability to tell us his name so we might call on him, capture his attention, pray to him, and worship him. It's an awesome privilege to know and to use the name of God.

I have a friend with an unlisted telephone number that rings directly in his office. He's a well-known public figure and he has given that number to a small group of trusted friends. Usually, a caller has to go through switchboard after switchboard, secretary after secretary, associate after associate, and with luck, might get to talk to him. Having that private unlisted number gives you the privilege of calling him right at his desk. He answers the phone himself. Those who know the unlisted number use it reluctantly, only in appropriate circumstances. Because he has trusted me with the number, I would never give it away to anybody. It's a privilege that I value highly.

But the Bible tells us that God has given us his name freely, and he invites us, implores us to call upon him at any time. "Call upon me in the day of your trouble and I will help you" (Ps. 50). Without the intervention of a receptionist, without the intrusion of a divine secretary or a long distance operator, we have the privilege of coming boldly through Jesus Christ to God's throne of grace. We can call him by name.

This third of the Ten Commandments in Exodus 20 is saying, Don't abuse that privilege. In fact, the biblical scholar Brevard Childs translates it this way: "You shall not abuse the name of the Lord your God." God has been generous to give us his name and make it available to us, so we are under a heavy obligation never to take that privilege casually or lightly. This commandment forbids us to use his name in vain, wastefully, emptily, unworthily, abusively, untruthfully, frivolously. It is a call to be careful and wise in the use of that great privilege.

Specifically, what does the commandment, "You shall not take the name of the Lord your God in vain" mean to us in the twentieth century? What actions violate this commandment today?

Cursing, profanity? That's certainly included. Profanity is a very unusual sin. It's a sin that doesn't have any real temptation. It relieves no pain. It gratifies no appetite. It's certainly not desirable or attractive. Profanity, it is said, is a tongue gone berserk on the basis of an intellect that is out of gear.

When an inarticulate person, bereft of vocabulary, wishes to impress others, he uses profanity, but it quickly ceases to impress and soon becomes boring, wearisome. Profanity is a vulgar habit, and its most nauseating expression is when a Christian drops a profane word occasionally in the mistaken belief that he must prove what a regular fellow he is or how much in tune he is with modern culture.

This commandment does forbid cursing, but that's not the deep-seated basis of this commandment. God would not, I think, place among these noble and profound moral concepts a rather petty prohibition against cursing. The Ten Commandments are not given by a petulant God who's oversensitive to minor infractions of protocol in the use of his name. You don't violate this commandment merely by a slip of the tongue. It's something more serious than that.

Does this third commandment prohibit perjury? Leviticus 19, which is something of a commentary on Exodus 20, says "you shall not swear by my name falsely." Consistently and repeatedly in Scripture, God calls us to integrity and honesty. Taking this concept to its ultimate expression, Jesus reminded us that we shouldn't swear at all. Our yes ought to be yes and our no, no. Since Jesus himself answered under oath before the court of the high priest, it seems clear he was not forbidding the taking of judicial oaths. Instead, he was admonishing us to keep our promises, to be dependable, to keep our word, to be trustworthy. With our contemporary cultural landscape littered as it is with broken promises, contracts, marriage vows, and promises to God, it's obvious we need this call to honesty from the Decalogue and the words of our Lord.

While the commandment clearly forbids profanity and perjury and such practices as the magical or superstitious use of God's name, there is more to the commandment than these. More than anything this command is a prohibition against hypocrisy and insincerity in the use of God's name. It's a warning against not taking God seriously. If you turned it around into a positive form, the commandment says, "You *shall* take the name of God in earnest." Don't give just lip service to the Lord, calling on his name but refusing to serve him. To talk about God but not live like God is a profanity worse than vile language or lying.

It's interesting to note that none of the commandments is a commandment against atheism. You don't find God anywhere in the Decalogue saying "you shall not be an atheist." That doesn't seem to be the real danger. An atheist is not so much dangerous as pitiful. According to the Bible, the real danger is a mild, innocuous form of religion that does not take God seriously. That's what bothers God, a cheap, empty faith. God commands, "None shall appear before me empty" (Exod. 34:20).

So we break this commandment when we profess to live in subjection to his sovereignty, but refuse to obey his command. If we call him Father and don't honor him as obedient children, we violate this commandment. When we call him King but refuse to seek his kingdom, we are guilty. When we say we love him but refuse to yield our lives to his guidance, we have violated this commandment. An even more serious violation is when we claim divine authority for our own actions and will, labeling our own views and convictions as God's.

As preachers of the gospel, we may come close to violating this commandment when we claim to preach in the name of Christ and yet our message is little more than a string of chatty anecdotes and entertaining illustrations that are really more self-glorifying than they are God-glorifying. Listeners in the pews violate the commandment to take God's name in earnest when they slouch back, listen, and draw out of the sermon only those little entertaining thoughts they want to hear. Like junk food, they munch on confections, letting all the meat of God's word go by unheard. We break the commandment when our prayers are glib formalities without half desiring the things we ask for. When we pray empty prayers and then close the prayer "in Jesus' name," we have disobeyed God's law.

Or worse, we break the commandment when we avoid using his name altogether. I know some people, reacting to a childhood experience of bitterness, turned off to religion, who refuse to have anything to do with God at all. They never call upon him. That's certainly taking God's name in vain.

If I believe in the skill of a certain mechanic and I go around telling everybody about the best automobile mechanic in the city but take my car to somebody else every time it needs repair, that's hypocrisy.

If I believe in a doctor and I tell everybody about this most skillful physician in the city but go to another doctor when I'm sick, that's hypocrisy.

Likewise, if I say I believe in God, but I never pray, I never worship, I never witness, I never serve him, I never call his name, then I'm guilty of the kind of empty hypocrisy this commandment forbids.

So, the positive expression of this third prohibition in the decalogue is, "You *shall* take the name of the Lord your God in earnest." It's an invitation to recover a sense of urgency in our relationship to God, to restore integrity, sincerity, faithfulness, seriousness in our relationship to God. We are to reverence his name in deed and in truth.

God is a spirit, just and wise,
>He sees our inmost mind.
In vain to heaven we raise our cries,
>While leaving hearts and souls behind.

Nothing but truth before his throne,
>With honor can appear.
The painted hypocrites are known,
>Whatever mask they wear.

Their lifted eyes salute the skies,
>Their bending knees the ground,
But God abhors the sacrifice,
>Where not the heart is found.

Lord search my thought and try my ways,
>And make my soul sincere,
Then shall I stand before thy face,
>And find acceptance there.

The Old Testament says, "You shall not take the name of the Lord your God in vain." Going beyond this, the New Testament teaches that in his final revelation God has given us a new name by which we are to address him. It is his ultimate name, above every name. That name is "Jesus," the name of his only begotten son.

We're told in the New Testament that there is none other name given among men under heaven whereby they may be saved. We're told that those who believe on the name of Jesus shall be eternally saved.

According to biblical thought, a person's name is vitally linked to reality. So we recognize that by calling on Jesus Christ, we are actually calling on the eternal God. He is the God who in power and majesty has graciously made himself available to us directly through his son. We can go about our daily routine today with the assurance that, as the hymn suggests, we can take the name of Jesus with us wherever we go. We will never be alone.

17. God Is a Woman and She Is Growing Older
Margaret Moers Wenig

Turn us, O God, back to you and we shall return.[1]

On Rosh Hashanah, I offered you
two different understandings of teshuvah.
Tonight, I offer you a third:
Teshuvah is turning, or returning, to God.

Who or what is God? Where shall we look for
    God's presence?
Our sages and philosophers are by no means
    unanimous in their response.
But they do concur on one matter:
Who or what God truly is
is ultimately unknowable.
God is the Hidden One (*El Mistateyr*),
the one who conceals His face (*hesteyr panim*)
or the Infinite, Unmeasurable One (*Eyn Sof*)
unknowable, unfathomable, indescribable.

Yet those same sages
also dare to try to capture
our people's experiences of God
in images we do know, can comprehend.

The Kabbalists went as far as to sketch God's form.
The Primordial Man (*Adam Kadmon*)—
each of God's attributes
associated with a specific part of his body:
head, arms, legs, torso, even male genitals.

Margaret Moers Wenig is Rabbi at Beth Am, The People's Temple in New York City. She is also a lecturer on homiletics at Hebrew Union College. A graduate of Brown University, Wenig was a contributor to *Womanspirit Rising*, edited by Carol Christ and Judith Plaskow, and *The Mishnah: A New Translation* by Jacob Neusner.

Midrashim gave us images of God
weeping at the sight of the Egyptians drowning,
bound in chains, forced into exile with his people,
laying *tefillin* each weekday morning,
and studying Torah with Moshe Rabbenu.

Our liturgy shows us God
as an immovable rock (*Tzur Yisrael*),
as a shield (*Magein Avraham*),
as the commander of a host of angels (*Adonai
    Tzevaot*),
as a shepherd (*Adonai roi*),
and on the Days of Awe, the *machzor* focuses upon
    the images of God as father (*Avinu*)
and God as King (*Malkeinu*).

All of these images are metaphors or allusions
never meant to be taken literally
merely meant to point us
toward something we can imagine
but never really see.

Tonight, I invite you to imagine God along with
    me.
Tonight I invite you to imagine God as a woman
a woman who is growing older.

God is a woman, and she is growing older.
She moves more slowly now;
she cannot stand erect;
her hair is thinning;
her face is lined;
her smile no longer innocent;
her voice is scratchy;
her eyes tire;
sometimes she has to strain to hear.
God is a woman, and she is growing older.

But she remembers everything.

On Rosh Hashanah,
the anniversary of the day on which she gave us
    birth,
God sits down in her kitchen
opens the Book of Memories on her table[2]
and begins turning the pages,
and God remembers.

"There, there is the world when it was new
and humanity when it was young. . . ."
As she turns each page of the book
she smiles as she sees before her,
like so many dolls in a department store window,
all the beautiful colors of our skin
and all the varied shapes and sizes of our bodies.
She marvels at our accomplishments:
the music we have written and sung,
the gardens we have planted,
the skyscrapers we have built,
the stories we have told,
and the ideas we have spun.

"They now can fly faster than the winds I send,"
she says to herself,
"and they sail across the waters that I gathered
    into seas.
They even visit the moon that I set in the sky.
But they rarely visit me," she thinks.

There, pasted into the pages of her book
are all the cards we have ever sent her
when we did not bother to visit.
She notices our signatures (*chotam yad kol adam bo*)[3]
scrawled beneath the printed words
someone else has composed.

Then there are the pages she would rather skip,
the things she wishes she could forget.
But they stare her in the face and
she cannot help but remember:
her children spoiling the home she created for us,
brothers killing each other
or putting each other in chains. . . .
She remembers seeing us racing down dangerous
    roads
and being unable to stop us.
She remembers the dreams she had for
    us—
dreams we never fulfilled.
And she remembers the names,
so many names, inscribed in the book;
names of all the children she has lost

through war and famine
earthquake and accident
disease and suicide. . . .
And God remembers the many times
she sat by a bedside
weeping that she could not halt the process
she herself set into motion.
Tonight, Kol Nidrei night
God lit candles—one for each of her children—
for the living and the dead[4]
millions and millions of candles
lighting up the night, making it bright as day.[5]
Tonight, God will stay awake all night[6]
turning the pages of her book.

God is lonely tonight
longing for her children
her playful ones (*yeled shaashuim*)
Ephraim—her darling one (*havein yakir li Ephraim*).
Her body aches for us (*hamu meay lo, rachem,
    arachem*).[7]
All that dwells on earth does perish
but God endures[8]
so she suffers the sadness
of losing all that she holds dear.

God is home alone tonight
turning the pages of her book.
"Come home," she wants to say to us, "come
    home."
But she won't call
for she is afraid that we will say, "No."
She can anticipate the conversation,
"We are so busy," we'd apologize.
"We'd love to see you but we just can't come.
Not tonight, not now. Too much work to do.
Too many responsibilities to juggle."

Even if we don't realize it, God knows
that our busyness is just an excuse.
She knows that we avoid returning to her
because we don't want to look into her age-worn
    face.
She understands that it is hard for us

to face a god who no longer looks the way she
    looked to us when we were children.
She understands that it is hard for us
to face a god who disappointed our childhood
    expectations:
She did not give us everything we wanted;
she did not defend us against all our foes;
she did not make us triumphant in battle,
successful in business, and invincible to pain.
We avoid going home
to protect ourselves from our disappointment
and to protect her.
We don't want her to see the disappointment in
    our eyes.
But God knows it is there
and she would have us come home anyway.

What if we did?
What if we did go home to visit God this Yom
    Kippur?
What might it be like?

I imagine that God would usher us into her
    kitchen,[9]
seat us at the table, pour two cups of tea.
She has been alone so long
that there is much she wants to say to us.
But we barely allow her to get a word in edgewise
for we are afraid of what we might hear
and we are also afraid of silence.
So we fill up an hour with our chatter
words, words, so many words.
Until, finally, she touches her finger to her lips
and says, "Shh. Be still. Shhh."
Then she pushes back her chair and says,
"Let me have a good look at you."
And she looks.
And, in a single glance, God sees us
as both newly born and as dying:
coughing and crying,
turning our head to root for her breast,
fearful of the unknown realm that lies ahead.
In a single glance she sees our birth and our
    death

and all the years in between.
She sees us as we were when we were young:
when we idolized her
and trustingly followed her anywhere,
(*zacharti lach chesed neuraich, lechtech acharai
   bamidbar*),[10]
when our scrapes and scratches healed quickly,
when we were filled with wonder at all things
   new—
a new dress,
our first pair of toe shoes,
a driver's license,
the new feelings in our body when we first allowed
   a friend to touch it.
She sees us as we were when we were young,
   when we thought there was nothing we could
   not do.

She sees us in our middle years too:
when our energy was unlimited
when we kept house,
cooked and cleaned,
cared for children,
worked,
and volunteered
when everyone needed us and we had no time for
   sleep.

And God sees us in our later years:
when we no longer felt so needed,
when chaos disrupted the bodily rhythms
we had learned to rely upon.
She sees us sleeping alone
in a room that once slept two.

God sees things about us we have forgotten
and things we do not yet know.
For naught is hidden from God's sight.

When she is finished looking at us
she might say, "So tell me, how *are* you?"
Now we are afraid to open our mouths[11]
and tell her everything she already knows:[12]
whom we love,
where we hurt,

what we wanted to be when we grew up,
what we have broken or lost.
We are afraid to speak now, lest we begin to cry.

Instead we change the subject
"Remember the time when . . ." we begin.
"Yes, I remember," she says.
Suddenly we are talking, both at the same time,
never completing a sentence
saying all the things
the greeting cards never said:
"I'm sorry that I . . ."
"That's all right, I forgive you."

"I didn't mean to . . ."
"I know that, I do."

"I was so angry that you hit me."
"I'm sorry that I ever hurt you—but you wouldn't
    listen to me."
"You are right, I wouldn't listen. I should have. I
    know that now, but at the time I had to do it my
    own way."
"I know," she nods, "I know."

We look away from her now, our eyes wander to
    the calendar on her kitchen wall
"I never felt I could live up to your expectations,"
    we say.
"I always believed you could do anything," she
    answers.

"What about your future?" she asks us.
And we stammer out an answer
for we do not want to face our futures.
God hears our reluctance and she understands.

After many hours of sitting and drinking tea
when, at last, there are no more words to say or to
    hear,
God begins to hum,[13]

Ai ai ai ai ai   ai ai ai ai ai   ai   ai ai ai ai ai   ai ai

And we are transported back to a time before
    memory

when our fever wouldn't break
and we couldn't sleep
exhausted from crying but unable to stop.
She picked us up
and held us against her bosom
and supported our head in the palm of her hand
and walked with us.
We could feel her heart beating
and hear the hum from her throat,

Ah Ah ba – by   Ah ah ba – by   Ai ai ai ai ai

Ah yes, that's where we learned to wipe the
   tears.[14]
It was from her we learned how to comfort a
   crying child,
how to hold and sing to someone in pain.

Then God reaches out and touches our arm
bringing us back from our nostalgia for a time
   long ago
bringing us back to the present and to the future.
"You will always be my child," she says.
"But you are no longer a child.
Grow old along with me
the best is yet to be
the last of life
for which the first was made."[15]

We are growing older, as God is growing older.
How much like her we have become.

For us, as well as for God, growing older means
   facing death.
Of course, God will never die
but she has buried more dear ones than we shall
   ever love.
In God, we see
'tis a holy thing to love what death can touch.[16]
Like her, we may be holy
(*kedoshim tihiyu, ke kadosh ani Adonai*)[17]
loving what death can touch

including ourselves—our own aging selves.

God holds our face in her two hands and
    whispers,
"Do not be afraid (*al tira*)[18]
I will be faithful to the promise I made to you
when you were young
(*vezacharti ani et brit otach bimey neuraich*)[19]
I will be with you (*ki imanu el*)
even to your old age I will be with you
(*ve ad zikna ani hu*)
when you are grey haired still I will hold you
I gave birth to you, I carried you
I will hold you still
(*vead seva ani esbol
ani asiti, vaani esa, vaani esbol, vamalet*)."[20]
Grow old along with me. . . .

Our fear of the future
is replaced now by curiosity,
understanding
that the universe is infinite,
unlimited possibilities are always arrayed before us.
Though the sun rises and sets just as the day
    before
no two days are the same.

We can greet each day now with eagerness,
awakening to wonder:
What shall I learn today?
What can I create today?
What will I notice that I have never seen before?

It has been a good visit.
Now we are tired and need to go to sleep.
Before we leave
it is our turn to look at her.
The face that time has marked
no longer looks only frail to us now
but wise as well.
For we understand that God knows
those things only the passage of time can teach:
that one can survive the loss of a love,
that one can feel secure even in the midst of an
    ever changing world,[21]

that there can be dignity in being alive even when
every bone aches.

God's movements no longer seem only slow to us
now
but strong and intent—
unlike our own
for we are too busy to see beneath the surface;
we speak too quickly and too loud to truly listen;
we move too rapidly to feel what we touch;
we form opinions too soon to judge honestly—
but God moves slowly and with intention.
She sees everything there is to see
understands everything she hears
and touches all that lives.

Now we understand why we were created to grow
older:
Each added day of life
each new year
makes us more like God
who is ever growing older.

That must be the reason
we are instructed
to rise before the aged (*mipney sevat takum*)
and see the grandeur in the faces of the old
(*vehadarta p'nai zakein*).[22]
We rise in their presence
as we would rise in the presence of God
for in the faces of the old we see God's face.

Looking at her now,
we feel overwhelmed by awe
(though embarrassed to say so).
This aging woman now looks to us
like . . . like a queen
her chair a throne
her house dress an ermine robe
and her thinning hair, shining like jewels in a
crown.

Tonight we sit here in the house of prayer
far from home
holding in our hands
pages of greeting cards

bound together like a book—
thousands of words
we ourselves have not written.
Will we merely place our signatures at the bottom
and drop the cards in the mail box?

God would prefer that we come home.
She is sitting and waiting for us
as she has waited every Yom Kippur
waiting—ever patiently (*erech apayim*)[23]
until we are ready.
(For she will not run out of time.)
Tonight God will not sleep.
She will leave the door open
and the candles burning
waiting patiently for us to come home.

Perhaps this Yom Kippur
by the time of Neilah[24]
we will be able to look into God's aging face
and say,
Avinu Malkeinu, Our mother our queen
we have come home.

NOTES

1. *Hashiveynu Adonai elecha venashuva.* Lamentations 5:21. We sing these words when we return the sefer Torah to the ark.

2. See Psalms 139:16 and 56:9 and especially the Unetane Tokef from the Musaf Amidahs of Rosh Hashanah and Yom Kippur, below:

> Let us tell how utterly holy this day is and how awe-inspiring. It is the day when thy dominion shall be exalted, thy throne shall be established on mercy, and thou shalt occupy it in truth. True it is that thou art judge and arbiter, discerner and witness, inscribing and recording all forgotten things. Thou openest the book of records and it reads itself; every man's signature is contained in it.

3. See note 2.

4. S. Y. Agnon, *Days of Awe* (New York: Schocken Books, 1948), 143:

Two Kinds of Candles

There are two kinds of candles, "candles of health" and "candles of the soul." "Candles of health" are for those who are alive and, according to custom, only for those who are married, one candle for each couple. It is not the custom to make separate candles for sons and daughters, even if they are grown up, so long as they are not married. The "candles of the soul" are for dead parents, whether both are dead or only one—only one candle for both. A woman too can make this candle.

The "candles of health" are large and the "candles of the soul" are small. But they must be so made as to burn until the close of Yom Kippur. There are some whose custom it is to burn "candles of health" in the House of Prayer, and "candles of the soul" at home. But that is not the proper way, because they are ceremonial candles, and the place for them is the House of Prayer. [Mateh Efrayim]

5. Some say that Yom Kippur is a day without any night.

6. It is the custom among some Jews to remain awake throughout the night on Yom Kippur.

7. From the Zichronot section of the Rosh Hashanah Musaf Amidah:

> I remember the loyal love of your youth, the affection of your bridal days, how you followed Me through the wilderness, through a land unsown.

> I will keep the promise I made to you in the days of your youth; I will make an eternal promise to you.

> Is not Ephraim my dearest child, my playful one? I often speak of him. I remember—yes, I remember him. My heart longs for him, my womb aches for him.

> (Jer. 2:2; Ezek. 16:60; Jer. 31:19)

8. Over and over again the liturgy on Rosh Hashanah and Yom Kippur (in Union Prayer Book II) emphasizes our mortality in contrast to God's immortality.

9. Syd Lieberman in "A Short Amidah," siddur *Kol Haneshamah*, page 184, offers the image of sitting in a kitchen drinking schnapps with God.

10. See note 7.

11. UPB II translation of Ribbon Kol Haolamim, "What are we? What is our life? What our goodness? What our power? What can we say in Thy presence?"

12. Psalm 139 (see UPB II, page 157) and UPB II translation of *Ma nomar lefanecha and Atah yodeah razey olam,* from the Selichot section of the Yom Kippur liturgy:

> What shall we say before Thee, who art on high, and what shall we recount unto Thee, who dwellest in the heavens? Dost Thou not know all things; both the hidden and revealed? Thou knowest the secrets of eternity and the hidden thoughts of every living being.

> Thou searchest the innermost recesses and probest the deepest impulses of the heart. Naught is concealed from Thee nor hidden from Thine eyes.

13. This motif is used repeatedly on Yom Kippur.

14. Hannah Senesh begins her poem, "To My Mother," with the words, "Where have you learned to wipe the tears?"

15. From Robert Browning, "Rabbi Ben Ezra."

16. This is the first line of a poem. Someone gave me a handwritten copy of it. I never learned the author's name.

17. From the Torah reading for Yom Kippur afternoon (Reform tradition): "You shall be holy, for I Adonai your God, am holy."

18. From a paragraph added to the Mourners' Kaddish during Rosh Hashanah Musaf and Mincha:

> Be not afraid of sudden terror, nor of the storm that strikes the wicked. [Enemies,] form your plot—it shall fail; lay your plan—it shall not prevail. For God is with us.

> Even to your old age I will be there; when you are grey-headed, still will I sustain you; I have made you, I will carry you; I will sustain you and rescue you.

> (Prov. 3:25; Isa. 8:10; 46:4)

19. See note 7.

20. See note 18.

21. Al Carmines, in his song "Many Gifts One Spirit":

> God of change and glory
> God of time and space
> When we fear the future
> Give to us your grace
> In the midst of changing ways
> Give us still the grace to praise.

22. From the Yom Kippur Afternoon Torah reading (Reform Tradition).

23. Central to the Selichot section of the Yom Kippur liturgy is the name of God revealed to Moses on Sinai: *Adonai, Adonai, El rachum vechanun, erech apayim....*

24. When Yom Kippur falls on Shabbat, Avinu Malkeinu is not recited until the Neilah (Closing) service.

A few words on the delivery of the sermon: I did not say aloud the Hebrew phrases that appear throughout the sermon in parentheses—except for the names of God that appear on pages 1 and 2. I felt that inserting the Hebrew would have interrupted the flow of the narrative.

Thus, *Hamevin, yavin*—those who caught the quotations or allusions, caught them; those who didn't, didn't.

This sermon was written for the three women who raised me: Mary Moers Wenig, Anna Wenig, and Molly Lane, and for the older women of Beth Am, in whose faces I have seen God's face.

I am grateful to my colleagues and friends, Rabbi Judy Shanks and Dr. Janet Walton, for their constructive criticism of early drafts of this sermon.

18. The Universalism of the Gospel
Calvin De Vries

The global context for this morning's celebration of World Communion may well prompt us to move beyond pleasant sentiment about Christians being gathered around a common table. In many ways the world has out-distanced our often timid and beleaguered ecumenism.

I should not want to diminish the importance of Christian ecumenism or its symbols. I believe that the New Testament espouses it and asks us to pray for it. We celebrate its advances. The 1982 report of the World Council of Churches, *Baptism, Eucharist and Ministry,*[1] is a landmark. It marks the first time that so many Christian groups have spoken together about their views on the sacraments and ministry, even if to acknowledge some persistent differences alongside confluences. That is significant!

But must we not say that the world situation today needs to elicit something more from our churches than a symbolic act of Protestant togetherness? How shall we relate appropriately to stunning developments in global affairs, to an escalating world culture that gives us all a sense that what happens in Tiananmen Square or Johannesburg or Baghdad happens to us all? In the June 1990 issue of *Atlantic Monthly,* writer Raymond Gastil comments that a world culture has penetrated everywhere since World War II. "This culture," he writes, "no longer accepts discrimination for reasons of ideology, religion, gender, or ethnicity."[2] Think of the reluctance of Eastern European Communist leaders to resort to

Calvin De Vries is Pastor Emeritus of First Presbyterian Church in Cedar Rapids, Iowa. De Vries has served pastorates in Washington, DC, New York, Illinois, and Iowa and has lectured at a number of seminaries. He is a graduate of Hope College and New Brunswick Theological Seminary.

brute military coercion in the face of peoples' desire for sovereignty. There is the encouraging unanimity among major United Nations powers regarding Iraqi aggression.

How interrelated we are! Daily we benefit from a global weather monitoring system. We all face together the universality of environmental problems. We exchange medical information with scant regard to boundaries. Native Iowan Dr. Norman Borlaug, through his "green revolution," made China the biggest food producer in history during the 1980s. Not least of all is the momentous interface among the world's monotheistic faiths, Judaism, Christianity, and Islam, not only in the Middle East but here in the cities of America's heartland.

Is there not a universal vision in both the Bible as well as in our current history that beckons us beyond Christian ecumenism to a gracious and compassionate outreach to all men and women and children everywhere? Marcus Borg in his recent book, *Jesus: A New Vision,* is saying that when he writes, "As an image of God, Jesus mirrors the care of God for what happens to humans in the world of history."[3]

Christian faith has generally been particularistic in practice. The New Testament was written in the context of strident confrontation with other world views. It is important, for instance, not to let its antagonism toward Judaism become our attitude today. In 313 C.E. Christianity became an approved religion in the Roman empire, later on securing favored status. It was not long before some segments of the Church began oppression of other religious perspectives. Even within the Church points of view at variance with those of ruling bishops were often savagely repressed.

Church history is hardly inspirational reading on this matter of openness to religious diversity. Most of us of middle age and beyond were raised in contexts of religious parochialism. Our own denomination was favored by God, we were often told, and others were marginal at best. Catholics and Protestants were separated by a theological Grand Canyon.

Thank God that has changed and continues to change! Yet, how inadvertently we suppose that the Bible is really on the side of religious exclusiveness. A well-meaning friend reminds us that St. Paul wrote, "What has a believer in common with an unbeliever?" (2 Cor. 6:15) and applies it to a minor religious difference. And then Christ reverts to Michelangelo's cosmic judge towering above the Sistine Chapel's altar: great art but spurious theology.

Such images must not become the controlling images of Christ that meet us in the Lord's Supper. World Communion can be the carrier of a will to work with men and women of all faiths to the end of human understanding and well-being.

I am not asking that we forgo Christian distinctiveness, even uniqueness. I believe in the presence of Christ with us at this table, powerful in our inner selves where he shapes and saves us. But he is not pointing us back in upon our beliefs and predilections. He is inviting us to bring the good news of God's grace and compassion to everyone, and more than that to live such an affirmation in our relationships. "God was in Christ reconciling the world to himself . . . entrusting to us the message of reconciliation" wrote St. Paul (2 Cor. 4:19).

There is in Scripture, despite its admitted parochialisms, a universal vision, present like a soprano descant high above the minor keys of the chorus. Think of that amazing vision in the later Isaiah, scripture close to the mind of Jesus, when he wrote: "And the foreigners who join themselves to the Lord . . . their burnt offerings and their sacrifices will be accepted on my altar; for my house shall be called a house of prayer for all peoples. Thus says the Lord God who gathers the outcasts of Israel, I will gather yet others to him" (Isa. 56:6–8).

What an amazing and soaring prophetic testimony against exclusiveness for the universal inclusiveness of divine grace from the sixth century B.C.E. When Jesus "cleansed the temple" he quoted, according to the Gospels, from this passage: "My house shall be called a house of prayer for all peoples."

The New Testament scholar E. P. Sanders says in his study, *Jesus and Judaism,* that the distinctive quality in Jesus' vision of God and his godliness was his acceptance of moral and religious outcasts.[4] There is a miracle of grace that goes from Jesus to Zacchaeus and Mary, to the very human disciples, and to all those thirsty for the healing of the human spirit but repelled by the self-serving pretensions of the powerful, the politicians, yes and even many of the "religious." Jesus was not setting aside the Torah but saying that that scripture is wrongly used when it excludes people from the concerns of God.

I am convinced that St. Paul inherited that vision, ambivalent as it may have been at times. He led the debate in the apostolic church for dropping cultic religious particularities as conditions for Christian discipleship, making Christianity a faith for Jew and Gentile alike. He wrote, "There is neither Jew nor Greek; there is neither slave nor free; there is neither male nor female, for you are all one in Christ" (Gal. 3:28).

Several years ago Stephen Montgomery, writing in *The Presbyterian Outlook,* commented on a paper that had been submitted to the national legislative body of the Church earlier in the year. He said of Muslims, "Do we worship the same God? If we do then are not both (of us) ultimately witnesses to the same source of truth? How is it possible to be faithful to Christ without falling into the superiority that has marred Christian-Muslim relationships in the past? There has been a rise in bigotry and prejudice in our country against Muslim peoples which is clearly contrary to the universality of God's love. When the Church remains silent on this matter it lends credence to such prejudice."[5] How much to the point! It can be said of Christian-Jewish relationships, of Protestants and Catholics in many places. Indeed, there are fellow Christians within the same communion of belief who need to hear that.

This morning I plead for a vision of World Communion that is more than ecumenical: for one that is world-wide and universal. "We must renew the sense that the breath of life in all human beings is the divine Spirit or Word," says theologian John Cobb.[6] This morning, Christ stands among us in the symbolic act of World Communion. It is biblical thought that leads us to be confident that Christ is reminding us of the largeness of God's grace and mercy, going not only to all Christians but as well to all of the world's women and men and children. The figure of Christ does not turn away but invites. The purpose of Christ is not to exclude but to include. If that is a formidable challenge then let us remember what Jesus says, according to John's Gospel: "[They] who believe in me will also do the works that I do; and greater works than these will [they] do" (John 14:12).

Religious diversity and the claims of our own faith are a vast and unsimple matter. The answers require our study, our dialogue, our understanding, our regard for those of persuasions other than our own . . . and our unceasing modesty before God. What we should not permit ourselves to do is to project a limited image of the divine goodness upon God. God is more inclusive than the farthest reaches of our most generous compassions. We truly honor God and celebrate the presence of Jesus among us when we come to this table with all of our human sisters and brothers in our compassion, intercession, and regard.

In 1985 Richard Drummond, a former missionary to Japan and professor of comparative religion at Dubuque Theological Seminary, wrote a book of great understanding and compassion about religious diversities. It is titled *Toward a New Age in Christian Theology* and concludes with lines from a great hymn, words with which we may fittingly conclude.

> There's a wideness in God's mercy, like the
>   wideness of the sea. There's a kindness in his
>   justice which is more than liberty.
> For the love of God is broader than the measure
>   of man's mind;
> And the heart of the Eternal is most wonderfully
>   kind.[7]

NOTES

1. World Council of Churches, *Baptism, Eucharist and Ministry,* Faith and Order Paper #11, 1982, Geneva.

2. Raymond Gastil, "What Kind of Democracy?" *Atlantic Monthly* (June 1990): 96.

3. Marcus Borg, *Jesus: A New Vision* (New York: Harper & Row, 1987), 192.

4. E. P. Sanders, *Jesus and Judaism* (Philadelphia: Fortress Press, 1985).

5. *The Presbyterian Outlook* (September 28, 1987): 9.

6. John Cobb, Jr., "The Earth and Humanity: A Christian View" in *Three Faiths: One God,* ed. John Hick and Edmund S. Meltzer (Albany, NY: State University Press of New York, 1989), 128.

7. Richard H. Drummond, *Toward a New Age in Christian Theology,* (Maryknoll, NY: Orbis Books, 1985), 202.

19. "... He Descended into Hell ..."
Patrick J. Willson

1 Peter 3:18–22; 4:6; Matthew 4:23–25

Like many pastors I learned to preach by preaching, inflicting my wares on small rural churches with more patience than members. As might be expected, I seldom preached anywhere twice. I wandered the back roads of the South, one Sunday preaching here, the next Sunday somewhere else. Before the service began I anxiously checked unfamiliar orders of worship and sized up the sanctuary. An elder would graciously lead me around, directing me to the bathroom, getting me a cup of coffee. We would chat about the church, and in the middle of our conversation I would inevitably slip in one question: "Oh, by the way, do you descend into hell?"

Most people listening to the conversation would have found that an odd thing to ask, but elders knew what I needed. Not all churches do "descend into hell" when they say the Apostles' Creed. You can imagine how embarrassing it is for a preacher to descend into hell all alone while the congregation romps on ahead rising from the dead and ascending into heaven!

Though most churches do "descend into hell," not all churches

Patrick J. Willson is Pastor of St. Stephen Presbyterian Church in Fort Worth, Texas. A graduate of the University of Texas and Columbia Theological Seminary, Willson also serves as a Supervisor in Preaching and Worship for the Columbia Theological Seminary Doctor of Ministry program. Willson is a member of "The Moveable Feast," an ongoing study group of preachers that meets annually to work through the lectionary texts.

recite that phrase of the Apostles' Creed. We remember that the creed was not handed down by the apostles carved in stone but rather developed over about four hundred years as a precis of what the Church believed and taught. The phrase "he descended into hell" was one of the last portions of the creed to gain wide acceptance. Many churches still don't accept it, or at least they don't say it. We do say it, but what on earth can we mean by such an odd-sounding assertion: Jesus "descended into hell"?

One thing is clear. We do not mean the same thing when we say it that early Christians meant when they said it. We just can't. Too much has happened over the years for that to be possible.

If we imagine hell at all we may conjure up visions of scaly demons torturing the damned; we may think of a kind of split-level, many-tiered hell, with the thermostat turned up higher for sinners of greater wickedness; we imagine punishments ironically fitting the contours of people's iniquities. Such a vision of hell is our legacy in Western civilization. We have learned what hell is like from paintings: from Michelangelo's *The Last Judgment* and Hieronymus Bosch's *The Garden of Earthly Delights*. We have heard of the levels of hell and the ironic punishments from Dante and John Milton. All of this is wonderful and awe-full, and I am grateful for this heritage, but it is not what Peter had in mind when he wrote his little congregation in Asia Minor about Christ's descent into hell, when "the gospel was preached even to the dead."

What Peter thought of was not Dante's hell or Milton's hell, but the Jewish idea of "Sheol," the place of the dead. Greeks spoke of it as "Hades." It wasn't hell in the sense of Dante's hell. It wasn't hell in the sense of "heaven and hell." All the dead of the human race wound up in Sheol: the good as well as the bad, the wise and the foolish, saints and sinners, Jews and Gentiles. All the dead gathered there. If Jesus was "crucified, dead, and buried," where else would he go but the land of the dead? Modern translations of the Apostles' Creed even say it that way: "he descended to the dead"[1] (not to hell, in the sense of a place of eternal torment). Like everyone else, Jesus went into the place of the dead. People did not "live" in Sheol, they "deaded" there, existing in a shadowy un-life where the darkness and silence were never broken by joy or laughter or praise of God or memory of life on earth. Or at least that is how Peter and other first-century Christians would have imagined Sheol. It may not be how we imagine hell, but that's OK.

Another reason we cannot mean the same thing early Christians meant when they said, "He descended into hell; the third day he rose again from the dead; he ascended into heaven," is that we just don't think of hell being literally, geographically down, and heaven, up. We need not condescendingly assume that all early Christians thought of heaven as up and hell down, but some surely did. Their universe had three stories: heaven, earth, and Sheol. When we think of heaven and hell we may not know precisely where to locate them geographically but we don't think of them as literally up and down. What John Calvin wrote of Christ's descent into hell is one of the most marvelous and moving passages of his *Institutes,* but the notion that hell is a prison under the earth he dismissed as "childish."[2] Even the most literal-minded fundamentalists no longer believe that hell is down under the earth. The language, we understand, is poetic and metaphorical. We understand the meaning. Someone is depressed; we say, "You look really down." We see someone excited, enthusiastic: "Boy, you're really up today!" Up and down can be useful metaphors to speak of spiritual life, but we don't think of heaven as literally up and hell, down.

Still we say, "He *descended* into hell . . . he *ascended* into heaven." But what does it mean to say that? It's a strange notion and sometimes a controversial one, but its meaning is simplicity itself. In Christ's descent into hell we see the fullness of Christ's embrace of human life: He not only lives the life we live, he dies our death, and then follows that well-worn trail to stand in solidarity with all of those who die. "He did not shrink from taking our weakness upon himself," says Calvin.[3] And because Jesus has walked among the dead we can have hope, even for the most deadly and god-forsaken times of our living and dying. That's what it means.

But even after saying what it means we are left a little empty. Is that all there is? Something seems missing. And something is. When Peter reminds his congregations that Christ "preached to the spirits in prison," he is not just asking them to remember a *meaning,* he is calling to mind a *story.* They know the story already, Peter only reminds them. When we say "He descended into hell," we are speaking of part of the Christ-story. He was "conceived by the Holy Ghost, born of the Virgin Mary, suffered under Pontius Pilate, was crucified, dead, and buried; he descended into hell"—it's a story

and the descent into hell is part of that story. Remember Matthew's
little summary of Christ's work:

> And he went about all Galilee, teaching in their
> synagogues and preaching the gospel of the
> kingdom and healing every disease and infirmity
> among the people. So his fame spread . . . and
> they brought him all the sick. . . . And great
> crowds followed him.

Even after Jesus' death that story goes on. What Jesus did in his
earthly ministry he does in the place of the dead. That's the story
Peter points to when he says, Christ "preached to the spirits in
prison." That's the story we are meant to remember when we say,
"He descended into hell."

Peter's congregation knew that story. All he had to do was remind them. Early Christians knew the story but we do not. Though
we may not know exactly how the story was told in Peter's church,
we do know how it was told during the second and third centuries.
A little masterpiece of Christian literature has been passed on to
us. This is part of our inheritance. The story is very dramatic, so
think of it as a drama.

The curtains draw back to reveal a stage soaked in thick darkness. The dark is heavy, oppressive, not just the absence of light
but a thing itself. All has been darkness as long as anyone can
remember. The silence is unbroken, and it too lies like a weight on
the stage.

This is the land of death, ruled over by Death himself, under
the supervision of the Prince of Darkness, Satan.

Suddenly the darkness is shattered by an explosion of light.
Stage lights come up to reveal a vast crowd of people, literally a cast
of thousands, millions.

The unexpected light breaking into the darkness creates confusion. All of a sudden something is happening in a place where
nothing ever happens. In hell, all hell is breaking loose.

The prophet Isaiah stands up, center stage. He is balding and
bearded and his eyes flash with the tensions of craziness and holiness, which is to say he looks exactly like Walter Brueggemann
who teaches the Hebrew scriptures at Columbia Theological Seminary. No one seems to quite know what is happening, but Isaiah

says he knows. "This is what I said would happen," he says, "The people who sit in darkness have seen a great light" (Isa. 9:2).

John the Baptist is there in the crowd too. As always, John is eager to prepare the way. He comes forward to say, "Yes, that's right. He's coming. He's coming. Be ready. Be ready to kneel before him."

Adam is there also. Adam is old and sick. He tells everyone he has been waiting for all these years and was ready to give up, but now he can feel it in his bones. It is coming: healing from the tree of life, healing from that other tree of that long ago garden.

Wild cheering breaks out from all of those who for so long have been silenced by death.

Just then, Death and Satan enter, stage left. (In this drama "death" is not only a place and a state, but a person and character in the drama.) Death and Satan talk together.

Satan is smooth and sleek and sure of himself, cocksure—I imagine him played by Jack Nicholson, talking through clenched teeth. He brags to his henchman Death about his latest triumph. "I am bringing one down for us," he sneers, "a Jew named Jesus. Was he ever a pain in the neck while he lived! He cast out all my lovely demons, he healed people of all the diseases I'd cursed them with, but now I've got him. He was a powerful man, but only human after all. Like anyone else, he was afraid. I heard him praying in the garden: afraid to suffer, afraid to die. But he did suffer and die, and now I've got him. He'll kneel before me as they all must, and then we'll bind him up with the rest."

Death is not so sure about the whole business. Death is played by Dom DeLuise: short, fat from the many souls he has devoured, and a little hysterical. Like a nervous suburbanite, Death seems worried about property values in hell with this new tenant coming in. Death says he doesn't feel good about this, and as a matter of fact he hasn't been feeling exactly himself since he devoured that fellow Lazarus. No sooner had Lazarus been swallowed in a single gulp than someone from above had summoned him back to life, leaving Death with a terrible case of indigestion.

"If this is the same fellow you're bringing here," he says to Satan, "it could be the end of everything we've worked so hard for."

Satan tries to assure him that everything is under his control, that there is nothing to worry about, but just then a voice like thunder interrupts their conversation saying: "Lift up your gates, O rulers, and be lifted up, O everlasting doors, and the King of glory shall come in."

"Now you've done it," says Death, "now you've done it. I tried to tell you, but would you listen to me? Noooooo!"

Death shouts to his demons to make fast the great doors of hell: to keep this One out, to keep the others in. The doors of hell are enormous, made of brass reinforced with bars of iron, the most durable metals imaginable when this story was told. It was over the gates of hell that the poet Dante envisioned the inscription:

> I am the way into the city of woe.
> I am the way to a forsaken people.
> I am the way into eternal sorrow. . . .
> Abandon hope all ye who enter here.

The doors grind shut and are bolted. Hell is now safe and secure.

Again the voice thunders: "Lift up your gates, O rulers . . . and the King of glory shall come in."

Terrified and confused, Death turns to the audience to ask, "Who is this King of glory?"

The answer comes from offstage: all the angels of heaven singing: "The Lord, strong and mighty, The Lord, mighty battle." With that song the bars of iron bend inward and the great brass doors are wrenched from their hinges.

Jesus kicks in the doors of hell. Doors are nothing compared to the fury of his determination. He strides into hell as if he owned the place. Death and Satan fall back in silence. Jesus stretches out his hand to Adam and lifts him from his bed of sickness to stand erect on shaky legs. Jesus looks out on the vast crowd that death has assembled over so may years, and he blesses them all: the patriarchs and prophets, the wise and the foolish, the priests and philosophers, the great and the lowly—he blesses them all and signs them with the cross.

Jesus calls them to follow him, and together they walk out of hell, stepping across the rubble he has made of the doors and striding up an enormous staircase for a destination in paradise.[4]

"He descended into hell," we say, and "he ascended into heaven."

Hell? What is "hell"? Where is "hell"? It's hard to say. We speak of hell often enough: the hell of war, the hell of prisoner of war camps, the hell of Auschwitz and Buchenwald and Dachau, the hell of crushing poverty, the hell of nuclear holocaust. We may even speak of personal suffering as hell: the hell of broken and tortured relationships, the hell of loneliness, the hell of confusion and mental illness, the hell of cancer and slow pain, the hell of being abandoned, the hell of being afraid.

Our public hells, our private hells, we speak of hells on earth as well as whatever ultimate hell there may be. However we speak of hell, however we picture hell, the Bible and the story of Christ's descent into hell invite us to imagine hell as a place where the doors have been kicked in from outside.

Those powerful doors—doors that bar out light and life, doors that stand as a barrier against all hope, doors that mock us in our futility, doors that we may think of as impenetrable—are kicked in and swing to and fro on twisted hinges. That sign, "Abandon hope all ye who enter here," lays in the dust and is scuffed with the footsteps of people leaving a place of despair on their way to a place where hope can be fulfilled.

We know something of hell. At one time or another we have all seen that sign, "Abandon hope all ye who enter here." In the midst of our days we have felt death's power. We have heard the doors slam shut on what seems like forever. We know what it is to feel like hell.

But whenever we describe our situation as hell, we do well to remember that in hell the doors have been kicked in from the outside. Sartre wrote a play about hell called *No Exit,* but the drama of the Church's story of Christ's descent into hell promises that there is indeed an exit, there will always be an exit. However dark it may seem, however hopeless it may appear, there is an open door. It has been kicked in from the outside by One whose design for human life is not that we remain in hell, even hells of our own making, but that we live with him in abundant life.

"Who is this King of glory?" His name is Jesus and "at the name of Jesus every knee should bow, in heaven and on the earth and *under the earth,* and every tongue confess that Jesus Christ is Lord, to the glory of God the Father."

NOTES

1. The English Language Liturgical Consultation, trans., *Praying Together* (Nashville: Abingdon, 1988), 29.

2. John Calvin, *Institutes of the Christian Religion*, II, xvi, 9 (Philadelphia: Westminster, 1960), 514.

3. Calvin, *Institutes*, 518.

4. This telling of the story is loosely adapted from: "The Gospel of Nicodemus, Acts of Pilate and Christ's Descent into Hell," trans. F. Scheidweiler, in Wilhelm Schneemelcher, *New Testament Apocrypha, Volume One: Gospels and Related Writings* (Westminster, 1963), 470–76.

IV. ETHICAL

20. The Untidiness of the Kingdom
Harry B. Adams

1 Corinthians 4:1–13; Matthew 13:24–43

There is always a certain trauma in taking a child for the first year of college. When we arrived at the college with our son, we found the usual helpful people who told us where his room was and pointed us in the right direction. In due time we found the room, and when we opened the door a look of dismay came over the face of our son. His roommate, whom he had not met, had obviously been there before him and actually finished the process of moving in. The bed was neatly made. Every item of clothing was hanging in its proper place. The desk had everything carefully set out. It was all quite neat and tidy, and it was obvious that our son was having something of a panic attack.

There is much to be said for neatness and orderliness and tidiness in life. For one thing, there is a certain aesthetic satisfaction in having everything in its proper place. At least, mothers seem to think so. It is characteristic of mothers that they have a decided aversion to dirty clothes in heaps on the furniture, sheets and blankets rolled in the middle of the bed, magazines and books strewn on the floor, bats and hockey sticks and catchers' mitts and footballs forming an obstacle course through the room. Somehow mothers seem to think that rooms are much more attractive when everything is neatly in order and in its proper place. There is something aesthetically satisfying about coming into a space in which everything is rightly placed and well organized.

Harry Baker Adams was born in Stanford, Kentucky. He received the B.D. degree from Yale University Divinity School, where he served as Professor of Pastoral Theology and from 1967 to 1987 was Associate Dean. Since 1987 he has been Chaplain of Yale University and Master of Trumbull College at Yale. He is the author of *What Jesus Asks: Meditations on Questions in the Gospels.*

There are practical gains when things are orderly and tidy. It is easier to move around when we don't stumble over objects that are not where they are supposed to be. We can find things we are looking for when they are in their proper places. Many an amateur carpenter spends an inordinate amount of time looking for the tool that was thrown down somewhere. We can get things accomplished when we get our time, our surroundings, our selves organized.

As well, external neatness often seems to be related to internal orderliness of thought. It is important to be careful and precise in the ways in which we think, and in the ways in which we order our lives. We need to develop the ability to analyze situations and to sort out the relevant from the irrelevant. We have to develop the capacity to make discriminations that are meaningful and significant, to develop a line of thought that is orderly and rational. Surely it is important to learn to think neatly, carefully, precisely.

We helped our son get moved into his room and to get everything arranged. When we left him, the room was neat and orderly and tidy. After we returned home, we restrained ourselves for a whole week, but then had to call to find out how things were going. Things were going very well indeed. And when we asked how things were going with his roommate, our son responded happily: "Oh fine. He's a real slob." We got the picture.

I don't know that one has to be a slob to qualify for the kingdom of heaven, but it is clear that there is a grace of untidiness about the kingdom. Jesus told the story about the man who sowed the good seed in his field, and about the enemy who came at night and sowed weeds among the wheat. When the plants came up, the servants of the householder couldn't understand how the weeds had gotten there. The householder explained that an enemy had done it.

Then the servants asked: "Do you want us to go and gather them?" Do you want us to pull out the weeds? Clearly the servants were upset and offended that there should be weeds growing among the wheat. They were quite prepared to tidy up the field, to get rid of the weeds that didn't belong there, to sort out the weeds and the wheat and get the field all cleaned up with only the good stuff left.

But the householder wouldn't let the servants tidy up the field. When they asked if he wanted them to gather up the weeds, he answered: "No, lest in gathering the weeds you root up the wheat along with them. Let both grow together until the harvest; and at harvest time I will tell the reapers, Gather the weeds first and bind them in bundles to be burned, but gather the wheat into my barn."

The Kingdom of God as we know it now, as we experience it, as we try to be faithful within it, is not precise and neat and orderly. There is a grace of untidiness about the kingdom. Do you want us to gather up the weeds, sir? No, let them grow in the midst of the wheat for now.

I have allowed and even insisted that there is virtue in neatness and orderliness and tidiness in the way we live. We recently underwent a renovation in our office, and the mess and confusion almost did me in. I am a clean desk person. I like to put things back where they belong. I dislike clutter. But the parable of Jesus alerts us that neatness and orderliness and tidiness do not define the kingdom of heaven. Furthermore, Jesus warns that if we identify the kingdom with tidiness, the harvest we hope to bring to fruition will in fact be destroyed.

Thank God the kingdom isn't such a tidy place. For the untidiness of the kingdom comes as a grace to us. Consider the graces of the untidiness of the kingdom. First, that the kingdom is untidy frees us from an awful compulsion to neatness and orderliness. An article in *The New York Times* described the terrible stress persons live under when they are trying to sell their home. "When Connie Hayes was trying to sell her house in Spring Valley, New York, she found her days a continuous whirl of cleaning. At night she often lay awake, mentally tidying the house all over again. 'I was crazy when it was all over,' Mrs. Hayes said. 'It was a tremendous strain. I am very house-proud anyway, but I found I was cleaning all the time. Not a thing could be out of place because you never knew when someone would arrive to look.' "

Another person reported: "I scrubbed, vacuumed, plumped up cushions, ate snacks at the sink so traces of food could be quickly disposed of, and became almost hysterical at the thought of anyone taking a shower because that meant repolishing the shower doors. My daughter and husband hardly dared move in case something got out of place, or a finger mark was left on a clean surface. You become quite manic and completely unreasonable."

We are not justified before God by our neatness; that is not what the kingdom is about. The kingdom is more about a child finding love and care than about keeping the house neat. The kingdom is more about relationship and communication with an adolescent than about keeping the room orderly. The kingdom is more about a home in which persons find identity and healing than about keeping everything in place in the living room. The kingdom is more about a church ministering to the people in its community than it is about keeping the walls spotless. " 'Do you want us to go and gather the weeds?' 'No, lest in gathering the weeds you root up the wheat along with them.' "

Second, that the kingdom is untidy frees us from having to maintain our purity by isolating ourselves from "the corrupt." I recently came across the minutes of a Christian church (Disciples) in the midwest in the 1860s. It appeared that the church board spent most of its time and energy putting people out of the church. People were expelled for such sins as drinking, dancing, smoking, card playing, and "fraternizing with the Methodists."

The issues are different for most people in our day, but there is still an inclination on the part of many Christians and many churches to separate themselves from those who see things differently, whether it be over the interpretation of scripture, the ordination of women or homosexuals, the stance on a woman's right to make a decision about abortion, or the formulation of certain doctrines of the Christian faith such as the virgin birth or the physical resurrection.

Surely careful thought must be given to the articulation of Christian doctrine and the exposition of Christian behavior. But the grace of untidiness allows us to keep those who differ with us within the concern of the kingdom and the care of God. " 'Do you want us to go and gather the weeds?' 'No, lest in gathering the weeds you root up the wheat along with them.' "

Third, that the kingdom is untidy saves us from having to make the judgments that are beyond our competence. We do not have to take upon ourselves the judgments that belong to God. We must make our judgments about good and evil, about right and wrong, as clearly as possible. But the ultimate judgment upon others and upon ourselves is not ours to make. Because we don't have to sort out now who is and who is not in the kingdom of heaven, we can live with openness and freedom toward others.

Surely it is the task of the Church to set standards of right belief, of loving behavior, of proper order. But when the Church has demanded too much tidiness, and has taken upon itself the absolute judgment of God on the heretic or the free spirit, there has been all too evident what can only be called the corruption of precision. When we get too rigid and precise in our judgments of others, we inevitably cast out the wheat with the weeds.

Paul set the present untidiness of the kingdom in this way: "Therefore do not pronounce judgment before the time, before the Lord comes, who will bring to light the things now hidden in darkness and will disclose the purpose of the heart."

" 'Do you want us to go and gather the weeds?' 'No, lest in gathering the weeds you root up the wheat along with them.' "

Finally, that the kingdom is untidy lets us know that the kingdom somehow is for us. Life is untidy. The church is untidy. The world is untidy. Children teach us many things, but surely nothing more crucial than the fact that life is essentially and inherently untidy. There is nothing neat and tidy about a baby. They are messy. We haven't grasped reality when we have everything neatly organized. We haven't grasped reality when our thoughts are precisely articulated. We haven't grasped reality when we have explained everything clearly. For life and reality and the kingdom of heaven are always beyond our efforts to make them neat and tidy and orderly.

The kingdom of heaven is like weeds sown by an enemy growing in the midst of a wheat field. And the neat, precise servants wanted to pull them out. But the householder said, "No, lest in gathering the weeds you root up the wheat along with them." Thank God for the grace of untidiness.

21. The Lion and the Lamb
Paul D. Duke

Isaiah 11:6–9

Last week a celebrated retirement occurred. Gunther Gebel-Williams, the world famous animal trainer, gave his last performance with the Ringling Brothers Barnum & Bailey Circus. His farewell tour brought him through St. Louis a few weeks ago, and some of us saw him. He does amazing things, especially with tigers. They snarl and scowl and hiss hatefully—then slink to where he sends them. His body is covered with scars. It's taken more than 500 stitches to sew him up where he's been bitten and clawed. The circus bills him as The Greatest Wild Animal Trainer of All Time.

Scripture tells of a taming of wild animals that Gunther Gebel-Williams will never do. Twice in the book of Isaiah we're given a picture of predators and their prey lying down beside each other in perfect peace. In Isaiah 11 and again in Isaiah 65 we read that when the Messiah comes the wolf, the leopard, the bear, and the lion will lie down with the lamb, the calf, the goat, the ox. And a little child shall lead them. A child will play at the den of the asp. The lion will eat straw like an ox. When the Messiah comes, says the Lord, they will not hurt or destroy on all my holy mountain.

What do we make of such a text? It would be nice to take it literally. It would be wonderful if God's eternal reign of peace should include all sorts of animals, none of them killing, none of them afraid. What if in paradise you could bury your face in the golden mane of a lion and pet him till he purred? What if goats are best friends with grizzlies in heaven, and the lamb and the wolf have conversations while munching clover for breakfast? I for one

Paul D. Duke is pastor of the Kirkwood Baptist Church in Kirkwood, Missouri. He was born in Montgomery, Alabama, and received his B.A. degree from Samford University and the M.Div. and Ph.D. degrees from The Southern Baptist Theological Seminary. He is the author of *Irony in the Fourth Gospel.*

have my hopes. I've known animals worth sharing eternity with. Scripture even says the final redemption is not of humankind alone, but of all creation. But who knows what this means? If God has plans for animals, they are secret to us, and the beasts themselves aren't saying a word. As for these texts about the lion lying down with the lamb, they want to do more with us than set us dreaming of paradise as a petting zoo.

This vision is a poetic picture of the peace God will make in the world. It's the promise of radical transformations. This world's instruments and agents of death will be remade into instruments and agents of God's peace: swords beaten into plowshares; talon and claw transformed into healing hands; nations no longer devouring each other but feeding together on God's bounty. Imagine Saddam Hussein and George Bush doing lunch, or Louisiana's David Duke kneeling to take communion beside Jesse Jackson. When Messiah comes with power there will be such peace.

It's hard to hope in that vision when so many fangs are bared and so many nations and factions are growling and snapping at each other. It was easier to believe last year when God gave us peace for Christmas. Last year the sound of the season was the music of hammers against a doomed wall. This year we hear the sound of snarling, the cries of victims being tortured or killed, the volleys of incendiary, self-righteous words. We may get war for Christmas. Jesus warned us never to be naive about peace. He said we'd be at each others' throats till the end. In such a world it's hard to hope for much peace.

In nineteenth-century America there was a Quaker painter named Edward Hicks who painted today's text over and over again. In all, he painted over eighty versions of the Peaceable Kingdom, the animals at peace led by a child. Study those paintings and you'll notice that over a period of years as Edward Hicks became more and more disappointed with the conflicts of his age, the predators in his paintings look more and more ferocious. Painting by painting the miracle looks harder and harder. He kept painting the vision, but at the end of his life he confessed he wasn't satisfied with his work.[1] It's hard to get it right. It's hard to trust ourselves to this vision when so many adversaries are so deadly. Woody Allen said, "The lion and the calf shall lie down together, but the calf won't get much sleep." We know what he means. Christ has called us to pray for peace and work for peace and to live as peaceably as we can with all people. But we know very well that the Peaceable Kingdom has not yet come as God wills it to come and as one day it will surely come.

But in the meantime, as we pray and seek that day, we can let the promise have more power in us. For the existence of violence and rage isn't just the problem of the snarling political world, it's the problem of my own snarling heart and your heart too. Carl Sandburg wrote a poem called "Wilderness" in which he said, "There is a wolf in me, fangs pointed for tearing gashes. . . . There is a fox in me . . . I nose in the dark night and take sleepers and eat them and hide the feathers. . . . There is a fish in me . . . a baboon in me. . . . There is an eagle in me and a mockingbird. . . . O, I got a zoo, I got a menagerie inside my ribs, under my bony head, under my red-valve heart . . . I am the keeper of the zoo."[2]

The first great work of God's Messiah is to come to the bloody zoo in me and you and to teach the lion and the lamb to live together. Christ has come to tame and integrate and harmonize our many warring selves to a whole self at peace. Do you remember how he came one day to a self-destructive crazy man, a man who howled at night like a beast and cut himself with rocks? Jesus asked him, "What is your name?" And the man said, "My name is legion for there are so many of us inside of me." And Christ drove out of him what was at war in him and gave him what the Gospel calls his right mind. Is there a howling zoo at war inside your ribs? There is, if the peace of God has not finished its work of taming and integrating all the beasts in you.

Which is not to say we're all alike. The menagerie in each of us is different. In some of us the angry lion is dominant. We tear at others, we tear at ourselves. For reasons we don't fully understand we lash out even at those we love. There's an untamed aggression in us, a raging hunger that destroys relationships. In others of us, the passive lamb is predominant. We're timid and afraid. We're never willing to roar, even when roaring is called for. We live like victims, without the power and the courage and the lion-hearted love of Christ. But what the peace of God gives is the integration of all these together. The work of Christ is to take the aggression in us and make it a more peaceable strength, to take what is gentle in us and make it more brave. Which do you need—the gentling of the lion in you or the roaring of the lamb in you? Some of us need both. It's both that Christ gives, who makes lion and lamb live in harmony.

Carol Gilligan is a teacher and writer who researches how children make decisions. She's noticed in particular how boys and girls often resolve conflicts differently. She tells of one instance she observed in which a girl said to a boy, "Let's play next-door neighbors." "I want to play pirates," said the boy. The girl said, "Okay, then you can be the pirate that lives next door!" That girl was onto something. Many of us, especially us boys, might have said pirates and neighbors don't mix. Let's divide them and play pirates for a while then neighbors for a while. The girl was more creative. She suspected that a pirate would be transformed if he were also a neighbor and that a neighborhood might be richer with a pirate next door.[3] This is the integrating way of God. The pirate in me and the neighbor in me, the lion in you and the lamb in you are no longer split off and in conflict but brought together in surprisingly creative relationship.

And if you ask, But how—how do I find such peace between my separate selves?—the answer I'll give is not a strategy or a therapy or a program, but a Person. The answer is deep friendship with the One scripture calls both Lion of Judah and Lamb of God. God's Messiah has come, his name is Jesus, and in his life the lion and the lamb dwell together. One of our crimes against him is to make him one without the other. To some people God is all lion— all strength and judgment and wrath. To others God is all lamb— all gentle and weak and meek. But Jesus the Christ has shown us the face of God, the face of lion and lamb together. Wasn't Jesus like a lion? Didn't he roar with judgment and strength? Wasn't he fierce and terrible to the powers of darkness? Isn't he unpredictable, majestic, and free as the wind? In *The Chronicles of Narnia* C. S. Lewis wrote of Christ as a lion named Aslan and one of the characters says of him, "He is wild, you know. Not like a *tame* lion."[4] And at the same time he is the gentlest lamb who cares for the weak, who forgives all sin, who suffers in terrible silence and for our sakes goes even to death like a lamb to the slaughter. Behold the Lamb of God who takes away the sins of the world.

In the Book of Revelation the question rings from heaven: Who is worthy to open the scrolls that tell the meaning of all history? The answer comes, Do not weep, for the Lion of Judah has conquered. And we turn to see this great lion, and what do we see? A lamb, standing as though slain. And all heaven sings, "Worthy is the Lamb"—the lion slain like a lamb—"to receive honor and glory and blessing."

And worthy to receive our poor conflicted lives, to put us at peace and make us whole. If the beasts in you are raging or if they're afraid, give them to the care of Christ. Let him dwell like a child at the center of them all. And he will call them by name and gather them into himself, until the lion and the lamb in him become the peace in you.

Madeleine L'Engle has written a wonderful children's book called *Dance in the Desert.*[5] It's the story of a young man and woman who long ago traveled through the desert with their child. They traveled with a caravan on their way to Egypt through a desert filled with ferocious animals. Some of their companions were afraid of the beasts, afraid especially that they might harm the child. When night came and they were all sitting around the fire, a great lion appeared at the edge of the camp and everyone trembled. But the child held out his arms and the lion rose up on his hind legs and, of all things, began to dance. And then from the desert came running little mice and two donkeys and three eagles, a snake and great clumsy ostriches, a unicorn, a pelican, and even two dragons. And they all bowed to the child and they all danced together round and round him as he stood at the center and laughed with delight.

You know the name of that Child. Let him stand at the center of your desert. Let all the beasts in you bow to him. And the Child will lead them. Eyes on him, they learn to dance together around him, God's peace and God's pleasure.

NOTES

1. John Dillenberger, *The Visual Arts in America* (Chico, CA: Scholars Press, 1984), 130–32.

2. Carl Sandburg, *The Complete Poems of Carl Sandburg,* rev. ed. (New York: Harcourt Brace Jovanovich, 1970), 100–101.

3. Carol Gilligan in an unpublished paper, cited by Sharon Parks, *The Critical Years* (San Francisco: Harper & Row, 1986), 39.

4. C. S. Lewis, *The Lion, the Witch and the Wardrobe* (New York: Collier Books, 1970), 180.

5. Madeleine L'Engle, *Dance in the Desert* (New York: Farrar, Straus & Giroux, 1969).

22. Keeping Up with the Joneses

David Albert Farmer

Exodus 20:1–2, 17; Romans 7:7–13

Recently, I was flipping through a magazine when I gradually began to feel very inadequate. For a good long while, I didn't know why, but before canceling my subscription, I thought I'd try to figure it out. And I finally did. There was no problem with the content of the magazine, but the advertising was getting to me. It was very well done—elegant, alluring, persuasive. Subtly and not so subtly, the message kept coming through that what I and my loved ones had wasn't quite up to par; that, of course, could be corrected by making the right purchases.

You've been drawn in by these kinds of ads too, I'll bet. For a compact stereo component system, the ad read: "For people who want everything but have no place to put it." And for jewelry: "Like poets or magicians . . . those masters of imagination, [our artists] interpret . . . dreams and desires for a clientele which, like [our company] itself, is unique in all the world." Then, a really classy ad for an automobile: "Owning [one of our cars] will not make you a different person. Yet you won't be the same, either. [Our car] defines its own class. Which gives an owner the singular distinction of attaining a goal all but abandoned in today's homogenized society. Individuality."

David Albert Farmer is pastor of the University Baptist Church, Baltimore, Maryland, and editor of *Pulpit Digest*. He was educated at Carson-Newman College and at The Southern Baptist Theological Seminary, from which he received the Ph.D. degree and at which he taught during his graduate studies. He has also taught at the Baptist Seminary in Rüschlikon, Switzerland. He is coeditor (with Edwina Hunter) of *And Blessed Is She: Sermons by Women.* "Keeping Up with the Joneses" was the ninth in a series of sermons on the Ten Commandments.

Advertisers get us because we want more and better *things*. They also get us because we have become technology-crazed. I was thinking about this when I saw my first television set that lets you watch, not just one program at a time, but two. This wave of the future is really going to frustrate some of you because of the joy you've been getting these last few years changing, every few minutes, from station to station with your remote control while your family sits helplessly by. You've had to be quick as you've kept up with the scores of several ball games at once, but—still—you've only been watching one program at a time. Now, you can actually watch two games or two movies or two sit-coms or two completely different kinds of shows at the same time; this is a wonderful innovation especially for those times when we just can't decide what mood we're in. Two events at once. A comedy *and* a tragedy. Something intellectually gripping *and* something utterly mindless. Incredible! And you can see how very much this kind of thing is needed in all our homes, can't you? It's important enough to extend your monthly credit a bit more, and it's important enough to choose over having a little something left at the end of the month to help those who have nothing at all.

If you can resist the temptation to wear the trendiest clothes, drive the priciest cars, live in the most prestigious neighborhoods, send your children to the preppiest of schools, then you have convictions of steel. Let's face it. Most all of us have bought in to an attitude toward *things* that drives us to buy the most expensive ones we possibly can, and, for many of us, this means we are buying items that cost a good deal more than we can actually afford. Forget the fact that there are quality items—maybe just as, or more durable, functional, fashionable—available for less money. That isn't the point at all. The point is, when others have *things* that cost more than the *things* we have, we're jealous. Some of us are so status conscious, in fact, that we wouldn't dream of buying even our personal care products at a discount store. Why, we know people who spend lots of money on these kinds of items. Can we do less? Name brands are everything to us; we must have a designer toothbrush! And it just happens to sit out in the bathroom for our guests to notice.

In the extreme, our jealousy of what others have and the desire to possess it for ourselves, becomes *covetousness*. To covet is to desire inordinately, and what we have—no matter how much it is—is never, ever enough.

The powerful preacher of the fourth century, John of Antioch—who, because of his eloquence, was given the title *Chrysostom* meaning "golden mouth"—once observed that there was a great difference between a genuinely wealthy person and a covetous person who might have a good deal of money. He saw it this way:

> The covetous [one] is not rich . . . can never be
> rich. The covetous [one] is a keeper, not a master,
> of wealth; a slave, not a lord.[1]

Reese Newbury is a purely southern bad guy in Pat Conroy's *The Prince of Tides*. If you've ever lived in a small town in which one wealthy, sleazy, and not-necessarily smooth person controlled, by economics, the destinies of the rest of the citizens, then you know Mr. Newbury. Young Tom Wingo found himself, under unpleasant circumstances, in Mr. Newbury's home study with Newbury's pathetic son, Todd. Wealthy, friendless Todd is trying unsuccessfully to establish a friendship with Tom whose family barely eked out a living. There is a large map of the county on the wall of the study, and Tom happens to see a red push pin at the South Carolina island on which the Wingos lived, the island being the only thing of value they had.

"Why is there a red pin on our island?" Tom asked.

Todd explained, "Dad places red pins on all the places he plans to buy. The green pins represent all the property he owns."

"He owns the whole . . . country. . . . [But] that's one piece of land he'll never own. I promise you that much," Tom insisted.

But Todd told the truth that all of who have been there understand: "He'll get it if he wants it bad enough."

In contrast with this push to amass *things*—especially *things* owned by a neighbor—is a much less practiced virtue: being satisfied with having what we need, just what we need. It's so seldom practiced that I can hardly point you to an example of this kind of living apart from a cloister of those who have taken vows of poverty.

When we covet, we begin by wanting what our neighbor has, but—in time—we want, not simply, some*thing* like what our neighbor owns, we want the very items she or he has. And, sometimes, whatever this power is within us causes us to want more than the *things* that belong to others. Your neighbor is not just envious of your supportive, loving spouse—hoping to find such a relationship some day; your friend wants *your* spouse. To act on such a temptation is the most intimate way I can think of to try and keep up with the Joneses.

The tenth commandment speaks to these attitudes:

> You shall not covet your neighbor's house; you
> shall not covet your neighbor's wife [or husband],
> or male or female slave, or ox, or donkey, or
> anything that belongs to your neighbor. (Exod.
> 20:17, NRSV)

This commandment "prohibits the kind of desire for anyone or anyone else's property that would create jealousy, envy, and greed in the one desiring, and would set in motion plans to take what is wanted."[2] If we read carefully through the Ten Commandments, we will notice that this is the only one of the ten that "places primary emphasis on emotion . . . rather than on overt action."[3] None of the others really ask us to look beyond

> public . . . acts to private attitudes. Like all Hebrew
> verbs of mental activity, however, "to covet" also
> includes an element of enactment. It is action in
> rehearsal.[4]

The tenth commandment is an expression of the law about which Paul was speaking when he wrote to the Romans and said, "I would not have known what it is to covet if the law had not said, 'You shall not covet' " (Rom. 7:7, NRSV). This is to say, the Law of God gives the sin a name. We all know the impulse and the drive, but we might not have known what to call it apart from the Word of God. Swedish scholar Anders Nygren explains that

> just as the sun's rays call forth the possibilities that
> are in the seed and bring them to full growth, so
> the law calls forth the sin that slumbers. Now it
> has opportunity to develop its inherent
> possibilities.[5]

Paul went on to say: ". . . sin, seizing an opportunity in the commandment, produced in me all kinds of covetousness" (Rom. 7:8,

NRSV). When the law *named* the murky, anonymous impulse within Paul, he knew at once about all kinds of sinfulness in his life related to destructive desire—unhealthy, blind desire—that seems to be the root of all sinfulness as well as a sin in and of itself.

At the end of the list of ten, there is this commandment that speaks against covetousness. As I've suggested, it is different from the rest in its attention to attitude that may then become evil action. And its placement is not a matter of happenstance. Perhaps it is a kind of summary of the sin involved in breaking any one of the commandments. All of them warn against making choices based on an unhealthy desire, an almost uncontrollable appetite, to have what rightly belongs to another, even to God.

The Ten Commandments put us into touch with the great liberating God. They remind us—each one of them—that we are free in the first place because of God's gracious actions, and they tell us how to remain free people, where not to wander, if we are serious about being personally and spiritually free. If you want to remain free people, you make peace with what you need in contrast to the ways of a society gone mad with pushing people toward more *things* than anyone's household can contain; you make peace with what you can have and enjoy it through honest means, through genuine relationship, and through who, at your best, you really are.

I ran across a helpful paragraph in Rabbi Kushner's book, *When All You've Ever Wanted Isn't Enough.* He wrote:

> Our souls are not hungry for fame, comfort,
> wealth, or power. Those rewards create almost as
> many problems as they solve. Our souls are
> hungry for meaning, for the sense that we have
> figured out how to live so that our lives matter, so
> that the world will be at least a little bit different
> for our having passed through it.[6]

A sense that we are really OK people and that we honestly have some real contribution to make to our world is hard to come by for many of us; this often leads us into various attitudes and acts of covetousness. In a recent issue of *The New Yorker,* there is the latest in a series of cartoons on the Seven Deadly Sins; this one happens to deal with envy, which is a part of covetousness. One panel shows a woman watching television, and the name of the show reads: "Lifestyles of Fortune's Favorites (i.e., Not You)." Another shows a man lying down, saying to himself, "Why bother moving from this sofa—my life will never be as good as Henry's anyway." And in another panel of the cartoon, a very articulate and angry man is saying, "It *INFURIATES* me to know that there are people who are better off, smarter, and more attractive than I am."[7]

To covet is to be controlled by some*thing* outside ourselves, and that is slavery. The Ten Commandments talk to us about not selling ourselves into any kind of slavery because slavery ultimately means oppression no matter how good it looks on the outside. At a very basic level, covetousness can be a slavery to materialism and status, but in its expanse it becomes more destructive even than this. Covetousness is a slavery to exterior supports for self-esteem and self-worth. Covetousness is slavery to an unhealthy sense of competition and the need to be controlling; it is slavery to a willingness to gain—through devious means—what another person has won through respectable means.

Make no mistake about it: Covetousness is slavery. And the tenth commandment points us in place of this taskmaster to God, to ongoing freedom in relationship with God. Relationship with God is worth desiring. And, dear friends, that is what we really need.

NOTES

1. Chrysostom, "Homily 20," *20 Centuries of Great Preaching,* Vol. 1, eds. Fant and Pinson (Waco, TX: Word, 1971), 86.

2. Marvin E. Tate, "The Legal Traditions of the Book of Exodus," *Review and Expositor* (Fall 1977): 498.

3. Ibid.

4. "The Ten Commandments," *Harper's Bible Dictionary* (San Francisco: Harper & Row, 1985), 1034.

5. Anders Nygren, *Commentary on Romans* (Philadelphia: Fortress, 1949), 279.

6. Harold Kushner, *When All You've Ever Wanted Isn't Enough* (New York: Summit, 1986), 4.

7. "The Seven Deadly Sins," *The New Yorker* (October 29, 1990): 124.

23. Friendships
Peter J. Gomes

And from generation to generation, passing into holy souls, wisdom maketh us friends of God and prophets.

—Wisdom 7:27b

When I was brought up in a staunchly Protestant and biblically minded home, I was thoroughly unaware that there was a portion of the Bible known as the Apocrypha. And I suspect that there are similarly situated ignorant people among you this morning. The text is taken from this unknown collection of biblical books, this wisdom literature, this Apocrypha literature that has been a part of the Orthodox canon from the ancient days of Christendom. And it is from this odd source that this odd text might have something to do with our lives. It is the twenty-seventh verse of the seventh chapter of the Wisdom of Solomon, these words: "And from generation to generation, passing into holy souls, wisdom maketh us friends of God and prophets." An odd text from an odd place, but at this time of year no excuse needs to be offered to talk about the most important subject of friendship: friendship with one another, friendships in the world, and most important, friendship with God. But of course those of you who know texts of this sort and who listened carefully as Mr. McAfee read the text this morning, will note that friendship is not where the text begins and neither can we. The text does not appear to be very much concerned with friendship at all. It is concerned very much with something else called wisdom.

Peter John Gomes was born in Boston, Massachusetts, and educated at Bates College and Harvard Divinity School, where he received his doctorate. A Baptist, Dr. Gomes has served since 1974 as minister of the Harvard Memorial Church and Plummer Professor of Christian Morals at Harvard University. He is the author of several books and was recognized in 1980 by *Time* as one of the outstanding preachers in the United States.

I must say that when I was eight years old in this environment that I just described to you, I had to memorize 100 verses from all of the verses of the Bible in order to win a prize in Sunday School to go off to camp. I won the prize but I hated camp so I didn't go. But this verse was, alas, not one of the verses that I was required to memorize. It would be many years later before I heard it. And I heard it for the very first time in this pulpit, in this church, twenty-five years ago a week last Wednesday. You wonder, "How would he know with such absolute precision and detail?" I can almost tell you what time I heard it and where I was sitting when I heard it. The details are clear to me because it was the Convocation Service of the Faculty of the Divinity School on the first Wednesday of the term in September of 1965. Twenty-five years ago I was a member of the entering class in that year, and with my fellow M.B.D.'s, as we were called in those days, B.D. juniors, sat under the gallery in respectful distance from the higher-ups and the mighty of the land and I listened to the sermon. The address was given by George Williams. And I'm looking out here to see if George is here this morning, and I don't see him. But he will hear what I've got to say. I remember very well, it was given by George who was then the Hollis Professor of Divinity and he had just come back from the Second Vatican Council where he was one of the servants. Now, I must confess, and I'd do so even if he were here, that I don't remember a thing that he said. And I'm sure that I didn't understand it when I heard it. After all, I was a mere B.D. junior. But I did remember this text and I remained fascinated by it ever since and resolved that sooner or later, I should preach a sermon on it. Twenty-five years later, almost to the day, this is it.

It is really not about friendship. I want all of my biblical mavens out there to know that I acknowledge this straightaway. This is not a text about friendship. It is a hymn to wisdom. And wisdom is a glorious, alluring, compelling, compassionate she: feminine, full of grace, full of miraculous power. She is described in a variety of ways. She is described as a teacher. At verse 22 it says: "For wisdom, which is the worker of all things, taught me." At verse 23 she is described as, "Kind to man, steadfast, sure, free from care, having all power, overseeing all things, and going through all understanding." She is described as, in fact, "the breath of the power of God . . . the brightness of the everlasting light, the unspotted mirror of the image of God and the very image of the goodness of

God." If you would see God in all the majestic, godly wisdom and power, you must first look upon the face of wisdom; and when you see her, you've seen it all. The whole book goes on and on and on, chapter after chapter, attribute after attribute about the qualities of wisdom. They heap up and accumulate. Every chapter begins, she is this, or she is that. Solomon is obviously infatuated with wisdom and his book is a love poem to her. Maybe that will entice you to read it. You've read some of the love poems of Solomon and they are pretty salacious; you might try this one out and see if it equals the others. Wisdom is his subject, and a mighty one she is.

But having said that and acknowledged that, I now confess very quickly that it is not wisdom that particularly draws me to this passage. It is not wisdom that at this stage turns me on. It is not wisdom that fascinates my mind or tickles my fancy here. I've preached many a sermon on wisdom and doubtless will probably have to do many more before my time comes. It is not what wisdom does here, it is not so much even who wisdom is. It is what wisdom enables me and you to become. It is the transforming, transferring power of wisdom. It is *not* that wisdom makes us wise, though that is a happy consequence, a by-product of wisdom. It is that wisdom enables us to be *friends* of God. Friends of God, what an extraordinary phrase. But not only friends of God but prophets. It is not the abstract qualities of divine wisdom and human knowledge at work here. This is not a hymn to the clever *summa* graduates of the college or the members of *Phi Beta Kappa*. This is an almost inadvertent testimony to friendship, to intimacy, to the delicate, to the perilous enterprise of being close to another person. What we might call in the jargon of the day, a hymn to "meaningful relationships."

But friendship with God, what a strange notion. It is almost a conundrum, almost an oxymoron. My notions of friendship and my notions of God do not easily square with one another. They do not easily go together, at least at first. God is either that great venerable figure of indeterminate age whose beard is of indeterminate length and who hurls thunderbolts at justly deserving mortals. Or, after three years at Harvard Divinity School, God is that implacable, absolute idea: awesome, moving, guiding force of the Universe. But neither of these: powerful idea or grand, eloquent old man, suggests intimacy, friendship, companionship, or relationship. And friendship, why friendship is something else entirely.

A friend is somebody you can trust. A friend is somebody you can borrow money from without ever being fearful of ever having to pay it back, or at least of ever being asked to pay it back. A friend is someone who would do the same thing for you. Someone to whom you can talk without fear of rebuke or recrimination.

But being friendly on the one hand, and being friendly with God on the other does not sound like a good idea. It sounds like being forward with the queen or something of that sort. It makes you a little nervous. Moses, for example, didn't dare look God in the face. In fact, Moses was more attracted to God's hinder parts as you may recall from the Book of Exodus. And none of the prophets seem particularly matey or chatty with God: angry yes, beseeching yes, trusting yes, dutiful and obedient yes, but not particularly intimate or friendly. And even Jesus from time to time has that awkward father-son relationship that is so constantly problematic.

But the text suggests that wisdom makes us God's friends. That's what it says, "friends of God," and it enables us to see, do, and know things in the world. That is the prophetic part. This is of course what prophets do—see, do, and know things in the world—and wisdom enables all of these. I recall our preacher of next Sunday, Harvey Cox, speaking at Morning Prayers a few years ago on the recovery of the notion of friendship with God. Harvey, like me, is a Baptist, and we both grew up on the gospel hymns that were full of intimate, syrupy, almost embarrassing hints of intimate relationships with God in the garden while the dew was still on the roses and things of that sort. And the stand-by hymn of our time and our youth was *What a Friend We Have in Jesus*, for example. Now, most of you are too sophisticated either to know it or to acknowledge that you know the hymn. *What a Friend We Have in Jesus*, to which a friend appended the subtext: "What a friend we have in Jesus, Christ almighty, what a pal!" That is the kind of feeling some of us grew up with, and we're embarrassed about it. And then there was *Jesus Is All the World to Me* which ends every verse with the line, "He's my friend." Then there is the great hymn that probably none of you know, *I've Found a Friend, O Such a Friend*.

None of these are found in this or any other edition of the *Harvard University Hymnal*. And Harvey Cox said something that reassured me mightily. He said that as he grew older, he grew more comfortable and grew more to like the notion of a God with whom one could be on friendly terms. Because I think he said he hoped to spend a great deal of time with God after he finished his course here; he hoped that it would be on friendly relations. God as a friend is not such a bad idea after all.

Why? Why is it not such a bad idea? Because friendship invariably means relationship, relating. I've never really accepted the recent convention where someone will say to you, "Oh, we don't have a relationship anymore, we're just friends." I've never understood what that meant. For being in friendship is in a relationship, and if it is a good friendship, a meaningful friendship, then the relationship is full of meaning, which means that it is meaningful. Relationship therefore must mean something else that has escaped my bachelor state. Friends relate to one another at an intimate, perilously dangerous, and wonderfully fundamental level. Friendships are precious and precarious. We all know when we have found one. What an extraordinary experience it is to discover as a little boy or a little girl that that person you like, likes you, and wants you to like him, and she wants to like you. What an extraordinary universe has opened up in the schoolyard playground when that moment of recognition takes place. And you go home, and you are asked what has happened in school and you say, "I've found a friend." Or you say, "So and so is my friend," or "my best friend." "I have thirty best friends." Who could ask for anything more?

We know what that discovery is like and we know what it is like when at the end of life one doesn't have thirty best friends, but one has one or two. Friends that will care for you despite all that you have become. Friends that love despite all that you haven't become. Friends who will love you not because they don't know you, but who love you in spite of the fact that they know you terribly well indeed. We know what friendship is in youth and in old age, and we are torn by the formations of friendships and all of their intimate burdens in this particular place in this particular season of life when everything from seventeen to twenty-two has the intensity of ten plus ten. We know what that is like.

And we also know what it is like to lose a friend: to lose them by death or by absence. We also know what it is like to lose them by neglect, not to pay attention to the little things upon which most friendships are ultimately based. And we know what it is like to lose them in anger when they are furious with us for something or they have betrayed us and we have dropped them, dropped them as if they never were. We know the passion, the intimacies of friendships formed and we know the pain and the pathos of friendships lost. But in every level of that knowledge we are dealing in a series of intimate engagements, one with the other. There is no friendship in isolation. There is no friendship in principle. There is no abstract notion of friendship. There is only friendship in exchange between one another: friendship in communion, friendship in relationship, friendship in community.

And so this notion of friendship when we think of it in terms of relating to God reminds us that what we are engaged with in a relationship with God is an intimate relationship, an intimate, total, and consuming relationship. To be a friend of God, and to have God as our friend is to enter into a relationship of unimagined wonder, power, love, and intimacy. And if one thinks of this image from the Wisdom of Solomon it begins to transform all of the other images with which we think of God. There is that God who is the law-giver, the stern father, the nurturing mother, the judge, the sovereign, the ruler of the Universe, all of that. But all of that gets transcended, transformed, and enabled by the figure of God as friend. And it is wisdom that enables us to know that friendship.

But to this arsenal of images the text opens up a possibility that by wisdom and over time and through generation to generation, age to age, we are able to relate to God and God to us in terms both of companionship and compassion. Companionship and compassion: The two words combined together form the notion of joy. You may recall from the second lesson that it is Jesus' prayer that our joy might be full once we have become no longer his servants but his friends. The notion of God enriched by the notion of compassion and companionship equal joy, and we share then what friends always share: everything.

What is it that Albert Camus says?

> Don't walk in front of me,
> I may not follow.
> Don't walk behind me,
> I may not lead.
> Walk beside me and just be my friend.

Camus did not write as a Christian, we know that. And he could not bear even the thought of the notion of God. But his line describes the notion of an intimate relationship between the human and the divine as we are daring to infer from our text. And lest you think the *Harvard Hymn Book* entirely bereft, in hymn number ten where we sing the last verse of the hymn, *O Worship the King*, perhaps you will remember the next time you sing it, that it ends in these phrases:

> Thy mercies, how tender,
> How firm to the end,
> Our Maker, Defender,
> Redeemer, and Friend!

It's not chosen just to make a good rhyme. It's chosen to make a good point.

And can that mutual intimacy, can that meaningful relationship, can that friendship ever be summarized better than it is in St. John's Gospel when he says so simply, "We love God, because he first loved us." To be a friend of God, then, to be the beneficiary of wisdom, is to be more than the mere object of creation, more than a subject in God's great sentence, more than a moral pawn in the great game of life. It is a sharing indeed in the identity, the work, the hopes, the ideals, the loves, the works of God. And it is not purely what friendship with God can do for us, but it is also what our friendship with God can do for God.

You may think that even stranger than the text. What can our friendship possibly do for God? What do you give the man who not only has everything, but *is* everything? You can give him yourself. I like to think that God takes pleasure in the friendship of his creatures. We love God because God craves love. And God craves us even as we crave after him. In a strange and wondrous way God needs us to serve and represent him, even as we need him for guidance, for judgment and mercy. And it is that mutuality of need, among many other qualities, that suggests the kind of both ultimate and intimate relationship that we celebrate in our prayers and in our lives.

And this puts the lesson home, for friendship with God is the means by which we learn and express and model friendships with others. Who among us in this church is so sufficiently self-satisfied, so sufficiently independent, so fully equipped in every way that he or she does not long for the satisfying experience of a true and genuine friendship? Who of us is so rich, so powerful, so effective that we find there is no one in whom we wish to or can rely? And who of us here in this church does not aspire at our very depth to be that reliable friend on whom someone else can depend in a moment of joy, or a moment of sadness, or a moment of great need? Who of us is willing to deprive ourselves of joy? Who of us is so selfish that we would not be willing to give joy to one who can receive and from whom you are willing to receive joy? Who of us is not in that category?

It falls to me very frequently in this enterprise to give some form of counsel to young couples preparing for holy matrimony. I assume that they are in love, but I always ask, and they tell me in endearing and sometimes in embarrassing terms that they are indeed, very much, deeply and sincerely in love. "That's all well and good," I say. "But, do you like each other? Do you trust each other? Ultimately, are you good friends? If you saw one another across the room after marriage, would you choose to join the other across the room?" You fall in and out of love many times. I know no relationship founded upon love in which that is not the case. You are in love, you are out of love, you are on your way out, you are on your way in. It's a topsy-turvy enterprise just like the subway. But if you cease to be friends, if your friendship is ultimately fractured beyond repair, then you are in trouble and so is your marriage. You can't fall in and out of friendship; it is a lifelong enterprise.

The art of living, we are told, is the cultivation not of great eco-systems, or of great systems of justice, or even of great systems of sharing. The art of living is the cultivation of friendships. They are the building blocks of society. How precious are those of our friends we know, who bother to keep up with their friends, who know them not as they ought to be but as they are. Those who have such friends are truly blessed and those who are such friends are among the blessed. And they model the relationship that exists between us and God.

For friendships at their essence, even the friendships that are formed in college, partake of godliness: knowing all, forgiving much, sharing everything, caring beyond cost. That is what godliness is, and it is the foundation of friendships that count. Such is the intimacy that we seek with a God who is described as "weeping with us" and who laughs with us. Such is that relationship to which we aspire in this life and on this earth.

To be a friend of God is to make *all* relationships in which we are engaged meaningful, full of meaning. And that divine friendship, the gift of wisdom, makes it possible for us indeed to achieve the ultimate ambition anyone can aspire to. And that is to be the friend we seek. Wisdom makes it all happen and from generation to generation passing into holy songs, "Wisdom makes us friends of God and prophets," and the result is nothing less than love.

24. At the River's Edge
Anna Carter Florence

Exodus 1:8–2:10; Romans 8:22–25

You can tell a lot about a society by looking at its children. Take the United States, for example. These days, we have day care, Sesame Street, Nintendo, and Bart Simpson. We also have crack, street gangs, homeless children, and babies with AIDS. One out of four children in our country lives below the poverty line, and for African-American families, that number increases to one out of two. In 1989, 53 percent of our tax dollars went to military defense. That tells you a lot about us, doesn't it? Children are more than wet cement; they are spokespeople for our values, our choices, our circumstances, and our lifestyles.

By all rights of the law, baby Moses should have been dead. That tells you a lot about Egypt. Moses didn't start life with many advantages. He was born in the equivalent of a Hebrew refugee camp or the Hebrew slave quarters on an Egyptian plantation. He was a boy baby, and the pharaoh, sounding an awful lot like King Herod in Jerusalem two thousand years later, had ordered that all male infants were to be thrown into the Nile River to drown. That tells you a lot about the pharaoh. He'd even gone so far as to instruct the midwives and anyone else who might happen upon a woman in labor to kill those boy babies as soon as they appeared, and if things had gone as he had ordered, that ought to have taken care of Moses. But in baby Moses' case, there were three people the

Anna Carter Florence is Associate Minister for Youth and Young Adults at Westminster Presbyterian Church in Minneapolis, Minnesota. A graduate of Yale University and Princeton Theological Seminary, Florence has been published in many magazines and journals and has written a book entitled *Free Will and Determinism: A Dialogue.*

pharaoh didn't count on: the midwife, the mother of Moses, and the daughter of pharaoh. They wouldn't play ball. The midwife feared God, the mother loved her baby, and the pharaoh's own daughter had compassion on the abandoned child; there was no question but that they each had to break the law in order to save the life of that baby. That tells you a lot about them. And they weren't saints. They were ordinary people acting under extraordinary circumstances, whose faith, love, and compassion made them more than they were.

Now, there are those theologians who will argue with you six ways to Sunday that this story is just a legend about a national hero, just a parallel version of a tale that exists in many other cultures, and they have a point. There are also theologians who will insist that it was the providence of God, not a handful of scared human beings, that saved baby Moses from the fate of a thousand other Hebrew boy babies; they have a point as well. But what interests me about this passage is more than questions of literary criticism or symbolism or predestination; what interests me is the action of the story itself, the characters who labor between right and wrong at the river's edge. That's what interests me, because I know that I've been down at the river's edge almost every day of my life, sitting on the bank, watching stuff pass: the boats, the dead logs, and sometimes the babies in baskets. You can learn a lot about a culture by watching what floats by on a river, because some of it belongs there and some of it doesn't. This is a story about our ability as human beings to know the difference between those two things. It's a story about how God works among us in the most daring and vulnerable ways to break down stereotypes. And we can learn a lot from it. We can learn a lot from the baby, his mother, her midwife, and the pharaoh's daughter.

When I was in New York last month, I went to see the new production of *The Grapes of Wrath,* John Steinbeck's classic novel of the Great Depression. It's a story about an Oklahoma sharecropper family, driven off their land by big agricultural interests and, like thousands of other desperate families, lured to the promised land of California in hope of finding work. Of course there isn't anything there but dirt poor wages and strikes and corruption and starvation. They lose everything, everything except their dignity and will to survive. In one of the last scenes of the play—and the novel, too—the daughter, who has been pregnant throughout the story, goes into labor in the middle of a flood and delivers a still-born baby. Her uncle John is sent out to somehow bury the baby in spite of the rising waters. Listen to what Steinbeck writes:

> Uncle John . . . put his shovel down, and holding
> the box in front of him, he edged through the
> brush until he came to the edge of the swift
> stream. . . . He held the apple box against his
> chest. And then he leaned over and set the box in
> the stream and steadied it with his hand. He said
> fiercely, "Go down an' tell 'em. Go down in the
> street an' rot an' tell 'em that way. That's the way
> you can talk. Don' even know if you was a boy or
> a girl. Ain't gonna find out. Go on down now, an'
> lay in the street. Maybe they'll know then."

You can learn a lot about the Great Depression from that scene. I know we all have stories about that period; my own family lost everything and went to California on a hoax, too. Migrant workers, farmers, factory workers, and so many others suffered without a voice then, and no one seemed to hear. Steinbeck's grim scene makes a strong statement: What does it take for us to realize that things are skewed and wrong? What does it take for us to realize that we can do better, we can *be* better? If a starving migrant worker doesn't spark compassion in us, then will a baby in a box, or a basket, floating down the river? If a statistic won't do it, a statistic that tells us that one out of every two black children we meet in this country doesn't get enough to eat, then what will? We need to know what our breaking point is, don't we? Especially when we're at the river's edge. What does it take?

The pharaoh's daughter came down to the river with her entourage of servants for a swim. Who knows what she'd been brought up to believe about the Hebrews, those coarse foreigners who multiplied like rabbits in their filthy ghettoes? Presumably she'd seen them working at a distance on yet another enormous building project. But it's hard to imagine that she'd ever actually had a conversation with a Hebrew girl her age or broken bread with a Hebrew family. That tells you a lot about her, about her life.

So here she is, the princess of Egypt, taking her daily dip at the river's edge, when she sees this basket floating in the reeds and hears something that sounds like a faint cry. One of her maids goes to fetch it, and lo and behold, what should be inside but a real, live baby, a squalling, hungry, frightened infant. Her first thought must have been, Whose baby is this? And then: Why would any mother put her baby in the river in such a carefully constructed little ark if she wasn't desperate for it to live? She looks to see if it's a boy or a girl; it's a boy all right. And then it dawns on her: "This must be a Hebrew child."

We can imagine how her mind must have been racing. "One of *them*," she thinks. "An actual Hebrew baby, who's going to grow up to be huge and ugly and a threat to my life, according to my father! What am I going to do? I'm supposed to kill it; I can't do that. What if I just leave it here? But then it will die anyway; how long can a baby go without milk?" And before she can decide what to do, a young girl comes bounding out of the bulrushes, saying, "Shall I go and get you a nurse from the Hebrew women to nurse that baby for you?" Obviously this is more than a coincidence; the girl means the baby's mother; she's probably his sister. And she's talking as if the baby belonged to the pharaoh's daughter now, as if the princess, not the mother or the sister, were responsible for it! The girl is talking as if they have a connection beyond the fact that they all just happen to be here together down at the river's edge: the baby, his sister, the princess, and her maids. And everyone is waiting for the princess to make a decision, everyone, that is, but the baby, who just wants to be held, and fed, and given a warm place to sleep.

We know how the story ends. The princess has compassion on the baby, and probably on his family, too, and decides to save it. She tells them that she will pay them to take care of him and that they should bring him back to the palace when he is older, so that she can raise him as her own son. It's a huge risk for her to take, to disobey her father's law, but I think what happened is this: When she actually saw this Hebrew baby at the river's edge and stepped into the shoes of that mother, all the things she'd been taught to believe since childhood, and all her fear and ignorance about this other group of people, just evaporated. She had a connection with someone, a relationship. No law was more important than that. It tells you a lot about her.

What does it take for us to realize that things have to change? What does it take for us to meet our prejudices head on? I believe it takes a connection, a relationship. Sometimes I think it takes a baby in a basket floating at the river's edge. But I think it also takes an awareness that we're laboring at something that isn't finished yet. Learning to be truly open to people who are different than we are takes time, and *un*learning our prejudices and fears can be painful. But we have to remember that when we stand at the river's edge, God gives us the strength to do what we have to do. God gives us the gifts of compassion and love to overcome our fears and pull that baby out of the water.

The Apostle Paul, as always, has something to say about this in his letter to the Romans. You're right, he concedes: Christ may have come into the world, but things are definitely not perfect yet. That's because we're in labor; we're giving birth to a new creation, a new vision of how to live together. God is the midwife, we're the mother in question, Christ is our labor coach, and the waters have broken. Ask anyone who has ever given birth before; when your water breaks, there isn't a midwife or obstetrician on earth who can hold that baby back; it's going to *come*. And I don't care how many Lamaze classes you've had: it's going to *hurt*. Even Paul knows enough about labor to say that the whole creation has been groaning. And he's right: We still let things like race and religion and nationality and sexuality get in the way of real people. We are groaning. But down at the river's edge, we may meet someone who is different than we are and have the opportunity to listen more than we speak, and give more than we take, and love more than we judge. We may get a peek at the empty tomb and at the baby in the manger and the baby in the basket who are waiting for us there.

There is a scene from the film *Gandhi* that I will never forget. India is groaning in its labor pains to be an independent nation, and, once again, it is the tragic conflict between Hindus and Muslims that is tearing things apart. The slaughter goes against everything that Gandhi, their beloved leader and the promoter of nonviolence, has worked for. And so despite the great risks to his health, he goes on another hunger strike, vowing not to eat until the violence between Hindus and Muslims ceases. Many days go by; the fighting rages on, and Gandhi's physicians tell him that given his frail state of health, if he does not eat soon, he will die. One morning, a ragged Muslim man makes his way into Gandhi's bedroom, hurls a piece of bread at him, and says, "Here; eat this! I'm already going to hell, but I don't want your death on my conscience too!" Gandhi asks him quietly, "What do you want?" And the man says, "Last night, my only son was killed in the riots by a Hindu. And I was so full of grief and rage that I went out and took a baby Hindu boy, and I smashed him against a wall until his head broke open. I know I'm going to hell. But you mustn't die for us, or we will have twice the torment." Gandhi thinks a moment, and then asks him, "You are a Muslim?" "Yes," the man says, "I am." "Then what you must do," Gandhi tells him, "is to go out and find a Hindu boy whose father was killed last night. Take him home and adopt him to be your only son, and raise him to be a good Hindu."

The groaning Hebrew people couldn't soften the hearts of the pharaoh and his daughter. But a mother who couldn't keep her own baby set him in a basket at the river's edge, hoping against hope that someone would see him and have pity on him, and failing that, at least see him and know why he had to be there. "Go down and tell 'em," said Uncle John. "That's the way you can talk. Maybe they'll know then." And someone did. Someone finally heard. The pharaoh's own daughter came down to the banks of the Nile and got her first real look at a Hebrew family, her first real taste of the miserable dilemma they were in, and she did what she could. She said, enough. Enough fear. Enough hatred. Enough ignorance. This baby is laboring to be somebody, to grow up and be *some*body, and I've got to labor at it, too. I've got to realize that the water has broken, and nothing can hold this baby back from coming: not the law, not the pharaoh, nothing. Somehow, I've got a connection with this baby because we're both here at the river's edge, and I can do something to help it. I can do that. And if I do, then I'll never be able to look at another Hebrew without seeing my own son.

What are we laboring for down at the river's edge? What old fears and stereotypes and worn out ways are we clinging to down in the bulrushes? Well, stand guard, because God is breaking the waters around us, the labor pains are fierce, and the baby in the basket is on its way. Nothing we can do to stop the pain, nothing we can do to push the baby back. We've got to reach in there and pick it up and say, "Yes, you're my son. You're my daughter. Doesn't matter what color you are; you're my sister. Doesn't matter what religion you are; you're my brother. I don't care what I used to believe, you can love anyone you want to, male or female. You don't have to grow up to be smart, or pretty, or strong, or perfect, because I don't care. It's all right. Don't you cry anymore. We'll just sit here together, down at the river's edge. We'll just sit here."

25. Remembrance Day
Catherine Sider Hamilton

There is a challenge before us on this Remembrance Day. It is a
challenge to do more than remember and mourn. It is a challenge
to face the problem of war that Remembrance Day raises. Especially this year we need to address the problem of war: There have
been some frightening events in the Persian Gulf in the last four
months, "wars and rumors of wars" as we heard in Matthew's Gospel last week. So we need to think about war and how we at St.
Matthias Church feel about war and react to war and live with the
fact of war. The Persian Gulf crisis may be the first time in twenty
years that the threat of war has touched us personally, but war is
a constant in the greater world. And perhaps as we think about war
and the Church we will find a connection with our own vision of
who we at St. Matthias Church are.

I will admit at the beginning that I dislike war. I see little redeeming value in it. I am also uncomfortable with Remembrance
Day. I am uncomfortable with Remembrance Day because it seems
to involve a justification and even a glorification of war. The
ceremonies of Remembrance Day have a way of rehabilitating
war, making it pretty and morally acceptable and perhaps even
glorious—altogether something war is not. The most telling example of this is the way the Church sometimes celebrates Remembrance Day.

In one church I belonged to, Remembrance Day was an occasion for a military parade. Part of a unit came out in full dress,
marched around the block, and filled several pews in church . . .
and then disappeared for the rest of the year. This disturbed me.

Catherine Sider Hamilton is a Candidate for Ordination in the
Diocese of Niagara, in Ontario, Canada. An Anglican, Hamilton is a
graduate of the University of Toronto, Queen's University, and
Toronto School of Theology. She has written numerous book
reviews and is the recipient of a number of academic awards. This
sermon was preached on Remembrance Day.

Why was "the army" officially in church? It linked the Church with the military in a way that I'm not sure we want. The army's official presence on that day seemed to say: "We, the military and the Church, are both part of the same establishment and we speak with one voice."

Does the Church really want to align itself with the military establishment and its job of waging war? If we do so we take on each other's values. The Church gives its support and a kind of moral respectability to the actions of the military establishment and, in turn, takes on something of the power-image of the military. I think this is a perversion of what both the Church and the army are really about. Jesus is no power symbol, nor was he part of the establishment. He spent his life challenging the values of power and establishment and he died at their hands. It does not make sense to link his Church with either one. Surely it would make Jesus lament as he lamented over Jerusalem.

God's people are called to stand apart from the vehicles of power and of the establishment so that we can challenge them and help those oppressed by them. We are the remnant people, called to be faithful to God alone, not seduced by the demigods of money or power or the respectability of the establishment. Listen again to the words of Amos that we heard today. Amos laments because God's people have turned away toward wealth and power and position, because they trample upon the poor and turn aside the needy while they build stone houses and plant pleasant vineyards. Therefore, says the Lord:

> I hate, I despise your feasts and I take no delight
> in your solemn assemblies. I will not accept your
> offerings. Take away from me the noise of your
> songs. But let justice roll down like waters, and
> righteousness like an everflowing stream.

Strong words! If Israel does not turn around and let justice and righteousness flow like a river, God's justice will roll down on Israel—and then "in all the squares there shall be wailing."

From the beginning God's people have been called to justice, to be the voice of the poor and the powerless who have no voice . . . even to be one of them, as Jesus was. This is why I don't like seeing the Church aligning itself with the military on Remembrance Day. I am quite sure that the poor and the powerless are not the main priority of the military machine, just as I do not think war is fought for their sake. War is too often an instrument used by the powerful to preserve their own power. World War II was not fought simply because Hitler was murdering Jewish people. It was fought also because Hitler's aggression was threatening the "balance of power" in Europe. Likewise, it has to be asked whether the world would be quite so upset about Iraq's annexation of Kuwait if all that oil were not involved. We could not preserve our standard of living or our current position in the balance of power without it.

I think we in Canada should be honest about our involvement in the Gulf. If war breaks out there, it won't be just because we're protecting or avenging the people of Kuwait or Saudi Arabia. We will also be protecting the oil fields and our access to them. This self-interest, as much as the carnage, is what I dislike about war.

Just to clarify: Although I don't like war because it is a tool of the powerful to preserve themselves, and so is opposed to Christ's vision, I am not exactly objecting to war itself here. I don't have to make that objection to you. I doubt that any of you like war. War is not a pleasant business, not least because it kills people. I am also not objecting to war for the very reason that war is pretty much a constant in our world. In this century alone the world has fought two world wars, the Korean War, the Vietnam War, the war in Afghanistan, in Iran/Iraq . . . and a host of invasions and guerilla wars. War seems to be built into the world's social and political structures and perhaps into human nature. War is an ugly fact of life, and it would be a platitude and probably fruitless to object to it.

But I do object to the falsifying of war. If we must have war, let us at least be honest about what we are doing. Let's not glorify war with pretty military parades and stirring hymns to victory. Let's not confuse our military, who kill and are killed for our standard of living and our security, with our Christ, who suffers and dies for those who have no security.

The reason Remembrance Day bothers me is that it has become a forum for just these sorts of falsehoods. And it's not only the implications of military parades in church and pretty uniforms. It is also what is said on Remembrance Day. One of the pious fictions I hear and read in the newspaper year after year is that we fought the world wars and the Korean War "to preserve the peace." How anyone can say this after the string of wars the world has fought in this century alone completely baffles me. We fight because our security is threatened, we fight for our power and sometimes for our lives, we fight for our houses of stone and second cars—we do not fight for peace. Peace will never come to us through war. War only breeds more war. If we really want to create peace the first thing we have to do is to stop uttering this kind of nonsense on Remembrance Day and stop doing all the other things we do that rehabilitate war and make it attractive.

I have been pretty negative about Remembrance Day up to this point. But Remembrance Day could be a good thing. There are ways we could use Remembrance Day to be honest about war and to actually promote peace. One way is to make Remembrance Day a time not for parades and pious falsehoods but for sorrow—sorrow for those who died in war and sorrow that war must be. It is a time to remember and to mourn those Canadians who were killed in the world wars and the Korean War—to mourn the waste of their young lives. It is a time to remember those who loved them and suffered when they died. And it is a time to mourn those they killed.

There is another way in which we could use Remembrance Day well, a way that is open especially to God's people. It springs from a vision that we found right here among ourselves last weekend when we gathered to try to articulate our dreams for St. Matthias Church. Near the end of the day someone summed up our list of goals by saying that above all we want to be one body. That is what we were, she said, at our beginning as the people of St. Matthias and that is what we want to rediscover. She hit the nail on the head. To be one body in Christ is the age-old vision and mission of the Church. God calls us to community, to a unity in diversity that recognizes and values the uniqueness of each individual, that loves and nurtures the uniqueness and knits it together into a whole.

This is an unusual vision and the world would say it is impossible—and so we wage wars. The exciting thing about the gospel is that Jesus says this vision of the one body is possible. It is possible in Jesus the Christ, whose body was broken and restored again to wholeness. Christ's cross and his resurrection are signs and guarantees to us that though we are broken apart in various ways as individuals and as a church, we will be made one body again. Every Sunday this begins to happen. We share in the breaking and the new wholeness each time we gather for Communion around this table to share one bread and one cup. This communion is the weekly acting out of the community God brings to life among us. It strengthens us, gives us grace to go out and live our unity with each other through the week and to carry our communion to the world.

And this is happening! I could see and feel it happening among us last weekend. There was a real feeling of love and unity (unity in lots of diversity!) at the end of the day on Saturday. Beware! God's grace is at work among us, molding us into the body of Christ.

I say "beware" because the vision we have found here is a radical one and it is likely to transform us until we find ourselves being and doing things we never thought possible. In fact, I can guarantee you that if we allow our vision of community to grow, if we abandon ourselves to God's vision for us, we will barely recognize ourselves ten years from now. The vision has a way of growing until our communion will burst out of the walls of this church and make itself felt out there. This is the gift that has been given to us, and we are called to accept it and nurture it and carry it out into the world.

It is this gift of loving community that we need to remember and celebrate on Remembrance Day, because in it lies God's answer to war. We can't stop war from occurring in the Persian Gulf or anywhere else. But we can build an alternative model. By our love for each other in all our differences and in our community that celebrates differences and uses them as its foundation stones, we can show that the world does not have to be a place of fear and hostility.

God gave us Jesus to show us the way. Jesus stretched out his hand in love and bore the pain that such an offering often brings. Now we who live in him can make the same offering. We can, and we are called to. And we are doing it! It was just such a stretching out of hands that founded St. Matthias and that happened last weekend. My prayer for us is that we will be given the courage to carry on, to continue building the loving community that we are already beginning to be, to continue reaching out in love to each other and with each other to Guelph and the world, so that people can look at us, at St. Matthias, and see the Kingdom of God.

26. God *Is* Concerned for the Oxen, Paul!

Jonathan Massey

Deuteronomy 25:1–6; 1 Corinthians 9:1–12

One of the hottest issues emerging in the 1990s is animal rights. No one, no matter what their position on the subject (if they keep up with the news) can dispute the truth of this.

One Sunday last month, *The Arizona Republic* devoted its entire Perspective section to the theme "Sacrificing Animals."

The article by Steve Twedt says,

> Key animal rights groups already have targeted with success the fur and cosmetic industries. In major cities, fur wearers are publicly confronted about their wardrobes. Since last January, Revlon, Avon, Mary Kay Cosmetics and Noxell Corp . . . have announced either a cutback, moratorium or outright ban on animal use for product testing, a practice animal rights activists charged was designed to limit a company's legal liability, not improve product safety.
>
> While animal activists hold little hope of similarly stopping animal research, they are maneuvering for the middle ground, hoping to influence how animals will be used and under what restrictions.[1]

Jonathan Massey is Pastor of Community United Methodist Church in Avondale, Arizona. A graduate of Asbury College, Massey received his Master of Divinity at Asbury Theological Seminary. Massey lives in Goodyear, Arizona, with his wife and two children.

Animal rights activists look at institutions such as the University of Pittsburgh, where various experiments claimed the lives of 55,439 animals in 1988 alone. Supervisor and veterinary technician Michael Maranowski, who works at Pitt, "admits to conflicting feelings of empathy for the animals and certainty that their loss will reduce human suffering." According to Maranowski, "the lab may lose one in ten new employees because of the emotional strain." He says that his own position is that, "God put the animals on the Earth and, if you've got to take them away from where they were intended to be, you owe them the obligation to take care of them. Once we become callous with animals, we may begin to treat people like that too."[2]

Well, so much for animal experimentation—only *one* part of the emerging animal rights battle. Let's look at another:

This week's issue of *U.S. News & World Report* tells how "Bruce Wargo hoped to bag a brace of pheasant or grouse, perhaps a few cottontails during a hunting trip last October to Connecticut's Paugussett State forest. What he got instead was a rude surprise. A covey of animal rights activists flushed him from the brush. They dogged his every move, hectored him about the evils of hunting and promised to annoy him until he left the woods."[3]

Although the ranks of hunters have dwindled by 700,000 since 1975, still nearly 16 million Americans—almost 7 percent of the population—bought hunting licenses last year. They paid $517 million in fees to hunt, which helps finance game research and management programs and purchase wildlife habitat, but also killed 4 million white-tailed deer, 21,000 black bear, 102,000 elk, 2,400 bighorn sheep, and 1,500 mountain lion among many other species in the 1988–89 season alone!

While 80 percent of Americans approve of hunting to put meat on the table, 80 percent also feel hunting for trophy heads is wrong. Sixty percent disapprove of hunting merely for sport or recreation. And, one in three Americans favor a total ban on hunting, which leads to the death of over 200 million animals every year.[4]

Animal research and hunting, and to a lesser extent factory farming are the practices that have fueled the animal rights movement. And these are the issues that Christians need to respond to. We are the people who claim to have a unique relationship with God and revelation from him concerning his will for this world and all within it. As with any human concern, we need to bring God's revelation and our sensitivity to God's will to bear on animal rights. We need to ask ourselves the question, Do animals have rights? And, If they do, how many?

Christians have taken different positions through the ages. Roman Catholic moral theology has generally seen no rights for animals at all. Thomas Aquinas, following the line he inherited from Augustine, who in turn got it from Aristotle and the Greeks, said "By divine providence" animals "are intended for man's use in the natural order" and therefore "it is not wrong for man to make use of them either by killing or in any way whatever."[5]

Now, although they were thinking out of a Greek philosophical mindset, I'm afraid they could take Paul's unfortunate comments in 1 Corinthians 9:1–12 to back up their case. Let's take a look again at what Paul said.

In arguing for the rights of apostles, and thereby pastors, to be paid for their work (a point I fully support, incidentally!) he says in verse 4, "Do we not have the right to our food and drink?" Verse 7: "Who serves as a soldier at his own expense?" (The answer, of course, is *no soldier!*)

Then Paul looks around for biblical evidence to support his position. Listen to what he says in verses 8 to 10 again: "Do I say this on human authority? Does not the law say the same? For it is written in the law of Moses, 'You shall not muzzle an ox when it is treading out the grain.' [Thereby keeping it from eating some of the grain.] Is it for oxen that God is concerned? Does he not speak entirely for our [that is, humanity's] sake? It was written for our sake . . ."

Well, like I said earlier, the point Paul was trying to make is correct: Those who labor full-time in Christian service should be paid for what they do. But the evidence he latched onto is entirely wrong. If you look at Deuteronomy 25:4, where Paul draws his quote from, you'll find that God *is* concerned for the oxen, and that commandment was written for the oxen's sake, not ours! The Old Testament is full of laws protecting the rights of animals, as well as of human beings.

The ancient Hebrews had a high view of animals, and respected them. Proverbs 12:10 says, "A righteous man has regard for the life of his beast, but the mercy of the wicked is cruel."

In a time when resurrection was not understood, the author of Ecclesiastes said in 3:19–21, "The fate of the sons of men and the fate of beasts is the same; as one dies, so dies the other. They all have the same breath [that is, spirit] and man has no advantage over the beasts . . . all are from the dust, and all turn to dust again. Who knows whether the spirit of man goes upward and the spirit of the beast goes down?" Here, Ecclesiastes shows the Hebrews realized animals have spirit, just like we do. The issue wasn't whether humans had something that animals didn't, but whether *either* would survive death![6]

Turn to Genesis chapter 2. The "breath of life" that made the man "a living being" in 2:7 is the same for the animal creation. Animals are also said to be living beings, or souls. Animals are classed with humans by being created on the sixth day (Gen. 1:24– 31). They are blessed with the same blessing with which humans are blessed (see 1:22, 28!). Humans are God's highest creation, according to Genesis, and are given dominion over all creation according to 1:28, but we are not a different *kind* of life than animals. It is the Spirit that is the basis of our common life.

As we discovered two weeks ago in our sermon on the environment, people have failed to realize that the dominion humans were originally supposed to have exercised over creation was *preservative*. There was to be no killing, not even to eat. Plants were given to humans and animals alike, not animal flesh (look at Gen. 1:30).

Only after people became alienated from God through disobedience do we find the beginnings of animal sacrifice (Gen. 4:4) and flesh-eating (Gen. 9:2–3). These things are part of the *curse* of the Fall. These things are looked upon as temporary and far less than God's perfect will.

The prophets looked forward to a time when the lion would lie down with the lamb, and Paul himself looks forward to a time when "the creation itself will be set free . . . and obtain the glorious liberty of the children of God" in Romans 8:21. Again, as we discovered two weeks ago, Christians have forgotten that there is a progressive aspect—here and now—that comes with the final salvation envisioned by the prophets and Paul. Just as we are being progressively made more holy in this life as we wait for the Resurrection (that is, just as we are being set free from the curse of the Fall), so we should be progressively returning to exercising the *good* dominion over the environment and animals, as envisioned by God in Eden! Here's where Christianity intersects animal rights, people!

If we are being restored to the full image of God we lost, we should be returning to God's attitude toward the animal kingdom surely and progressively, as we await the Resurrection and the new world to come!

Christians as a whole have been dead to this wonderful vision of salvation, but there have been wonderful exceptions. It is said that when St. Francis (the man behind our hymn *All Creatures of Our God and King*) "considered the primordial source of all things, he was filled with . . . pity, calling creatures no matter how small, by the name of brother or sister because he knew that they had the same source as himself."[7]

John Woolman, the early American Quaker saint who fought the institution of slavery his entire life, said he "was convinced . . . that true religion consisted in an inward life, wherein the heart doth love and reverence God the Creator and learn to exercise true justice and goodness not only toward all men but also toward the brute creatures."[8]

As a Methodist, I'm *so proud* of our own John Wesley, a man hundreds of years ahead of his time who recognized in his sermon "The General Deliverance" that although humans are God's highest creation, animals, too, have some measure of God's image stamped upon them.[9] Looking toward the world to come, he even says,

> May I be permitted to mention here a conjecture concerning the brute creation? What, if it should then please the all-wise, the all-gracious Creator to raise them higher in the scale of beings? What, if it should please him, when he makes us 'equal to angels', to make them what we are now,—creatures capable of knowing and loving and enjoying the Author of their being? . . . Consider this, consider how little we know of even the present designs of God; and then you will not wonder that we know still less of what he designs to do in the new heavens and the new earth.[10]

In that same sermon, Wesley destroys the keystone argument used by those who deny any rights of animals: that they are not rational. (The same argument, incidentally, that has been used to take rights away from women, blacks, children, and retarded people!) He says *of course* they can reason, and of course they have emotions and can love!

Again, he was so far ahead of his time! Has anyone read about Koko the gorilla? She was raised by a developmental psychologist like a human child.

In October 1978, when she was seven years old, *National Geographic* reported she looked at herself in a mirror and signed the word "woman." She had, at that time, a working vocabulary of 375 signs. Koko can respond to and ask questions, tells people when she's happy or sad, refers to past and future events, comes up with original definitions for objects, occasionally insults her human companions and sometimes lies to avoid blame! She lives independently in her own trailer, adopted a pet kitten, and was interviewed by *Life* magazine a few years ago. Does God care nothing for Koko, and can we do whatever we want with her and her kind, according to Aquinas? (I'll never forget watching a gorilla family in the Cincinnati zoo. The male was obviously hungry, but passed the first carton of milk given them to his nursing mate.)

The December 5, 1988 issue of *The Arizona Republic* told how, "for two days, a herd of elephants nursed a wounded elephant calf after nudging him along the road to the nearest human protection in the forests of eastern India.

"It took the elephants six hours to cover the two miles to a forest ranger's office. The staff administered first aid . . . but he later succumbed to head wounds inflicted by a tiger.

"Tears rolled out of the mother elephant's eyes as the rest of the herd formed a circle, raised their trunks and trumpeted over the body. . . .

"The elephants apparently thought the proximity of people would keep the tiger from returning for the kill, according to the news agency."

Does God care for the elephants? Does the Christian faith have anything to say about the slaughter of these creatures to increase the supply of ivory baubles?

These are the higher animals, but *The Arizona Republic* has also reported that even birds have thinking ability. According to University of Iowa scientist Edward A. Wasserman, "Pigeons commit new images to memory at lightning speed, but the remarkable thing is that they organize images of things into the same logical categories that human beings use when we conceptualize."[11]

Does God care for the pigeons? You will have to answer that for yourself, as I have to. We live in a world that is only partially redeemed, and how much we are redeemed from the curse of the Fall (and, therefore, how much we should be redeeming God's creation) is something you will have to decide in your own heart. I have no sure message from God on this.

I'm grateful for the polio vaccine, but feel bad that so many primates had to die to test it. I've flirted with a vegetarian diet, but returned to eating meat even though I'm certain this was not God's original, best intention for us. I live in a lot of contradictions, feeling my way forward.

One thing I have given up forever, though, is hunting for sport. Once while hunting over near Snowflake in 1976, I shot a hummingbird on impulse, wounded it, and watched as this beautiful creature died a miserable, senseless death. Why did I kill it? Why did I want to kill anything? I looked inside that day and saw something so horrible (and I'm speaking for myself here—no one else!) I've never hunted since. What did I feel? What do I still feel? It is expressed well by a poem by Robert P. Tristan Coffin, which I found in the March/April 1985 issue of *alive now!* magazine:

Forgive My Guilt

Not always sure what things called sins may be,
I am sure of one sin I have done.
It was years ago, and I was a boy.
I lay in the frostflowers with a gun;
The air ran blue as the flowers. I held my breath.
Two birds on golden legs slim as dream things
Ran like quicksilver on the golden sand.
My gun went off; they ran with broken wings
Into the sea; I ran to fetch them in,
But they swam with their heads high out to sea.
They cried like two sorrowful high flutes,
With jagged ivory bones where wings should be.
For days I heard them when I walked that
    headland
Crying out to their kind in the blue.
The other plovers were going over south
On silver wings leaving these broken two.
The cries went out one day; but I still hear them
Over all the sounds of sorrow in war or peace
I ever have heard. Time cannot drown them;

Those slender flutes of sorrow never cease.
Two airy things forever denied the air!
I never knew how their lives at last were spilt,
But I have hoped for years all that is wild,
Airy, and beautiful will forgive my guilt.

Amen.

NOTES

1. *The Arizona Republic* (January 14, 1990).
2. Ibid.
3. *U.S. News & World Report* (February 5, 1990): 30.
4. Ibid.
5. Andrew Linzey, *Christianity and the Rights of Animals* (New York: Crossroad, 1989), 22.
6. Ibid., 78.
7. Ibid., 32.
8. Ibid., 15.
9. John Wesley, "The General Deliverance," Vol. VI of *Wesley's Works*, 250.
10. Ibid., 250–51.
11. *The Arizona Republic* (December 25, 1988).

V. PASTORAL

27. Standing on the Banks of Tomorrow

Kenneth L. Chafin

The Lord spoke to Moses and said, "Send men out to explore the land of Canaan which I am giving to the Israelites; from each of their fathers' tribes send one man, and let him be a man of high rank." . . . After forty days they returned from exploring the country, and came back to Moses and Aaron and the whole community of Israelites at Kadesh in the wilderness of Paran. They made their report to them and to the whole community, and showed them the fruit of the country. And this was the story they told Moses: "We made our way into the land to which you sent us. It is flowing with milk and honey, and here is the fruit it grows; but its inhabitants are sturdy, and the cities are very strongly fortified." . . . Then Caleb called for silence before Moses and said, "Let us go up at once and occupy the country; we are well able to conquer it." But the men who had gone with him said, "No, we cannot attack these people; they are stronger than we are." Thus their report to the Israelites about the land which they had explored was discouraging: "The country we explored," they said, "will swallow up any who go to live in it. All the people we saw there are men of gigantic size . . . we felt no bigger than grasshoppers; and that is how we looked to them." Then the whole Israelite community cried out in dismay; all night long they wept. One and all they made complaints against Moses and Aaron: "If only we had died in Egypt or in the wilderness!" they said. "Far happier if we had! Why should the Lord bring us to this land, to die in battle and leave our wives and our dependents to become the spoils of war? To go back to Egypt would be better than this." And they began to talk of choosing someone to lead them back.

—Numbers 13:1–31, 25–28a, 30–32, 33b; 14:1–4

Kenneth L. Chafin is a native of Oklahoma. He was educated at the University of New Mexico and at Southwestern Baptist Theological Seminary, where he received his doctorate. Dr. Chafin was Carl Bates Professor of Christian Preaching at The Southern Baptist Theological Seminary in Louisville, Kentucky, and until his recent retirement served as pastor of the Walnut Street Baptist Church in Louisville. This sermon was preached on the occasion of the one hundred seventy-fifth anniversary of that historic church.

I never read this passage—but what I wonder, "What if?" Have you ever read a story and tried to give it a different ending? I have tried to give this story a different ending many times, because it didn't have to end this way. It shouldn't have ended this way. This is not what God wanted to happen but it happened. This is a wonderful passage from the Word of God to serve as a backdrop as we stand on this day to celebrate our one hundred seventy-fifth anniversary, as we stand on this day to look to the future we have as a congregation.

The anniversary committee said to me six months ago, "We've thought of having guest speakers, we've thought of various approaches but we think that nothing would be more appropriate on the day we celebrate our anniversary than for the pastor to preach." My mind immediately went to this text. And I was drawn to it because there is an obvious parallel between Israel and this church. Israel was at that place she had dreamed about for forty years. Ever since she came up out of Egypt, she had been thinking of the Promised Land. This is the place God had in mind when he spoke to Moses on the backside of nowhere. They had begun as slaves. Now they luxuriated in God's freedom. They had been a "no people;" now they lived in covenant with God and God called them "my people." They had experienced the hand of God in their lives, in deliverance from pharaoh, in guidance in the wilderness, in provision of good, and in the leadership of Moses and Aaron. Now they were positioned to go into the Promised Land fulfilling of his promise to Abraham. I see Walnut Street Baptist Church today getting ready to experience what those who have gone before us could only dream of.

If we could take the accumulated dreams of the pastors and lay-leaders of this congregation whey they began this church or at any phase in this church, we are standing where they longed to be and will never see. We've come from a handful of people in a rented house in 1815 to become a great congregation in this place. We've spanned most of two centuries and are poised to move across this decade to the twenty-first century. We've come from an infant congregation to a people of influence, and while other congregations have fallen by the wayside, it has been this congregation's privilege to birth congregations, to nourish an infant seminary when it moved here from Greenville, South Carolina, to start orphanages, to launch ministries, and to participate in the development of a denomination.

When we voted this summer to set up a committee to keep an eye on the denomination, it bothered a few, but you need to remember that we were already a church when this denomination was formed and we may still be a church when the denomination is not there. We are a blessed people. And on this day, we stand where God has brought us seeking with anticipation to know and to do his will. So I see Israel and I see this congregation in the same way—a blessed people "standing on the banks of tomorrow." And that's where we are.

I know, as I read the passage, you may have thought, "I wonder if Dr. Chafin realized that Israel, in this story, turned their back on their future?" Yes, I remembered that. And to me there is not a sadder story in the Bible than the discouraging report that the leaders who had been sent to spy out the land brought. It is the classic picture of what happens to a people who have frightened leaders. It will happen to our country if our leadership does not discover courage. They are so afraid of not getting re-elected that they sometimes do not lead us in the direction that courage would send them.

Today, from our vantage point, we can understand what happened. Monday morning quarterbacking is always easy. They overestimated their enemies. This is easy to do. Often we are defeated not by enemies but by our imaginations of our enemies. They underestimated their own resources. They had become a great people and, with God's hand, a great nation. They caricatured their future and distorted it. They idealized their past. Can you imagine a people who had been rescued from slavery remembering fondly those days as good old days? They forgot God's purpose for them and his promises to them, and they condemned the whole people to aimless wandering and death.

After this experience, God sent them back into the wilderness—for forty years they wandered, waiting for everyone over twenty years of age to die—except Joshua and Caleb. When a people turn their back on God's future, the only thing that allows God to give a future is a bunch of funerals. And so Joshua and Caleb had to wander around with them for forty years until everyone had died except those two who had been twenty years old or older.

This is what happens to persons and to a people when they turn their back to the future and try to return to whatever their Egypt was. It's not a pretty sight—weeping, complaining, frightened, re-membering, accusing people. But it is the story.

The story serves to remind me that the future is never auto-matic for a person or a nation or a congregation. That when God calls us, he doesn't put up on an escalator where the just stand, look around, wave at our friends, as it delivers us at the next floor. We participated with God through our obedience, through our faith, through our sacrifice, and through our commitment. The future of this congregation is not just a matter of God's plan for it and God's purpose for it and God's vision for it. The future of this church is in your hands and mine and in your heart and mine and in your obedience and mine.

The story also contains a reminder that in the midst of pessi-mism and discouragement there are always those who have a vision for God and for the future. That's the role of Joshua and Caleb in the story. With the same set of facts, they came to a totally different conclusion. The speech that almost got them stoned to death is a classic speech. Listen to what they said, "The country we pene-trated and explored is very good indeed. If the Lord is pleased with us, he will bring us into this land which flows with milk and honey and give it to us." Lots of people think that people who have faith are not in touch with reality. Joshua and Caleb saw the giants. Joshua and Caleb saw the fortified cities. They saw the problems that were there, but faith gave them a different perspective.

Today as your pastor I stand as the spokesperson for all the Joshuas and the Calebs in this church. And to say to you, "I have no intention of leading you back to Egypt. I will not lead you back to Egypt. I will fight you if you try to go back to Egypt." I see my task as your pastor for as long as God leaves me here to call on us to deal openly and honestly with what faces us in the future: Who are the giants that must be confronted, what are the fortified cities that we must lay siege to, what forces that destroy the lives of people must we address? These cannot be glossed over, and we must not gloss them over.

But it is my task, also, to remind you of the resources of God and of what is available to us for that future; to call forth the gifts of the membership and to call on us to be as faithful in our day as our forefathers were in their day; to stand here and say to you, "We are well able to possess the land."

This is a powerful story, this story I read from the Scriptures. And each time I read the text I understand a little bit more the anxiety of those leaders as they entertained a very uncertain future. I guess when I was very young, I would read a story like this and say, "I'm Caleb. I don't understand this bunch of pessimists. I'm Joshua. I'm full of courage." But I've lived a little longer and I am a little more honest about the kind of people we are, and I think it's the story not just of Israel but of each of us who comes to the place where we must embrace an uncertain future.

It's the story of this church—as God leads us out into an unknown future where we need to say "yes" to God's tomorrow for this church. And yet I realize that both emotions in this story are in each of us. Each fall I watch six-year-olds start to school. And this fall, I noticed it especially. You could almost see on the expression of each child a desire to be free of family and out in the big world *and* a desire to get back into the car with momma or daddy and go home and take a nap. Both of those emotions are there. And whether you are leaving home to go to school or leaving singleness to get married or changing jobs or considering retirement, anytime you come up against a future where you are not sure what is going to happen, those emotions are there. There's a part of each of us that's excited by the challenge and the potential, the adventure and the newness of the unknown.

There are a lot of Joshuas and Calebs in this church. As a matter of fact, last Wednesday night after prayer meeting I was with fifteen Joshuas and Calebs as this group dreamed about the future for this church. And there was so much energy in that room and so much excitement in that room that many of us who came into the room weary went out all charged up and found it hard to go to sleep when we got home.

And there are some discouragers. You know, it's hard to look at anything that is future oriented without someone standing up and seeing the giants and seeing the fortified cities and wondering if this land will not absorb us.

So, on this day as we deal openly and honestly with our mixed emotions, what I am calling us to do is to turn from our fear and our anxiety and give ourselves without reservation to God's tomorrow for our lives and for our church, to remember our common confession, "Jesus Christ is Lord." We are not a club, we are a church with this confession, "Jesus Christ is Lord." I call us to renew our covenant with God and with each other and to rededicate our lives to God's purpose and to lay on the altar of God our gifts and our interest and our influence and our dreams. The future of the church is tied to your response, to your life, to your commitment, to your faithfulness. God is ready to give this church a magnificent future, which God alone has planned. Are we ready?

I have done some reflecting this week on my own response to the call of the future for this church. When you called me and I was already sixty-one, I saw myself at best as a Pope John XXIII opening a few windows and letting a little light in, and at worst, a little longer interim than I had been before. But this week as I have looked at this time and this passage and I have reflected on the kind of response God wants from me, and I have thought about the kind of response that God needs from you, there has come to my mind a picture of a text.

It's a text that could well have been a text for this sermon from Hebrews 12:1. If you will recall, Hebrews 11 is made up of the call of the roll of the faithful—beginning with Abel and Enoch and Abraham and Sarah and moving down through the centuries in what one of my professors called, "the art gallery of the faithful." The author of Hebrews says, "But what of ourselves? With all of these witnesses to faith around us like a cloud, we must throw off every encumbrance, every sin to which we cling and run with resolution the race for which we are entered, our eyes fixed on Jesus on whom faith depends from start to finish." And to the art gallery of the faithful in Hebrews 11 I began to add the names of those who had gone before us here at Walnut Street who would have loved to have seen this day. And I dare not begin to call names.

There are some in our history that I never met. It would be wonderful if John A. Broadus could have been here. Every time I stand in this pulpit and realize that I am looking at the pew in which John A. Broadus—the president of Southern Seminary—sat, I am humbled. Or if W. O. Carver could have been on the committee to write the church history like he was on a previous one. W. O. Carver was probably the outstanding missionary philosopher that our denomination has developed in its history and was a member of this congregation. So there is a part of me that would like to have met those people well-known and those people unknown, but the truth is I have thought of people whom I have buried, who when Barbara and I came here as members of the congregation were active in the life of the church. And I would like for them to be here today.

What the Hebrew writer is basically saying is that all of these people who have gone before us are like a cloud of witnesses, like a great amphitheater looking on to encourage us to embrace God's tomorrow with all that means. What part do you think God wants you to play in this church's future? Are you willing to let God work in you and through you for this church's future? What change would it take in your commitment and in your availability and in your spirit and in your priorities and in your lifestyle? This day is a day for new beginnings for us as persons and for us as a people.

Maybe it needs to be between you and God where you are. When we stand to sing the hymn, you will say, "Father, I have been a part of this church's history and I want to be a part of its future. Take me and use my mind and use my thoughts and use my gifts and use my influence and use my money and use my time." It may be that some of you need to walk down this aisle for the first time in decades and let the walking down the aisle say, "I am a part of this church's past and now I commit myself to this church's future." And maybe as people in the pews and at the front of the congregation are recommitting themselves to the days ahead, maybe some of you need to walk down this aisle for the very first time and cast your lot with this people and become a part of this church's future.

I come to you this morning in a rededication of my life to Christ whom I preach and to this church whom I serve and I ask you to make that same rededication of yourself to this church's future.

28. What Does God Look Like?

Thomas H. Graves

". . . he was afraid to look at God."

—Exodus 3:6

Ray and I were friends. We were very good friends. Our friendship grew out of several trips that we took together. We attended
denominational meetings with one another. We traveled to Las Ve-
gas and then on to Los Angeles where we sat in the left field stands
to see a Dodgers game. We spent a week in Danville, Virginia, with
his family and had a marvelous time. We planned a trip this summer to Maine, just the two of us, a trip we were never able to take
because of his quickly progressing cancer. We spent a great deal of
time in conversation, not just while traveling but also at mealtime
in many restaurants in town. These last few months provided a
great deal of time for talking in hospital rooms and at the bedside
in his home.

Almost to the very end, Ray was able to keep on talking and for
that I thank God. It was that last conversation, just hours before his
death, that I'll always cherish and can never forget. It was very late
in the evening, but my friend wanted to talk. His wife called and
I drove quickly to their home. Ray had a question. We had had
some previous conversations about a particular passage in Scrip-

Thomas H. Graves is president of the newly founded Baptist
Theological Seminary in Richmond, Virginia. He was formerly a
member of the faculty of Southeastern Baptist Theological
Seminary, where he was also editor of *Faith and Mission,* a
theological journal. He went to his present post from the pastorate
of St. John's Baptist Church in Charlotte, North Carolina. He was
educated at Vanderbilt University, Yale Divinity School, and The
Southern Baptist Theological Seminary, from which he received the
M.Div. and Ph.D. degrees.

ture concerning the image of God, so his question did not come out of the blue, and it wasn't a childish or thoughtless kind of question and certainly not a cynical one. But he said, very deliberately, searching for just the right words, "Tom, I have a question." And he put the question into these slowly formed syllables: "What does God look like now, Tom? What does God look like now, for me?" Here was a man whose life was ebbing away. With his strength all gone, he looked to his wife, son, and friend, all standing by his bed, and asked, "What does God look like for me right now?"

That is an important question for us all to consider as we ponder the visitation of death. What does God look like for us right now? As we gather in the midst of a deadly world, in the face of the death of many gone too early, too early for us to escape the harsh questions of sorrow, what does God look like now for us?

To Ray that night, my immediate response was that right now, good friend, God looks like a man dying on a cross. That's one way God looks. A clear word to a dying man, a suffering family, grieving friends, a sorrowing church, is that God endures our pain as well. Not only has God been there, but he is there, mixing his tears with ours. God looks like a dying man on a cross, suffering and weeping. Our God shares our grief. Christ enters into our suffering as he says at the very beginning of his ministry, "I have come to heal the broken-hearted." He shares our sorrow as he stands by the graveside of his dear friend Lazarus and weeps. He shares in our suffering when he says, "Come unto me all ye who labor and are heavy laden and I will give you rest." He shares our suffering when he speaks those very last words, "Lo, I am with you always." That promise includes his presence at a death bed and a funeral service. Our sufferings belong to God. We are not alone in our grief. That is what Paul meant when he spoke: "There is absolutely nothing that can separate us from the love of Christ. Not life, not death, not anything else." What does God look like? God looks like a man dying on a cross.

Someday our conversations will resume. Ray will have more questions and many more answers to my questions. I look forward to that. Imagine, looking forward as we struggle with the reality of death. That is possible because of the Christian affirmation that God also looks like the risen Lord. That is the very core of our faith: We come even in the awful sadness of this deadly moment and speak of hope and of resurrection.

Ray knew when to die. He waited until dawn; his timing was perfect. We are now gathered on a Sunday, our faith's day of resurrection celebration, to ask about death. Here we are on the day that proclaims the dawn of a new hope. What does God look like? Today, especially on this day, God looks like the risen Lord.

I remember another conversation months before. I had lunch with Ray just prior to his doctor's appointment. We really didn't spend much time talking about his physical condition. But that very night, he pulled me aside, in the parking lot of our church. He'd gotten awful news from his doctor. The cancer had spread, it was a great deal worse than he ever realized. As he talked about it in his blunt and frank fashion, he assured me, "Tom, always know I'll be all right." And then he began to quote, like his mother could do so well, some poetry. Drawing from William Cullen Bryant's "Thanatopsis," the words came easily to his lips, so easily and heartfelt that I hurried to my office and read them again. Here are the words he remembered:

> So live, that when thy summons comes to join
> The innumerable caravan, that moves
> To the pale realms of shade, where each shall take
> His chamber in the silent halls of death,
> Thou go not, like the quarry-slave at night,
> Scourged to his dungeon, but sustain'd and sooth'd
> By an unfaltering trust, approach thy grave,
> Like one who wraps the drapery of his couch
> About him, and lies down to pleasant dreams.[1]

God looks like the risen Lord. That's the very core of our faith and that's why Ray left me written instructions concerning his funeral. At the bottom of the page he scrawled, "Go home and have a party when it's over!" I could not do that and I don't expect others to do that either. We can, however, gain a sense of the hope he held on to. We can gain a sense of the joy and peace he felt in the presence of the risen Lord. What does God look like? Like a man on a cross; like the risen Lord.

What else does God look like? One more thing Ray said to me that night. Realize how difficult the conversation was for him, struggling for words and only with difficulty forming them into understandable sounds. "God told us," he said, "God told us what he looked like. God told us he looks like love." That's the simplest, yet most profound, picture in all of Scripture. God looks like love.

I saw that in my friend's life. It was something beautiful for God. The kind word, the caring deed, the acts of ministry and care, flowers and phone calls for others, even as he was dying. God looks like love, and I saw a great deal of that through the life of Ray.

We see that supremely in the revelation of God's love in Jesus Christ. In Jesus we see God as one who embraces the sick, who soothes the anxious, who affirms the discouraged, and who forgives the sinner. In Jesus we see a God who loves.

What does God look like? Like a dying man on a cross, like the risen Christ, like love. The conversation ended as Ray said, "Yeah. Yeah. That's what God looks like." That was our last, but not our final conversation. What does God look like? Like a man on a cross, like the risen Lord, like love. I know that much more clearly because of a saintly friend, who taught me well what God looks like.

NOTE

1. William Cullen Bryant, "Thanatopsis," in *The Norton Anthology of American Literature* (New York: W. W. Norton and Company, 1986), lines 74–82.

29. What to Do When Your World Turns Upside Down
Gary A. Kowalski

The day will come when your world turns upside down. One minute the universe is revolving smoothly on its accustomed grooves, and the next it jumps completely off the tracks. The phone rings late at night and a voice says that there's been an accident. The routine physical examination turns up an unexpected cancer. Our spouse tells us that he or she wants out of the marriage. There are hundreds of ways for the carefully constructed worlds we inhabit to go flying utterly to pieces.

"There is only one question which really matters," writes Harold Kushner. "Why do bad things happen to good people? All other theological conversation is intellectually diverting; somewhat like doing the crossword puzzle in the Sunday paper and feeling very satisfied when you have made the words fit; but ultimately without the capacity to reach people where they really care. Virtually every meaningful conversation I have ever had with people on the subject of God or religion has either started with this question or gotten around to it before long."

The Gallup Poll conducted a survey not long ago. One of the questions asked people in churches what sermon topics they would find most helpful. At the top of the list, people asked for sermons on how to put their faith into practice. Right below that, they asked for sermons on death and dying. The results weren't too surpris-

Gary A. Kowalski is minister of First Unitarian Universalist Society of Burlington, Vermont, and former minister of the First Unitarian Universalist Church of Seattle, Washington. A graduate of Harvard College, he received the Master of Divinity from Harvard Divinity School in 1982. Kowalski won the Harvard Billings Prize for Excellence in Preaching in 1979 and the Clarence Skinner Sermon Award of the Unitarian Universalist Association in 1985. He is author of *The Souls of Animals,* published in 1991.

ing. People naturally turn to religion for guidance in how to respond to suffering and loss. They turn to religion for strength and comfort in bearing disappointment. They want a religion that addresses life's greatest problems and that does so in a practical way.

Ours is probably an average congregation. There have been three divorces this past year. One man is laid up in the hospital with an injured spine and facing an uncertain recovery. One man is looking at imminent kidney failure, one has Alzheimer's, two have been out of work for well over a year, there's been at least one suicide attempt, and several people are under a psychiatrist's care. No one here is invulnerable. Sickness and separation and death touch us all.

Why do bad things happen to good people? Like Harold Kushner, I was talking with a woman not long ago when our conversation turned to this question. She saw so much suffering and injustice in the world, she told me, that she couldn't believe in a righteous and merciful God. She couldn't love a God who could create such misery and allow such inequities to exist. The woman was ninety years old, and she told this to me as a kind of confession. She lived in a Methodist retirement home, and she'd never been able to tell any other human being that she didn't love God. She wanted to know whether she was crazy or a terrible person for feeling that way. I was glad to be able to reassure her that she wasn't crazy and that many people had the same doubts and questions.

In fact, every religion in the world has to wrestle with the same question, "Why do bad things happen?" There are some good answers, but none that are completely satisfying.

Some answer by saying that evil and sickness and death don't actually exist. Bad things are merely illusions. God is good and the universe is just, and when life appears otherwise, it must be the result of our own bad thinking and incorrect perceptions. This was the attitude of Socrates, who said that "nothing evil can befall a good man, in life or in death." It's an outlook shared by modern Christian Scientists and by many others in our society. In many ways, it's a healthy philosophy, since it encourages us to keep our vision focused on the flowers and not the weeds. It invites us to think positively and to remain the master of our own inner selves whatever slings and arrows fall our way. In other ways, however, this is an incomplete answer. Loss and pain are not fictitious en-

tities. Life is not always fair. There are shadows in life as well as
light. However much we might wish otherwise, tragedy is a part of
our experience.

Why do bad things happen? Another answer is that bad things
have a way of working for the good. Facing challenges and hardships may make us stronger individuals. Experiencing pain may
make us more sensitive and caring for the pain of others. If we
could only see it, everything has its purpose. As Alexander Pope
wrote,

> All nature is but art, unknown to thee:
> All chance, direction, which thou canst see:
> All discord, harmony not understood;
> All partial evil, universal good.

This answer also has merit. We often do learn and grow by wres-
tling with adversity. The best swords have to be tempered by
thrusting them into the fire. But again, this answer is incomplete.
Some suffering builds character, but sometimes its effect is the
opposite, as with children who grow up in violent and abusive
homes. How can we say "it will all work out for the best" to the
parent who has lost a child, or to the person with AIDS? In real
life, not every story can have a happy ending.

Another answer to the question "Why do bad things happen?"
is the belief in a system of future rewards. Though life seems unfair now, you can have faith that the accounts will be squared later
on. Though life is hard for the present, your suffering will be
repaid and rewarded in heaven. This answer also has some appeal.
In this life, at least, crime usually doesn't pay, lies usually have a
way of catching up with you, and mischief-makers usually come to
a bad end. It's equally true that virtue and integrity carry some
built-in rewards: peace of mind, recognition from our community,
the trust and confidence of friends. But whether or not a heavenly
reward really exists is a matter of faith, not knowledge. All we
know for certain is that this world is not always just or uniformly
equitable. There's no guarantee that you get what you deserve
from life.

One of the classic attempts to address the question of why bad
things happen is contained in the Book of Job. Job recounts the
story of a man whose world turned upside down. Actually, the
Book of Job contains two separate stories. The first story begins

with chapters one and two. These chapters are written in prose and tell how a righteous man named Job in the land of Uz became the object of a wager between God and Satan. God permits Satan to test Job by taking away everything he has—his wealth, his sons and daughters, and finally his health—in order to measure the depth of his loyalty to God. The final chapter of the book is also in prose and forms the conclusion of this story. After being tested, and found worthy, Job is restored to his former condition. He is given new cattle and new oxen, he has more sons and daughters to replace those he lost, all in double measure to what he had before. This prologue and epilogue in prose form one story of Job. The moral of the story is the conventional one that goodness will be rewarded in the end. "Patient as Job" and "long-suffering as Job" are phrases that have entered our language to convey this theological message. Don't complain about your troubles. Have faith. Sooner or later, you're sure to receive your due.

The second story of Job is contained in the central portion of the book. These thirty-nine chapters are written in poetry rather than prose, which suggests they may come from a different author than the one who wrote the preface and postscript. The Job portrayed here is not patient, not long-suffering, nor uncomplaining. Just the opposite. This Job is a man who knows he's been wronged. He knows that life has been unfair to him. He's outraged and angry, and he demands that God give some accounting or explanation for all the evil that's befallen him. "I would speak to the Almighty," Job exclaims, "and I desire to argue my case with God."

Onto this scene come Job's three well-meaning but bumbling friends. What do you say to someone who's lost his home, his livelihood, his family, who's covered with boils and sitting in an ashheap, scraping his sores with a broken pot? "I know just how you feel" doesn't seem right. "It is hard to know what to say to a person who has been struck by tragedy," writes Harold Kushner, "but it's easier to know what not to say. Anything critical of the mourner ("don't take it so hard, try to hold back your tears, you're upsetting people") is wrong. Anything that tries to minimize the mourner's pain ("it's probably for the best, it could be a lot worse, she's better off now") is likely to be misguided and unappreciated. Anything that asks the mourner to disguise or reject his feelings ("we have no right to question God, God must love you to have selected you for this burden") is wrong as well." Job's friends make all these mistakes and more. They're of small comfort to a man who needs compassion more than criticism, and who needs someone to hold him rather than scold him.

One of our most incurably human tendencies in the face of tragedy is to blame the victim. The woman who was raped must have done something to provoke her attacker. The man who has cancer must have brought it on himself with his "Type A" behavior and "cancer prone" personality. We reassure ourselves that we're different, and hence immune to the misfortune that afflicts our neighbor. Job reflects that before his troubles began, "Men listened to me, and waited, and kept silence for my counsel. . . . And now I have become their song, I am a byword to them. They abhor me, they keep aloof from me." But while Job becomes an outcast and an untouchable among his neighbors, he continues to protest his innocence before God: "Oh, that I knew where I might find him, that I might come even to his seat! I would lay my case before him and fill my mouth with arguments. I would learn what he would answer me, and understand what he would say to me. Would he contend with me in the greatness of his power? No, he would give heed to me. There an upright man could reason with him, and I should be acquitted for ever by my judge."

And Job gets his wish! For "then the Lord answered Job out of the whirlwind: 'Who is this that darkens counsel by words without knowledge? Gird up your loins like a man, I will question you, and you shall declare to me.' " There follows the great epiphany that I read to you earlier this morning. God appears in overwhelming majesty and might: Lord of stars and sunlight, Lord of the dark and damp, Lord of the strange creatures, the hippopotamus, the crocodile, the fiery stallion. And Job, chastened and humbled, confesses that "I have uttered what I did not understand, things too wonderful for me, which I did not know," and repents in dust and ashes.

It took me a long while to understand the ending to the Book of Job. It wasn't a satisfying conclusion. God never really answers Job. He doesn't reply to Job's reasoning. He rejects Job's petition for a redress of grievances. God doesn't even try to justify himself or to defend his own character. He certainly doesn't apologize. Everything he does, he says, is "executive privilege." He simply seems to say to Job, "I'm God and you're not!" He triumphs not by superior logic or argument, but ultimately by pulling rank.

Why does Job give in? Why is Job, who demanded justice and fair play and due process, willing to bow down before this arbitrary deity? The answer is that the encounter with God is not logical or rational. It is a religious experience. "I had heard of thee by the hearing of the ear," Job says to God in the final sentence of the book, "but now my eye sees thee." The faith we live by and that sustains us through the sad times and the glad times and the mad times is not based on rational demonstration, but on inner conviction. The power behind life is not ultimately logical or orderly or just. It is wild and untamed and full of rough edges. It rages as well as gently flows. It thunders and floods as well as softly rains. When our world falls apart, that is not a logical process, nor is it logical when it comes back together again. The redeeming fact is, however, that it can come back together. The darkness that seemed like it would never end gives way to light. Despair melts and hope is born. How this happens is a mystery . . . inexplicable . . . an act of grace.

What can you do when your world turns upside down? There are several things we can learn from the Book of Job:

1. Don't blame yourself or be hard on yourself. Don't allow yourself to be poisoned with guilt or self-hatred. Although his so-called friends try to convince Job that he must be to blame for his own problems, Job maintains a strong sense of his own inward goodness and worth. He knows there are some elements in his situation that are his responsibility but that others are beyond his personal control. When you're down on your luck, try not to get down on yourself.

2. Let your pain be pain. Job doesn't try to deny or minimize his suffering. Whenever we're feeling depressed or tense or angry or afraid, we have a strong tendency to move away from those feelings and to get rid of them as quickly as possible. For some reason, we believe that we're not supposed to feel tense; we're not supposed to feel disillusioned. We need to fully acknowledge our own pain in order for healing to take place. Instead of struggling to move away from painful feelings, try to express them and give them scope. They're a part of who you are and a part of being human.

3. Open yourself to change. Job is finally answered by God, but not in the way he expected to be answered. He is restored to life, but not in the way he thought he would be restored. When our world turns upside down, our first thought is always to bring back that lost world. We want to make things just the way they were before our world shattered. Yet there is no bringing back the past. We have to let go of that old universe. We have to loosen our death grip and open our hands to receive the new life that's offered.

To the question "Why do bad things happen to good people?" there may be no satisfactory answer. We do not always merit the misfortune that falls into our lives, any more than we merit each day's sunrise or the colors of the dawn. Life is a gift we have not earned, but that nonetheless is ours to accept or reject. When your world turns upside down, reflect that it is not your world at all. Rather it is God's world—a universe shot through with mystery and wonderful beyond human understanding. In spite of its pain and sadness, it remains an incredible creation. And when we realize that, like Job, we find the inner resources to go on living. Without ever becoming reconciled to the world's misery or injustice, we can welcome each new day as a reason to give thanks.

30. Table Talk
Hal Missourie Warheim

I will not leave you desolate;
I will come to you.

—Jesus of Nazareth
John 14:18

In the lives and ministries of Jesus Christ and his band of disciples, the Last Supper was celebrated at that strategic point in the drama where things had started to go badly and were soon to get a hell of a lot worse.

When they met together that night in the guest room of one of the houses of Jerusalem, they were climaxing a three-year ministry of teaching and healing that had become too popular, too prophetic and, therefore, terrifically dangerous. All over Palestine, from the shores of Galilee and the Samaritan towns and villages to the metropolis of Jerusalem, the Nazarene and his friends had won the hearts of the people but alienated the power elites.

By now Jesus had an unpublished price on his head set by those who could manipulate life and death to keep the status quo. The machinery behind the scenes had already begun to turn and was soon to produce a clandestine arrest, a kangaroo trial, and a blood-spattered cross.

This was pretty much par for the course in Judea or in any other society where prophets arose to challenge vested interests and idolatrous values. Jesus and his disciples were not naive about the fate of people who follow God in an ungod-like world, optimistic though they were about the triumph of their mission. Jesus had come to Jerusalem thoroughly familiar with this city's reputa-

---

Hal Missourie Warheim is professor of Christianity and society at Louisville Presbyterian Theological Seminary in Louisville, Kentucky. An ordained minister of the United Church of Christ and a member of the Kentucky Bar, Warheim is a graduate of Elmhurst College, Eden Theological Seminary, and the University of Louisville.

tion as a murderer of the prophets, and even the most unaware member of his band must have sensed the high probability of trouble. Indeed, Jesus had come to Jerusalem not because he was ambitious to preach in a big city church, but because this holiest of all places was also the citadel of everything that holds out against the invasion of God's kingdom. Jerusalem the holy, was also Jerusalem the harlot. Jesus had come here with his friends to struggle for God against all unrighteousness. But, like so many Christian prophets in our own time, while they had come upon the scene in triumph, they were soon to taste the bitterness of defeat.

By the time Jesus and the others assembled around the table that night, the lines of battle had been clearly drawn. Depending on which side of those lines one stood,

> the Temple of Jerusalem had been cleansed or violated;
> the Mosaic Law of the Sabbath had been broken or
> fulfilled;
> Israel was about to inherit the kingdom of heaven or in
> danger of losing its religious heritage;
> the Galilean was a blaspheming heretic or the Son of
> God.

As this storm of conflict for the soul of a nation gathered in Jerusalem, Jesus Christ gathered his disciples in an upper room.

Contrary to the belief of many American Christians as evidenced in their cultic behavior, what Jesus did with his friends up there around the table at this crucial point in the struggle was not to hold the first church dinner or to organize a bowling league. Christ gathered his friends around that table for a battle-briefing to prepare them for his own crucifixion and theirs.

This Prophet of Prophets knew how the warfare would go. He told them that this mission would cost him his life. He anticipated the suffering, the humiliation and death. In these predictions, Jesus was not clairvoyant; he simply perceived as realistically as anyone in history the radical, resistant strength of evil in the world, which will kill anyone who is determined to oppose it. Over the falsely optimistic protests of his followers who didn't want to believe it, he told them that he would be torn from their midst, that Jerusalem would have yet another victim, and that they who had built their hopes and centered their lives on him would know what it means to be disillusioned, dejected, and alone.

Jesus Christ was aware also of the mettle of those men who stood with him in the struggle. "One of you will betray me," he said.

"Which one of us, Lord?" they questioned, "Is it I?"

"Indeed, when the fat is in the fire, every last one of you will lose his nerve and give up the fight for it is written, 'I will strike the Shepherd, and the sheep of the flock will be scattered.' "

"No, not I, Lord," they said, "I can believe it of the others, but, even if I must die with you, I'll be faithful to the end."

"O, truly, I must say to you, before this thing is over, you will have prostituted everything I stand for seventy times seven. And, then, when Right is on the Cross and Love is in the tomb, you will realize just what you have done and who you really are, and your hearts will be hot with shame and your wretchedness from grief will heed no bounds."

But Jesus also believed that God is sovereign and holy. Against righteousness, evil could not have the final say. His own death would be the strategy of victory and, despite their timidity and weakness, his friends would be called again to follow him all the way. In continuing Christ's warfare against the forces of evil, each one of them would have his own trial and his own cross. As Jerusalem had hated him, the world would hate them. They would be stoned by the mobs and rejected by their friends, kicked out of the churches and dragged before the courts. For the rest of their lives, whenever they were faithful, they would be in trouble, suffering the hell of fighting for heaven in a world at war with its God.

In this manner Christ briefed his disciples for the struggle as they ate their last meal together:

> Evil will tear me from your midst, and you will be
>   disillusioned and alone.
> You will all betray me and suffer the grief of guilt.
> You must take up your cross and follow me to
>   victory by way of Calvary.

This is not the kind of speech that troops like to hear before going into combat even if they know the war is won. It is not the sort of message that is likely to become the gospel for any typical

American church. But, in every Jerusalem of the world, there is, perhaps, a tableful of people who will care enough about right and truth and love to want to follow in the way of Jesus Christ. For these, as for the first disciples, weak and fearful though they may be, Jesus Christ has something more to say, namely:

When the struggle is going badly and promises only to get worse,
  "I will not leave you desolate; I will come to you."
When you are broken-hearted and drowning in your guilt,
  "I will not leave you desolate; I will come to you."
When you have been obedient and are nailed upon the cross,
  "I will not leave you desolate; I will come to you."

These words proved to be no empty promise. Jesus was not just whistling in the dark. After their master's death, the disciples' world came crashing down. Sealed within his tomb were all their dreams and hopes. Everything they had worked for, believed in, lay in shambles of defeat.

And then he came to them!

While retreating down the Emmaus Road, hiding out behind locked doors, going back to their nets and boats, Jesus Christ, the risen, victorious Son of God came to them.

And by his presence these people who were dead were raised to new life. He breathed on them and their spirits felt fresh power. He spoke to them and their faint hearts lost their fears. He walked with them and their guilt was salved with peace. He broke bread with them and gave them of his life to eat. He filled their lives with song, and then he led them back to die.

For nearly twenty centuries of continual warfare against the forces of unrighteousness and evil, these have been the experiences of the men and women who follow in the way of Jesus the Christ.

By the wisdom of God it has been our destiny to be called up for service at a time in America and in the world when things are going badly and threaten to get a hell of a lot worse. In such an age, we have been summoned to be warriors of God and not sextons of a fort. Therefore, as we gather about this table to be prepared and sustained for the struggles ahead, let us all be clear about what to expect.

There will be countless crucifixions of all that is right and good and true. And, for anyone who deeply cares about these things of God, there will be bitter disappointments and the anguish of despair.

There will be, also, betrayal of these things of God among us and within each of us. And anyone who serves the Christ in earnest will feel the throbbing wounds of shame.

Furthermore, if and when we're faithful and are determined in what we do, we are bound to get ourselves in trouble, and a hostile world will run us through.

But, in all these things—despair and guilt, persecution and peril and sword—shall we be separated from the victorious God-in-Christ?

No! "I will not leave you desolate; I will come to you."

And this, as many of us know, is no empty promise. By Christ's presence, though we are dead, we will be raised to new life. He will breathe on us and our spirits will feel fresh power. He will speak to us and our hearts will lose their fears. He will walk with us and our guilt will be salved with peace. He will break bread with us and give us of his life to eat. He will fill our lives with song and then lead us forth to die.

And because God is sovereign and holy, against righteousness evil will not have the final say. The giving up of our lives in God's service will be the strategy of victory, and "in all these things, we will be more than conquerors through God who loves us."

31. Growing Down: A Sermon on Aging

Walter B. Shurden

Psalm 71

Why did my children—and now my grandchildren—prefer to hear my growing-up stories at bedtime rather than their book stories? Childish eyes sparkle as I tell stories about my first spanking at school; about the time Jody George and I went to "fist city" on top of the first grade tables and all because each of us was certain that Ann McGaugh loved one and not the other; about the time I swiped a watermelon and a policeman gave me chase until I found refuge under Buddy Garrett's darkened front porch; about the time I followed my fourteen-month-older brother to his first day of school and stood with my nose through the fence crying my four-year-old heart empty. Why did Sherry and Paula and Walt prefer those stories? And why now do Emily and Audrey have tastes for the same?

Because those tales cut me down to size. These bedtime slices of autobiography made me appear real and vulnerable, which is to say human. Big people are none of those things to little people. Kids want to hear stories about the people they love. And they prefer stories that reek with reality, stories filled with failure *and* triumph, with courage *and* defeat, with a dab of meanness *and* a

---

Walter B. Shurden is Callaway Professor of Christianity at Mercer University in Macon, Georgia. Shurden has also served as Dean of Theology at the Southern Baptist Theological Seminary and Professor of Religion at Carson-Newman College. Shurden is the author of many books, including *Not A Silent People: Controversies That Have Shaped The Southern Baptists* and numerous articles for publications such as *Pulpit Digest*.

pinch of goodness. Such stories tell the little ones that they are not alone with their feelings and tears and anger and selfishness and achievements.

But with all these growing-up stories, have you ever wondered, with the widower Will in A. G. Mojtabai's novel *Autumn,* why there are not also some "growing-down stories"?[1] Why don't our elder elders tell us what it feels like to grow down in the later stages of life as well as grow up during the early stages of life? Some of us "young people" who are in our thirties and forties and fifties would like to know what it feels like to start down the mountain now that we are almost finished with the ascent. There are thousands of growing-up stories, but very few growing-down stories. With each passing year and the dropping of a bit more sand, I find myself wondering about the ingredients of good, healthy, creative aging.

Maybe growing-down stories are seldom told because no one asks. Maybe those stories are perched on the edge of many an older tongue that thinks no one is interested. Or maybe there is a conspiracy on the part of all ages to avoid the confrontation with the end of life. For in one sense, every last one of us is doing precisely what Mattie Rigsbee, the seventy-eight-year-old heroine in Clyde Edgerton's wonderful *Walking Across Egypt* is doing: We are "slowing down" and "falling off." Maybe the absence of growing-down stories is a part of the great denial. Whatever the reasons for the reticence, we need to remedy the situation.

What would growing-down stories include? From what I have read and observed and heard, they would be rich and challenging, sad and sorrowful, joyous and exciting, replete with anger and anxiety, humorous and hopeful. In a word, they would be very much like the growing-up stories. And like the growing-up tales, I'll bet we would never forget them. Three words would dominate growing-down stories.

In these growing-down stories we would hear much about the need for *independence.* Do you remember the name Joseph Califano, Jr.? Once secretary of the Department of Health, Education and Welfare, he is now a national spokesman for "Project Independence for Older Americans." I don't know what the Project does, but I imagine the very name of the organization—Project Independence for Older Americans—brings the elderly of this country to their feet with cheers!

Growing-down stories, like growing-up stories, would be scary stories. They would have some fear in them. Fear of loss of health, fear of desolation through loss of loved ones and friends, fear of loss of usefulness, fear of not being taken seriously—these and other terrors stalk the steps of our elders. But probably none is greater than the loss of independence. Here is the big fear of the future for all of us—the fear of the loss of control! While a legitimate fear for the elderly, we non-elderly need to be slow to see it as an all pervading reality.

To equate aging with a lack of competence is simply another "ism," an ism as pre-judging and distorting as racism and sexism. A prerequisite to human dignity is the right to think and act for oneself. There is, after all, such a thing as "the priesthood of the elderly."

Psalm 71 is a lament from an older person. One of the slurs hurled at this one who is growing-down is that he is helpless. "God has forsaken him . . . there is none to deliver him." And right here, my friends, is the language of profanity: "senile old man," "helpless old lady."

Senile old man! Try that language on Pope John XXIII! At seventy-seven years of age he became the pope of the Roman Catholic Church, and in five years he revolutionized not only the Catholic Church but the whole of Christendom. Senile old man! Try that language on Claude Pepper. He took America by its shoulders and shook it to its senses about the elderly. Helpless old lady! Hang that phrase around the neck of Sister Teresa as she prepares in the early morning hours to hunt out the sick and dying on the streets of Calcutta. These are folks who not only took care of themselves; they took care of a good portion of their world! By word and life and deed they practiced the priesthood of the elderly!

If "helpless" and "senile" constitute the language of profanity, condescension is its posture. Older people chafe under the assumption that they no longer know anything. They are riled at the implication that they can no longer handle their lives. Longevity, it is now being said by specialists of every kind, is tied to individual autonomy. So after a year of counseling with an eighty-one-year-old woman, the counselor was given the ultimate compliment by way of a thank-you: "You never patronized me."[2]

Independence is a central word in growing-down stories. But growing-down stories will also, if they are real and true and human, have something in them about *dependence*. Dependence is not a four letter word; it is a human word. It is not a psychological deficiency; it is a spiritual reality. I stuck my nose through that fence and cried for my brother Bob for a very simple reason: I needed him! And I still do at fifty-three and I will at eighty-three.

No soldier soldiers alone. A rifle is necessary, but a buddy is every bit as important.

No wonder that inventive nut, Grady Nutt, created a new word: *togetherapy*. Comes from two words: *together* and *therapy*. And after reading and reflecting on the creation stories in the Book of Genesis, Grady came up with the following exegesis:

> You were not created a hermit or a lonesome pine:
> you were created
> as a person
> and that means
>   you need other persons
> like a fish needs water
>   a bird needs feathers
>   a child needs parents
>   a flower needs spring!

He went on:

> The Book of Genesis has a great way of putting it:
>   Adam is created
>   to caretake the garden
>   name the animals
>   enjoy creation.
> The giraffe had other giraffes
>   the whale had other whales
>   the aardvark had other aardvarks
>   the louse had other lice.
> God is pictured as saying:
>   "Lice have it better than Adam"
>   or, more scripturally,
>   "It is not good that man should be alone."
> Enter Eve.[3]

And Psalm 71, this old psalm from this old person, speaks of dependence. "Upon thee have I leaned from birth." No adequate interpretation of this confession of dependence could ever transform this phrase into some kind of radical "every-tub-sits-on-its-own-bottom" theology. This is not the voice of an individualistic, enlightenment-influenced Protestant. This is the voice of a Jew. To lean upon Yahweh was to lean upon the people of Yahweh. Communion with God always meant community with the people. Dependence on God meant someone was leaning on God's people. It is not irreverent but right in light of biblical theology to say that God is not enough by himself. God's everlasting arms find expression in our arms!

Human existence is always partly a gift from others. Love and friendship and togetherness and a shoulder to sob on are not the extras but the essentials of life. Even monks live in community. Where there is no community, there is no life. All of life is dependent on other life.

And so are the elderly. While defending independence, the elderly, and all the rest of us, will have to come clean about our dependency. It is not a sign of failure or of worthlessness to have to say, "I can no longer take care of this house. It is too much for me." It may be a sad day, but it is not the final day when I throw my keys on the table and say, "I cannot drive any longer; I've driven others all my life; now I must be driven."

The danger is that we shall make a cult out of either independency or dependency. Health and wholeness is not found in either extreme. The attempt at radical independence is clearly a dead-end street. It simply is not the way God made us; it is not the shape of reality. But neither is a paralyzing dependency the mark of the fulfilled and fulfilling life. Somehow the elderly, and all of us who are growing old, must find a better way. And the better way is that of interdependence.

And so growing-down stories, if they are to be Christian and creative and compassionate stories, must possess the note of *interdependence*. Henri Nouwen tells of a legend that comes from the island state of Bali where in a remote mountain village old men used to be sacrificed and eaten. A day came when there was not a single old man left, and with the disappearance of the elderly, the traditions were lost. Soon the people wanted to build a great house for the meetings of the assembly. However, when they came to look at the tree trunks that had been cut for that purpose no one could tell the top from the bottom. If the timbers were set the wrong way, it would set off a series of disasters in the proposed building. A young man came forward and said if they promised never to sacrifice another old man, he would show them a solution. They promised. And he brought forth his grandfather whom he had hidden; and the old man taught the community to tell the top from the bottom![4]

When we think of this mystery that we call aging, we young ones must be careful in thinking we are the care-givers and the elderly are the care-receivers. We must avoid an over-under relationship with our seniors. They really can help us tell the top from the bottom. Years do give perspective! Vision, for all the dimness of fading eyesight, is often clearer in the growing-down part of life than in the growing-up years. And another thing, the old folks need no protection from the truth. They have bumped into it long before the rest of us came along. Grandparents and great-grandparents are not easily surprised! No stereotype, in my experience, is further off base than the one that pictures the older folk as rigid, without understanding, inflexible, and unforgiving. They have known for years what it is to be hurt by those who are dearest and nearest in life; they, too, have been petty and petulant and have deliberately and premeditatively hurt others; they have had to forgive before, and they have sinned before.

Little wonder that this older person who put experience to words in the Seventy-first Psalm cried out: "So even to old age and gray hairs, O God, do not forsake me, till I proclaim thy might to all the generations to come." The elderly can help the rest of us tell the top from the bottom.

But it really is a two way street, older friends. While we wish for you as much independence as your years permit, we also, like the grandson in the Bali story, wish to help secure you from the dangers of the later years. What we need to hear from your growing-down stories is how to tell the top from the bottom of life. But we need something else. We also need to hear you say you need us. We need you to tell us how to love you best in these years in which you have so much to give.

Pat Moore, a twenty-six-year-old industrial design engineer, spent part of three years of her life disguised as an eighty-five-year-old woman. She wanted to know how to best design products to help the elderly. Once mugged, often insulted, and repeatedly ignored in her role as an old person, Pat Moore was also graciously assisted and loved. "If I could wish for any particular result from my work," she wrote, "it would be that people of all ages would learn that we live in a community, a society; that we are not isolated; that we are all connected, the baby, the child, the teenager, the young adult, and the senior citizen—and we are responsible *to* one another and *for* one another."[5]

"We are all connected!" The word is *interdependence.*

Morton Kelsey stood awed before the largest living creature, a giant redwood tree that had celebrated three thousand five hundred birthdays! Nearly three hundred feet high and a hundred feet around, it was thirty feet in diameter. But here is the most amazing fact: *it is still growing!* Each year it adds five hundred more board feet to its girth. Mused Kelsey, "What zest for life this tree has!"[6]

Thirty years from now, God willing, I'll be eighty-three years old. My granddaughters, who for reasons I need not explain call me "Wibis," will be thirty-three years old. Oh, how I hope that they will be able to look at me and say, "What zest for life ole Wibis has." And I'll say, "Girls, let me tell you a growing-down story about the time I . . . recognized my priesthood . . . about the time I . . . realized that no soldier soldiers alone . . . about the time I . . . celebrated the fact that we are all connected." I hope they will remember those stories for fifty years more. And then in the year 2070 I hope they tell them to their granddaughters.

NOTES

1. As cited in Kathleen Fischer, *Winter Grace* (New York: Paulist Press, 1985), 116.

2. Ibid., 64.

3. Grady Nutt, *Being Me* (Nashville: Broadman Press, 1971), 66, 67.

4. Henri J. M. Nouwen and Walter Gaffney, *Aging: The Fulfillment of Life* (Garden City, NY: Image Books, 1976), 23.

5. Pat Moore, *Disguised* (Waco, TX: Word, 1985), 167.

6. Morton Kelsey, *Reaching* (San Francisco: Harper & Row, 1989), 12.

32. God Wins
George C. Anderson

Mark 5:1–20

A two-year-old pulls every Kleenex out of a box when she knows good and well she is not supposed to. Who is at fault? The child, who knows she is wrong? Or the syndrome of two-year-oldness, which naturally leads normal children to test their independence and limits? Or is the father at fault for leaving the box of Kleenex where little hands can reach it?

A country is divided into filthy rich and miserably poor. It's been that way for generations. Who is at fault? Those who first created the division generations ago, or those who live divided now?

A group of congressmen are set up by the FBI in an illegal sting operation to take bribes. Who was in the wrong? The FBI for its illegal trap, or the congressmen who indeed did take the bribes?

A boy is beaten irrationally by his alcoholic father. He grows to be a man and beats his son irrationally. Whose sin is at work here; the father's, the son's, or the alcohol's?

A demoniac approaches Jesus and his disciples. The whole scene is ugly, especially for sensitive Jews. Nothing is kosher here. The man is demon-possessed, he lives in the tombs, pigs are everywhere, and this is Gentile country.

The story is strange, but also familiar. For who is to blame for this man's problems? How does someone in Mark's world become

George C. Anderson is pastor of Briarwood Presbyterian Church in Jackson, Mississippi. He is the recipient of a Sax Bradbury Scholarship to the Royal Academy of Dramatic Arts in London. A graduate of St. Andrews Presbyterian College, Anderson received his Master of Divinity from Union Theological Seminary in Richmond, Virginia.

demon-possessed anyway? Is he ambushed all of a sudden by de-mons hiding along the road? Or does he in some way invite them in? From one perspective, the demons are outside influences vic-timizing the man, causing him to torture and beat himself. From another perspective, the man displays a personal attachment to his demons when he begs Jesus to depart from him.

Our confusion grows as we try to figure out just who is talking when the man speaks; the man or his demons. We think it is the demons when he says, "My name is Legion; for we are many." But then we think it is the man when he begs Jesus not to cast *them* out into the country. But *then* we think it is the demons again when they beg to be cast into the swine. To distinguish between the man's voice and that of the demons is difficult because in one sense they are at odds, and in another, they are in harmony.

Discussing stories of demons is strange to the modern ear, but talking about what leads us to hurt ourselves and others is not. We often ask who is to blame for our sins and problems. On the one hand, forces do exist outside ourselves that make us do that which we should not do. "I do not understand my own actions," Paul says. "For I do not do what I want, but I do the very thing I hate. . . . " He concludes, "It is [not] I who does it, but sin which dwells within me" (Rom. 7:15, 20).

On the other hand, we all cooperate, willingly or not, with many of these powers of sin. We are not robots, after all. Ezekiel got fed up with people blaming their parents for their problems, and he minced no words when he declared, "the soul that sins shall die" (Ezek. 18:20).

Truthfully, the statements of both Paul and Ezekiel are right. We are both victims *and* coconspirators of our sins. Our problems are inherited *and* adopted. In some ways we can't help our faults and failings, in other ways we are self-made. Look in a brutally honest mirror, and one day you see the faces of other people and other forces that have shaped your life; another day, you see no-body's face but your own.

The ambiguity of sin and sickness intensifies when we turn from the difficulty of their diagnosis to the difficulty of their so-lution. The healing of the demoniac is tough because it is hard to tell whether the man wants to be healed or not. When the demo-niac sees Jesus, he runs up to worship him. But when Jesus com-mands the unclean spirit to come out of him, he says, "What have you to do with me, Jesus, Son of the Most High God?" The man both wants Jesus near and doesn't want him near.

The townspeople are equally difficult to understand. One would hope they would be delighted the man is saved from his lunacy. Instead, the healing scares them to death. The demoniac has been out of his mind for a long time, and no one could do anything with him. Clothing, chains, and fetters are mere annoyances with him. Then all of a sudden, they find the guy sitting quietly, fully clothed, and absolutely lucid. Something strange is happening here.

Further, their pigs have been destroyed. That the Jews raised pigs in the first place is a moral problem. But the Gentiles are willing to pay well for them. These valuable but "unclean" pigs, once peacefully rooting about, are now carcasses floating near the shoreline. To say the scene is eerie is an understatement. The townspeople are scared silly and quite angry about the loss of the herd. They certainly didn't want Jesus to cure them of their unholy means of money making. No wonder they ask Jesus to leave.

But though they beg Jesus to go away, they also want him to come near. The evidence of this can be seen in the way they later treat the demoniac. Jesus does not let the guy follow him, but sends him back home to witness to those frightened townspeople. And listen they do. Eagerly.

We would be too quick to label the demoniac and the townspeople fools. They are about as typical of our own lives as they can be. Picture right now someone you know with a severe personal problem. The problem causes pain and, just as the demoniac tormented himself, much of this pain probably is self-inflicted. But does the person really want to be healed or not? Am I off base in suggesting that the answer could be both yes and no? We want to be rid of our problems, and yet we hang on to them, too. We hang on because our problems become comfortable, even usable.

One question a good counselor often tries to get answered in dealing with people is, "What do you get out of your problems?" Or to put the question in different ways, "What are you gaining from your sicknesses? What are you afraid of losing if you are healed? Attention? The excuse to escape responsibility? A shield against the world?"

Joe can hang on to his bitterness about being fired without reasonable cause three years ago because it excuses his continuing unemployment. His bitterness lets him avoid being honest about the truth that he is unemployed not only because he was fired unjustly, but also because he is scared of taking another job where he might, again, be labeled a failure.

Laura hangs on to her resentment of her parents because it gives her an excuse not to take responsibility for her own life. She says they alone caused her to be socially crippled. Saying so keeps her from considering that she herself is afraid of the demands of relationships.

Therapy often is painful because it breaks old familiar chords of dependency, and that hurts. Though the process of therapy is not to be confused with conversion, they often are painful for basically the same reasons. We have struck deals with the demons of our lives, and to be rid of them is to be rid of the security, the familiarity, the escapes, the comforts they offer us.

C. S. Lewis's discomforting story *The Great Divorce* concerns a group of people who, having spent some time in dreary hell, are allowed to board a bus to heaven. They get off at a bus stop where a long walk to heaven awaits them. Residents of heaven are there to be their guides. Surprisingly, many refuse to go. They refuse because they have to give up something that would keep them out of heaven. One person won't go because his guide is a convicted murderer whom he can't forgive. Another would have to give up his discussion group in hell that argues moral and religious theories and resists any kind of practical application. There is a man who would have to give up his well-developed cynicism that refuses to be foolish in thankfulness, joy, and wonder. And there is the woman who would have to give up her need to control other people in order to have a relationship. All these poor souls cling to whatever is keeping them from entering heaven because they have grown dependent on their problems. They want to be included in the kingdom but not at the price of their liberation from their comfortable sins and sicknesses.

The demoniac and the townspeople are both attracted to, and repelled by, the grace of God. In kind, most of us want God to come nearer, but not too near. We know God has to come near to help us, but his coming near will also change us, and change can hurt. So, if we are going to be healed, it will be both because of our asking and despite our refusing.

In the Gospel of Mark, Jesus heals those who have faith and want healing, and will not (and, at least in Mark, maybe can not) heal those who have no faith. But here we have a story about most of us; a story about those whose faith lives ambiguously between following and fleeing. Can God help us in our confusion over blame and in our indecisiveness about healing? Will God give up on us before we fully want him to come near?

We can take much hope in the fact that the rejected Jesus doesn't give up on the townspeople who so fearfully ask him to leave. He sends the healed man back to the townspeople as living evidence of the power and grace of God. When a little time passes, and their fear subsides, the people are able to listen to the man tell how it is to be free of demons. The healed man does not tell of some greater demon casting out the lesser ones that had shackled his soul. Instead he tells of the mercy of God Almighty experienced in the man named Jesus. And the townspeople "marvel," the Revised Standard Version says. Maybe if we read a bit into such a wonderful word as "marvel," we will see a little predisposition to belief there, too. The very people who begged Jesus to leave now beg the healed man to stay and tell more.

In Mark's Gospel, God does not force miracles in the human heart. God will calm a sea and feed thousands, but will not coerce a heart to believe. Why? Because God did not create us to be robots. We can resist God's grace. But our resistance doesn't necessarily mean God is going to give up. God has other ways to win. The healing of the demoniac suggests that God may not accept our initial "no" and go away. God doesn't give up on the demoniac who both wants to be healed and doesn't want to be healed. Nor does God give up on the townspeople who want Jesus out of town, yet listen eagerly to the healed man tell of what God in Christ has done for him. God wins people over. He does so all in a moment as in the case of the demoniac, and through the slow means of testimony as in the case of the townspeople.

How God wins over hearts that both resist and invite him is a mystery. But I imagine God wins in something of the way one wins at romance. A guy asks a girl out. She says, "Get lost!" He sends her flowers. She keeps the flowers but never thanks him. He sings serenades under her window. She laughs but tells him to go away. He joins her on a walk and they talk. Finally, she agrees to dinner.

And they celebrate the anniversary of their first date with a wedding.

Some might think I am trivializing grace when I compare God winning us over with such a romantic analogy. But Jesus himself compared the kingdom to a wedding, a ceremony that joins two willing parties. Plus, there have been a number of church theologians who compared faith to falling in love. When someone falls in love it involves both a willing and a winning. Someone wins you over, but finally your heart is willing, too. When we can see beyond the pain that is usually involved in growing by grace, we realize just how beautiful the miracles are that somehow make us surrender to healing without coercion. How marvelous is the subtle power of God.

I realize I am talking mostly to the converted who, like the healed man, can give some testimony to what God has already done for us. But I also realize that every person in this sanctuary has hurts and needs still. We want to be rid of them, and yet we may be hanging on to them for their familiar "benefits" at the same time. The simple good news I affirm today in this confusing and rich text is this: God is perfectly willing to heal and won't necessarily wait until we are perfectly willing to be healed. God hears our weak calls for help. And God responds, refusing to be turned off by the resistance and barriers we contrarily put up against him. Though God will not force healing, God will not give up on us. Ultimately, God wins. Praise be to God! Amen.

33. Living with AIDS
Gary A. Wilburn

John 11:17–45

Last November during my annual physical checkup, I complained to my doctor about feeling unusually tired and exhausted. He did all the normal x-rays and blood tests and became a bit concerned about one of the tests on my liver. Since he could not find anything wrong, this respected internist suggested that I might want to think about taking a blood test for the HIV virus, which is connected with AIDS. "There is no reason to think that you need the test," he said, "but the only way you can be sure is to have it."

I shrugged my shoulders and said, "Sure, might as well. It can't hurt." Now I knew enough about AIDS and the HIV virus to know that it can only be contracted in one of three ways: high risk, unprotected sexual activity; contact with contaminated blood; or from an infected mother to her child. I knew that my wife and I have remained faithful to each other for the now twenty years of our marriage, so I was sure there was no possible way I would have contracted the disease through sexual activity.

I also knew that I had not received a blood transfusion and that neither of us had ever been an intravenous drug user who might have gotten hold of an unsterilized needle or syringe. I had absolutely no reason to think that I might have AIDS. But since I usually feel it's better to be safe than sorry, I gave my permission for the blood test.

Gary A. Wilburn is Senior Pastor of Immanuel Presbyterian Church in Los Angeles, California. He is a graduate of Princeton Theological Seminary and Regent College in Vancouver, British Columbia. Wilburn is the author of two books, *The Fortune Sellers* and *Visualize*.

As he was writing up the order, my doctor said, "I'll put this on a separate bill in case you want to pay for it yourself rather than putting it through on your insurance." I naively asked him why that would be necessary. He explained that many people are doing it that way because they don't want their insurance records red-flagged. "But it's just a test," I said. "It doesn't mean that you have AIDS."

"You know that, and I know that," he said, "but there is a lot of fear and paranoia about AIDS in this country. We don't even use a person's name on the test; we use a special code number to protect their anonymity."

For two weeks I thought a lot about that test and about a society that is afraid of the truth. I imagined how a person might feel if they were indexed on some list and ostracized from the rest of society. I remembered horror stories of people being shunned years ago in this country because of the "Big C"; they were afraid even to whisper the word *cancer*. Now it is not only fear but shame, and shame is a worse killer even than AIDS.

Thankfully, my test came back negative. The liver test was a fluke. My health is fine. I do not have the AIDS virus. But there are many who are not so fortunate.

One of those people is Elizabeth Glaser, the wife of actor Paul Michael Glaser of "Starsky and Hutch" fame. Elizabeth was a happy wife and mother until two years ago when she sat sobbing on the steps of the hospital where a doctor had just told her that her daughter, Ariel, had forty-eight hours to live. In 1981 Elizabeth had received a contaminated blood transfusion after the birth of Ariel. During breastfeeding, she unknowingly passed the virus to her daughter and three years later to her son. Ariel died in March of 1988. Today both Elizabeth and her son have the HIV virus. "One of the things that my life has taught me," she said recently, "is that I have nothing to lose by being honest. I don't have the time to play games."[1]

As your pastor, I feel the same way. It is unacceptable for a civilized society to act as though the problem will just go away if we keep pretending it isn't there or that it isn't our responsibility. We are so interdependent that what happens to one of us happens to all of us. How can we be silent when we live in a country that bars people with AIDS from entering it until they are documented? This is not Nazi Germany. This is America.

The Church has been silent for too long. We can be many things to many people. But if we cannot be the Church, the healing body of our Lord Jesus Christ, to those whose lives are destroyed by the tragedy of AIDS, then we have no right to call ourselves Christians.

I was outraged a few years ago when I read of a young man with AIDS who became a Christian through the chaplain's ministry at the Kaiser Permanente Medical Center here in Los Angeles. He wanted to be baptized by immersion at a local evangelical church. But the members of the church refused because of their fear that the virus would spread in the baptismal water. A doctor assured them that the disease could not be transmitted that way, but, just to be safe, they could baptize him last and the doctor would drain and sterilize the tank himself. The elders of the church still refused to baptize him. I wrote the chaplain and offered to baptize him myself. I received a letter of gratitude from him informing me that the new convert had finally been baptized in a county swimming pool. He said that his work with these young men with AIDS had taught him many things about love and compassion. "[They] suffer from many causes other than the disease itself," he said. "One of them is the smugness of the established church."

I received a sick letter last week from a person who heard about our concert this coming Saturday to benefit those persons with AIDS. He as much said that AIDS was God's judgment on homosexuals who should be put to death. That is an ignorant, arrogant, and evil thing to say. The story of Job and the entire life and teaching of Jesus stand in opposition to that view.

Suffering happens to people in spite of their goodness. Some catastrophes happen because of nature, others because of human action, and others because of our inaction. Do you realize that every minute twenty-four people starve to death somewhere in the world? What was the sin of those starving children? Episcopal Bishop Paul Moore of New York put it well. "If God punishes people through sickness, don't you think those who perpetuate nuclear war . . . would at least get herpes?"[2]

There is a word of judgment in the AIDS crisis—not upon people with AIDS but upon our society and our church. As Rev. William Sloan Coffin observed, "Can anyone doubt that if the primary group of victims had been from upper middle class heterosexual whites, funding from the government . . . would have been ten times what it is today?"

Recently President Bush told it like it is. "We're in a fight against a disease—not a fight against people," he said. "And we will not and must not in America—tolerate discrimination."

Still, the Church of Jesus Christ lags far behind its founder. As one activist put it, "We've seen many more calls for compassion from Hollywood than from the Church, and that's a scandal."

In John's Gospel reading this morning, Jesus demonstrates again his humble, loving compassion. Jesus' entire ministry is marked by his special love for and desire to be with the poor, the outcast, the marginalized, and the dispossessed. He not only announces good news to the poor and freedom to the broken victims of human indignities and oppression, but he acts in solidarity with them. He touches them, eats with them, and, as with Lazarus, unbinds them from the bandages of shame and death that keep them the victims of a fearful and uncaring society.

Jesus was not ashamed to be seen with those on the fringe of society. He even had the audacity to announce that they would have the seats of honor at his heavenly feast. How can you and I do less?

Sickness, like sexuality, always raises questions of human identity. Certain illnesses reveal the vindictive spirit in all of us. That spirit leads us to believe that the preservation of my identity requires the diminishment of yours. We feel safe when others are condemned, isolated, and quarantined.[3] There is no safety in ignorance, denial, and fear. There is safety only in the truth.

As we partake of the table of our Lord this morning, may God show us the latent fear in each of us that freezes our feelings into ideologies and prevents us from being agents of God's love and healing with those who suffer. In risking that love, we open ourselves to receive the love of God in the Christ who meets us in the person of the unloved as well as in the Holy Table. As Jesus' body on earth, we have no alternative other than to embrace the estranged and the outcast in open, caring ways of love.

We can become a "fellowship of unbinding." We can unbind the bandages of shame and death in this city. How? We can pray, individually and in services of public worship. We can welcome persons with AIDS into our fellowship, offering our assistance and our facilities to them and their families and friends for support group meetings. We can reach out and touch those with the HIV virus just as Jesus reached out and touched that man who was suffering from a dreaded skin disease. We can support our local AIDS service agencies. We can visit the sick and be present to those who have been abandoned by family and friends.

Finally, we can work for justice, speaking the truth, educating the ignorant, calming the hysteria of the fearful. "We can use this opportunity to make a powerful statement about the inclusive nature of the gospel. . . . The church could join, if not lead, the chorus of voices calling on government at every level to commit funds for research, personnel and facilities for treatment."[4] As Bishop Kelly asked recently, "What is the good of mourning those we have lost if we don't act to save those who have a chance?"

Some of you here this morning may be dying from AIDS. But there is not a person in this sanctuary who is not dying of something. We are all moving toward death. The challenge of Lent is for us to make friends with our own finitude and limitation, our suffering and our shortcomings, and thereby allow ourselves to embrace life.

At present there is no cure for the disease. But there is a cure for the despair. We can live with AIDS. We can live as ones who are suffering because life is lived not in years but in moments of love and caring and discovery. We can live with AIDS as members together of the body of Christ in this church because Christ comes alongside us in our struggle and offers us the opportunity to be love for each other. We can live with AIDS in our society because we share a common humanity and a common divinity in the image of God.

And finally, we can live with AIDS because of our faith that some day love will conquer fear. We are going to fight for hope, like Mr. Bush said. "America has a capacity for beating the odds— and astounding the world."

In December of 1988, Miss Pearl Bailey, that great woman of faith, addressed the World Health Organization at Geneva.

> I've heard it said, "Not in this century will there
> be a cure [for AIDS]," she said. But we must say
> and believe: "Oh yes there will be."
> In some *bosom* there is faith: In some *mind*
> there is a key to open the door. We must falsify
> the lie that AIDS is "unconquerable." Somewhere
> in the world a man or woman will, by the grace of

> God, become filled with the knowledge that will
> save humanity.
> Through our combined efforts it can and must
> be done. . . . God created mankind. We must not
> allow AIDS to destroy it, or force us to destroy
> ourselves.
> Time is not on our side. God is.[5]

I believe that. Do you?

A few months ago I stood in the hospital room of a young man who had everything to live for but was dying of AIDS. We held hands and talked about his joys and his fears and about his God. He was a baptized Christian, and he loved his Lord very much. We read Scripture and prayed and then took the bread and the cup of our Lord's undying love together. As we shared in Holy Communion, I asked him the opening question in the Heidelberg Catechism, "What is your only comfort in life and in death?" A twinkle came to his weary eyes and he responded, "My only comfort is that I belong—body and soul, in life and in death—not to myself but to my faithful Savior Jesus Christ."

Marty died a few days later. He died in the Lord and he lives today in the Lord. As Pearl Bailey would put it, "His eye is on the sparrow and I know he watches me."

NOTES

1. Geraldine Baum, "A Star in the AIDS War," *Los Angeles Times* (March 21, 1990): E-7.

2. Russell Chandler, "AIDS: Rigid Church View Is Fading," *Los Angeles Times* (June 12, 1986): 38.

3. Alan Jones, *Passion for Pilgrimage* (San Francisco: Harper & Row, 1988), 67.

4. Earl E. Shelp and Ronald H. Sunderland, "AIDS and the Church," *The Christian Century* (September 11–18, 1985).

5. Pearl Bailey, "We the Seekers Shall Be the Finders," statement delivered to the World Health Organization "On AIDS" at Geneva, December 1, 1988.

VI. DEVOTIONAL

34. The Problem of False Expectations
Victor J. Eldridge

Exodus 4:10

"But Moses said to the Lord, 'O my Lord, I have never been eloquent, neither in the past nor even now that you have spoken to your servant; but I am slow of speech and slow of tongue.' "

I want to take as my text seven words from that verse "Neither in the past nor even now" or, to give the sermon a title, talk about the problem of false expectations.

This story in Exodus 3 and 4 is told with the vividness that characterizes the compilers of the Yahwist stream of tradition. In it we see Moses on the spot. One pleasant afternoon he had been quietly enjoying the sunshine as his flock grazed contentedly nearby when into his line of vision had come that attention arresting phenomenon of the bush that burned and burned and burned yet was still there. His curiosity was too much for him, and it led him into a situation where he found himself in direct encounter with God. To his delight, and perhaps the easing of a still active conscience, came the news that God was about to take action on behalf of the people whom Moses had abandoned, but never entirely forgotten, forty years before. Then shattering his enjoyment of this great religious experience came God's demand that Moses himself spearhead the great mission of rescue from Egypt. As God's finger came down squarely on him, Moses squirmed. It was

Victor Eldridge is principal of Morling College, The Baptist Theological College of New South Wales in Eastwood, N.S.W., Australia. He was born in Maitland, N.S.W., Australia, and received degrees from Sydney University and Melbourne College of Divinity in Australia. His Ph.D. from The Southern Baptist Theological Seminary in Louisville, Kentucky, is in Old Testament studies.

a magnificent scheme, he assured God, but the choice of personnel was all wrong. "I'm not the man you want," he said, "and, even if I were, I know nothing about you anyway. Even if I did no one would listen to me." It is one of those delightful Old Testament conversations between God and man in which God always has an answer to every argument brought. Finally in desperation Moses introduced his clinching argument. "God," he said, "you're talking about what you're going to do. But what have you really done for me. I've never been a speaker and I'm no better since you've called me than I was before. The very least you could have done was give me an easy flow of speech that would enable me to charm pharoah into agreement and compel the Israelites into action. But I'm still stumbling and mumbling as I talk to you now."

"But Moses said to the Lord, 'O my Lord, I have never been eloquent, neither in the past nor even now that you have spoken to your servant; but I am slow of speech and slow of tongue'" (Exod. 4:10).

What is it that Moses is really asking for? An immediate and easy answer to his problems: God's instant equipment of him for his task, a minor miracle, a great religious experience that would enable him to become a minister overnight. The solution of personal limitations and inadequacies and weaknesses so that from that interview at the burning bush would have emerged not Moses the shepherd with a new task and a slow tongue but super Moses, the Chrysostom of the desert, the Billy Graham of the Burning Bush, the man to whom all things came easily and immediately.

Does the writer believe God could have done that? Of course he does, but in the story God does not choose to do so. And what emerged was a Moses who had to rely on Aaron as his spokesman; a man unable to do the task by himself but who is dependent on an inferior to act on his behalf.

I believe that this story mirrors what happens to many of us. We have a concept of what God should do for us and often it doesn't work out that way. There are people who come to seminary with high hopes. Ah, they think, when I become a student for the ministry I will overcome my present problems. Out here in the world with all its temptations I succumb so often, but when I live in the rarefied spiritual atmosphere of a theological seminary, when the only companions I have are the very saints of God and I alone am tainted with sin, when all my days are spent in the study of the Bible, then not only will I be able to answer every question anyone asks me about the Bible from the details of eschatology to the name of Cain's wife, but I will also leave behind the temptations and sins which so easily beset me. I, who could speak only to my own and the congregation's embarrassment, will be able to preach in the greatest churches of the land. God has called me, he will equip me. *But* somehow it isn't working out. That key that unlocks the door to instant Christian victory has not been found. There are still the same limitations, still the same struggles. I am still me and I don't want to be me. Some of us have to say as we look at our high hopes and the sad and disappointing realities of life "Neither in the past nor even now." All of which raises the question, why? Why does God not give that immediate victory, that dramatic equipment for life that we seek? I suggest four possible reasons why sometimes we have to learn to live with our limitations longer than we would like to.

The first reason is because even great religious experiences, even miracles have their limitations. Look at the story of Elijah at Mount Carmel. What a tremendous victory! What a stupendous miracle! Followed by what? A frightened man running from the anger of the queen, wishing he was dead, feeling himself to be alone, and having to learn that God made himself known not in the exciting and the spectacular, the wind, fire, and earthquake, but in the quietness of a still small voice. His miracle had done its job, but one can't live on miracles.

Moreover miracles convince only those willing to be convinced. The Bible writers make this point very clearly. Look at Moses in this story. In Exodus 4:1–9 we are told how his rod was changed to a serpent, a minor miracle that even the Egyptian magicians could duplicate, but enough to make Moses run for his life. Then his hand was changed to leprous and back again, but Moses was not convinced. Nor later were the Israelites to be convinced. They had experienced the terror of the plagues, the great event of the Red Sea, the overcoming by God's power of every barrier to their freedom, but once in the desert they wondered if the God who had got them there could possibly keep them alive, could possibly give them food and water, could possibly defeat those giants in their new land. Miracles only convince those willing to be convinced. You can't live on religious experiences. Their glory soon fades in the harsh reality of the difficulties and challenges of the new day.

The second reason we are not always granted the miracles we seek is that it requires a greater exercise of faith to live without them. Jesus said to Thomas, "Have you believed because you have seen me? Blessed are those who have not seen and yet have come to believe" (John 20:29). The first letter of Peter speaks of Christ as the one who "although you have not seen him you love him: and even though you do not see him now you believe in him and rejoice with an indescribable and glorious joy" (1 Pet. 1:8). In John 4 is recorded the story of a man's desperate request to our Lord to heal his son, but Christ's reply is to warn of the danger of demanding the spectacular before people were willing to believe. "Jesus said to him, 'Unless you see signs and wonders you will not believe'" (John 4:48). He went on to grant the request but not before his apparent refusal had elicited an avowal of greater faith from the suppliant. It is when our faith is put on trial and when the accompanying signs are not there that real growth occurs. What greater expression of faith could be found than that of the Hebrew boys in Daniel 3:17–18. "O Nebuchadnezzar, we have no need to present a defense to you in this matter. If our God whom we serve is able to deliver us from the furnace of blazing fire and out of your hand, O king, let him deliver us. But if not, be it known to you, O king, that we will not serve your gods and we will not worship the golden statue that you have set up." *But if not*—there is the real test of faith.

Third, I suggest that we often fail to see that God does not need to overcome our inadequacies before he can use us. It has been suggested that the reply given to Moses in Exodus 4:11 means that God was able to use Moses in all his stammering weakness. A Moses eloquent and polished may not have been as persuasive and useful in God's hands as one whose stumbling sincerity allowed God's power to shine through. Is that not what Paul says about his thorn in the flesh in 2 Corinthians 12:8–10? "Three times I appealed to the Lord about this, that it would leave me, but he said to me, 'My grace is sufficient for you, for power is made perfect in weakness. So, I will boast all the more gladly of my weaknesses, so that the power of Christ may dwell in me. Therefore I am content with weaknesses, insults, hardships, persecutions, and calamities for the sake of Christ; for whenever I am weak, then I am strong.'"

Finally, God's apparent refusal to grant us immediate victory over our deficiencies does not mean final defeat. It is only that victory is not to be given easily but won on the battlefield in strenuous and costly effort. In the story of Moses there is the record of Aaron as spokesman in Egypt, but as the story develops Aaron seems to fade from the scene. It is an argument from silence and a preacher's speculation, but it is possible that as life went on Moses gained through struggle what he had once expected as a gift. We do not know, but a modern parallel comes to mind. The college where I teach is named after the man who was its principal for forty years. G. H. Morling was in his final years of principalship when I was a student, but later he was a member of a church where I was pastor. He was known as one of the finest preachers in the denomination and indeed beyond it. Even in his eighties he had a command of language and power of eloquence that demanded attention. Yet as a young minister he was known as "Stammering George" so severe was his speech impediment. It was not overcome suddenly but by the severest discipline and control, and stories are told of times when he would spend hours talking to one of his closest friends with a marble in his mouth to help control his stammer. He wrote a spiritual autobiography that he titled *The Quest for Serenity* and in which he told of the lifelong struggle he had had with a more than usual nervous temperament. But it was here that the secret of his strength lay. And so often it is as we struggle— depending on Christ yet expending our spiritual energy too so that real qualities emerge in our character and victory is finally won.

To many this cry of Moses has never come, "neither in the past nor even now." They do not look with disappointment that there has been no miraculous conquest of weakness and failure. But to others it is a real experience. Despair or obsession with our failures is not the answer. An obsessive concentration on problems and a struggle to handle them on our own is self-destructive. Rather we need to accept them as Paul did, as qualities that force us to Christ. I heard an Anglican minister once describe his own struggles with nervous illness and his increasing frustration that led to breakdown. As long as he concentrated on his weakness he continued to sink further into despair and illness. But when he learned to let his weakness push him back to God, to accept it not as an enemy but as a goad to drive him to God, he started to climb toward victory.

Sometimes we ask of God what he knows it is best for us not to have. We need to accept ourselves for what we are and let our weakness become our strength in Christ.

"So, I will boast all the more gladly of my weaknesses, so that the power of Christ may dwell in me. Therefore I am content with weaknesses, insults, hardships, persecutions, and calamities for the sake of Christ; for whenever I am weak then I am strong" (2 Cor. 12:9b–10).

35. A Day of Falling Stars
Clyde E. Fant

Genesis 22:1–18

He rose before it was light and looked outside his tent. It was the darkest night, he thought, he'd ever seen.

Then he waked his son quietly, so as not to wake her. That would be the last thing he needed. He would have to decide how to tell her later.

He stood again at the flap of the tent and looked up into the black night and thought of another night at the same tent, when God had pointed him to the stars of the sky and said: "Abraham, do you see those stars? Your descendants will be as numerous as the stars in the sky."

But on this night there were no stars, and in the tent there was no laughter. The boy's name was *Isaac,* but for Abraham it would no longer mean "laughter."

For God had said something to Abraham he could not believe. Like a crack of thunder on a clear day, without preamble or warning, the words of God had come to him: "Take thy son, thine only son Isaac, whom thou lovest . . . and offer him for a burnt offering upon one of the mountains I will tell thee of." He had been in a kind of stupor ever since. But he obeyed. He knew nothing else to do. And so they went, three days journey toward the mountain.

When they reached the place, Abraham said to the servants: "You stay here with the animals. My son and I will go to that

---

Clyde E. Fant is O. L. Walker Professor of Christian Studies at Stetson University, DeLand, Florida. He was pastor of the First Baptist Church, Richardson, Texas, and has taught preaching at Southeastern and Southwestern Baptist Theological Seminaries, at Duke Divinity School, and at the Baptist Seminary in Rüschlikon, Switzerland. He translated *Bonhoeffer: Worldly Preaching,* was coeditor of the thirteen-volume *Twenty Centuries of Great Preaching,* and wrote *Preaching for Today.*

mountain and worship; and when we are done, we will come back to you." . . . And they went, both of them together.

The servants thought nothing of it; the customs of these people were all familiar to them. They followed an invisible desert God; they worshiped on top of mountains; they made sacrifices. So their master was going to pray, to make a sacrifice of some sort. They scarcely noticed his leaving.

The boy carried the wood, the father carried the fire, the knife; and they went, both of them together.

After awhile, as they climbed, the other words came, the words Abraham had dreaded—not like thunder, but soft and curious—the words of the boy: "My father, I see the fire and wood, but where is the animal for the burnt offering?"

Like a dead man, Abraham answered, his own heart already pierced through: "My son, God will provide a lamb for the burnt offering."

In our lives there are no voices—at least none that seem to come from beyond ourselves—no clear voices that articulate nouns and verbs, subjects, objects, in our ears, neither words of promise nor words of condemnation. Nonetheless, in the unpredictability of our existence, in the caprice of fate, life often seems absurd, as absurd as it ever seemed to Abraham: when life goes wrong, when hopes are cut down, when, in a word or a heartbeat or a flash of time, all the stars fall.

Abraham faced three tests in his life. The first was the test of Where? *Where shall I go, O Lord?* The second was the test of When? *When shall I have a child, O Lord?* But the third was the worst test of all—the test of Why? *Why, O Lord? Why must my child die?* Isn't Abraham's story our story?

Like Abraham, you and I first have to learn *where* we are to go in life, where our paths should lead, where to study, where to work, where to find a home. And even those of us who have found answers to those questions still ask, "Where do I go from here?"

Then, sooner or later, we find ourselves asking, "Lord . . . *when,* Lord? I've gone *where;* I've followed what I thought to be right for me; but *when,* O Lord? It doesn't seem to be in my hands yet. I have a family; I have a job; I have my plans; but *when?* When will life be as the stars of the sky? When will the promise be ours?"

But these two trials appear insignificant before the bitterest question of all, a question we all must face someday: "*Why,* O God?

Why did it have to be this way? Why did life have to take that turn? Why does this have to happen in my existence?" Neither in heaven nor on earth can we find justification for the seeming capriciousness of the tragedies that strike our lives.

For Abraham this test came in an absurd demand. Those words, *Offer your son upon an altar,* posed the ultimate test of his faith. It contradicted everything in Abraham: his common sense, his understanding of life, and, most of all, his understanding of God, the very God who had given him the impossible son. The very God who had stood at the door of his tent with twinkling eyes and said, *Surprise!* now stood at the door of his tent with a chilling stare, and an unrecognizable face, and words that froze his heart.

When Abraham heard God's words he could not think, just as you cannot and I cannot when the caprice of life strikes, when we are confronted with the unthinkable, the unimaginable, and we ask ourselves—*Why?*

I said that in our world we hear no voices. That is not so; there are many voices. There are the voices of the screech of brakes and the scream of metal; there is the telephone call in the dark of night; there is the friend standing at the door, eyes downcast, tongue fumbling for words; there is the hushed voice of the doctor in the hospital corridor. There are many voices in our world that test our faith and our obedience. How will we answer them?

And they went, both of them together. Then what? For Abraham, or for us? We can only climb with these words: *God will provide.* As parents have told their children, and one another, when there was nothing else to say: *God will provide.*

I'm sorry. I wish it could be more than that; I know it sounds too pat, too glib. Trust me, from the mouth of Abraham that day there was nothing glib about those words. He had gotten no answer to his *why?* All he knew was, he had to keep putting one foot in front of the other. It was the promise of his life. He had nowhere else to turn.

What could he have thought, as he climbed? You know what he thought: *I have sinned in God's sight. God is not taking away only my son, but the Promise.*

We are not seeing a story simply about a father losing a son, as poignant as that is. Abraham's psychology is not the focus here. We are seeing the ultimate insanity of the universe; we are seeing the irrationality of fate and life.

And blindly he walked, by what stumbling faith he had, and he mumbled those words again and again until his son looking at him, stopped smiling, and shook his head and only looked at the ground. *God will provide. God will provide. God will provide.*

They came to the top of the mountain. He took the knife, and the boy looked at him again: *Father!* The scripture moves slowly here, with uncommon detail, for the writer does not want to miss any of the pain of Abraham: the wood placed upon the altar; the boy bound around (thank God, spared more details of that); the knife flashing in the air. And again the booming voice of God: *Abraham! Now I know* . . . and behind him, the ram in the thicket.

As they went down the mountain there was laughter—wild, joyous laughter—somehow, someway, Isaac was "laughter" again, and Abraham had the knife taken out of his own heart. The dead were alive again. More than that, the Promise was alive.

When I read these words I thought, this is ultimate drama and surely somewhere, someone has written poetic words about this tragedy. But I could find nothing, so I offer these words:

The Sacrifice of Isaac

And they went, the both of them together.
Who knows what they thought, they said?
"Behold the fire, the knife; but where the lamb, my father?"
Choked anguish, able scarce to speak;
(Dost ask, my son, my little lamb,
My morning star in sunset years?)
"God will provide a lamb, my son."
And they went, both of them together.
(Oh, why my future now, O God,
My future from me take away?
My past already from me torn,
From Ur of Caldee sent away.
How now endure this loss most grave:
Tomorrow's promise, love most dear;
The path of godforsakeness to tread.
All lost; all lost; all lost;
All lost.)
He carried torch and knife most dread,
The wood alone upon the child,
In gentle love protecting yet

From accidental harm.
How strange:
The child with wood, the light knife his.
But which among us, who would say,
Who bore the heaviest load that day?
And they went, both of them together.
Still silent now, the summit reached,
Altar built, wood in its place,
The boy bound round, the knife now reached,
Eyes searching, searching: love unmistaked,
Yet how explain the awful act?
His own heart pierced already through.
"Abraham! The ram! Stay . . . I know."
With blinded, hope-crazed eyes he saw!
His fingers flew the bonds to loose,
His child embrace, the mount descend.
Their laughter echoed in the quiet—
Where on the mount, with pierced heart,
Another parent hid his face,
Another son to wood was bound.
And there God bore the awful grief
Another must not bear.
God will provide for us, as said,
A lamb our offering.
So Abraham and God, they shared
A parent's love forever;
And that is why through life they went,
The both of them together.

And if the brightest star of your life, the brightest hope of all your days, is extinguished, then hear these words: "I Jesus have sent my messenger to you with this testimony for the churches. I am the root and offspring of David, the bright and morning star. . . . You will do well to pay attention to this as a lamp shining in a dark place until the day dawns, and the morning star rises in your hearts" (Rev. 22:16; Pet. 1:29).

The Promise is alive.

Let us pray:

>We are not prepared for grief, O Lord,
>   ever:
>And sometimes children are not delivered from death;
>And sometimes we ourselves are the offering;

And sometimes stars do fall.
Remind us that you experienced the very
  loss
That Abraham never suffered;
And that the bright and morning star
Also was extinguished
Only to rise again,
In your plan, and in our dreams.
So for all of us this day,
Those who are the people sitting in darkness,
Place in our sky that light
That shall never again be extinguished;
So that when we cannot see anything,
The morning star may yet show the way.
In Christ's name.

Amen.

36. Like a Tree

James Earl Massey

He is like a tree planted by streams of water,
that yields its fruits in its season,
and its leaf does not wither.
In all that he does, he prospers.

—Psalm 1:3

The psalmist was talking about the steadiness, the strength, and aliveness of someone who keeps God first in all things. He was saying that there are rewards in being godly—the greatest of which are inward: The imagery speaks with an immediacy we all understand. The psalmist insists that God can make us like trees: The text offers more than a picture; it makes a promise about how we can live.

We can be like a tree—*steadied by a strong root system.* A deeply rooted tree can stand against the heaviest wind or storm. The wind might bend the tree, and a furious storm might destroy some of its branches, but the tree will remain. A true believer, rooted in God, is like that.

I have watched this in many lives and across many years. Again and again I have known and watched persons who had a strong root system of faith and prayer and Scripture-wisdom, stand tall against severe winds of pressure and tragic circumstance. These were godly folk who knew how to draw their strength from God.

James Earl Massey was born in Ferndale, Michigan, and received degrees from Detroit Bible College (now William Tyndale College) and Oberlin Graduate School of Theology. A member of the Church of God (Anderson, Indiana), Dr. Massey currently serves as dean of the Anderson University School of Theology. He has written sixteen books and hundreds of articles, and preaches and lectures frequently at colleges, universities, and seminaries throughout the United States and abroad. This sermon was preached on the Christian Brotherhood hour.

I was attached to trees from my early boyhood, and I especially remember three trees just in front of our family house. Two of those trees were cottonwoods just inside our yard, and the third tree was an oak just across the street. I played in and around those three trees as a boy, and I watched them grow as I grew. During a storm one summer day I saw lightning strike the oak tree across the street. I ran out to it after the storm, wondering if it would die, but that old oak persisted for many years afterward because its root system had remained strong and steady. The lightning did destroy some of its branches and left a large section at its top bare and flat, but new leaves finally came to those bare places because life was still at work in its roots.

A truly steady life needs a strong root system. The rootage must be deep and dependable because our lives must grow downward and outward if we are to grow upward with steadiness. If there will be life above, there must be a supportive life below. Like a tree, we will flourish or fail in keeping with our roots.

We can be like a tree—*renewed and sustained by resources necessary to our life*. The root system of a tree does something more than give it steadiness: The roots draw moisture and minerals from the soil in which it grows. Strong trees have more than roots to steady them; they have resources to sustain them—and they relentlessly search for those vital resources upon which they depend.

Yes, it does happen—because a law of recognized need controls its quest to be sustained. It is a common law of life.

> The tree that never had to fight
> For sun and sky and air and light,
> That stood out in the open plain,
> And always got its share of rain,
> Never became a forest king,
> But lived and died a scrubby thing.
> The man who never had to toil,
> Who never had to win his share
> Of sun and sky and light and air,
> Never became a manly man,
> But lived and died as he began.
> Good timber does not grow in ease.
> The stronger wind, the tougher trees;
> The farther sky, the greater length;
> The more the storm, the more the strength;

By sun and cold, by rain and snows,
In tree or man good timber grows.
Where thickest stands the forest growth
We find the patriarchs of both,
And they hold converse with the stars
Whose broken branches show the scars
Of many winds and much of strife—
This is the common law of life.[1]

There are resources necessary to our life, and apart from gaining them we can but die. If we would have leaves that do not wither and bear fruit in due season, then we must have working within us that desperate will that resides in roots; we must lay hold upon what we need from God to sustain us.

The psalmist pointed to God's word as one resource; he knew that renewal and strength come through listening to God in devotional study and prayer. Listen to those words again: "But his delight is in the law of the Lord, and on his law he meditates day and night" (v. 2). Meditation lets meanings do their work within us, granting perspective, patience, and deepening of principles. There is no resource like the Word of God. It generates within us a creative power that influences thought, aids decision making, calms our spirits, tames our wildness, and nourishes our souls.

Like many another struggling pilgrim, poet Joyce Kilmer had experienced this. Faith in God's Word kept Kilmer on his feet in 1913 when his daughter Rose, nine months old, was stricken with infantile paralysis. Yes, he took some comfort in the news that there was no reason to fear that she would die from that sickness and from the awareness that the infirmity of her body need not hinder the vitality of her mind; but his deeper comfort was drawn from a richer resource. The more he meditated on the goodness and greatness and grace of God, the steadier Kilmer became, so steady and strong in faith that his friend Robert Cortes Holliday dared to comment that "in spiritual force he was [an] oak."[2]

The psalmist rightly pictured the godly person as "a tree planted by streams of water." No one who takes in what God makes available will shrivel or be undernourished within.

I have said that God can keep us steady and sustained, two results that stand clearly before us in the textual picture of the one who "is like a tree." There is something more to be said, however, and it is also part of the picture in the text: *A healthy tree shares itself with its surroundings, giving back to the environment.* With God's help, we can be like that.

Like trees, we were made to give something back to the setting that nourishes our life. As for trees, they give back beauty, food, shade, shelter, fuel to warm us, timber for our dwellings, medicine for our ills, material for our clothing, and ornaments to decorate about us. But let me be a bit more specific about a few of these benefits. A mature shade tree that is fifty or more years old absorbs a lot of heat from our surroundings, cooling the scene in which we live. A mature shade tree humidifies the atmosphere around us, loosing into the air 75 to 100 gallons of water per day. But here is more: A mature shade tree supplies all the oxygen required by ten people in one year. A mature shade tree removes about one quarter pound of dust particles from the air per day, performing the service of an air filter. The same tree removes gases from the air, especially carbon dioxide, which would otherwise smother us.[3] Consider it: A mature shade tree can cool, humidify, restore, and clean the air around us, as well as give beauty, food, shade, shelter, medicine, and itself as timber and fuel. The tree does not receive without giving back. With God's help, we can be like that.

Until his death, George Washington Carver treasured the memory of Mrs. Moriah Watkins, a black midwife who opened her heart and home when he, a homeless waif, came to Neosho, Missouri, seeking a school to enter so that he could learn. She gave him his first opportunity to go to school. She had found him sitting beside the fence of her yard, waiting for the nearby school to open. He was but a stray creature; she rather saw him with eyes of concern. Her sharing of herself and her home blessed his young life and gave him resources for needed growth. Moriah Watkins was the one who gave Carver that Bible that was so dear to him, the leather volume already worn by much use but that he used until his dying day. She was to him like a mature shade tree to its setting, and Carver said so, remembering her as "a great shady oak tree, strong and cool and full of comfort."[4] That is how God makes and uses those who yield themselves to him, those who delight in his will, meditating and acting on what has meaning for day and night, for time and eternity, for self and for others.

> He is like a tree
>   planted by streams of water,

that yields its fruit in its season,
and its leaf does not wither.
In all that he does, he prospers.

The wicked are not so,
but are like chaff which the wind drives away. (vv. 3–4)

Prayer

O God our Father, we want to be alive, healthy, and fruitful in our time. We want to give back to life, and not just take from it. We want to be steady as we live, and grow as we should. Help us to experience all this by your grace, and to your glory, through Christ our Lord. Amen.

NOTES

1. "The Common Law," author unknown.

2. See Robert Cortes Holliday, ed., *Joyce Kilmer: Poems, Essays and Letters in Two Volumes*, vol. 1 (New York: George H. Doran Co., 1918), esp. pp. 48–52.

3. From "What's a Tree Worth?" by George Stritikus, Associate County Agent, Montgomery County, Alabama, The Alabama Cooperative Extension Service.

4. See Lawrence Elliott, *George Washington Carver: The Man Who Overcame* (Englewood Cliffs, NJ: Prentice-Hall, Inc., 1966), 34, 87–88.

37. God's Unfinished Pictures
Carroll E. Simcox

On this day as I enter my eightieth year there rings in the ears of my mind this text from one of the letters of St. John: "Beloved, now are we the children of God, and it does not yet appear what we shall be: but we know that when he shall appear we shall be like him, for we shall see him as he is" (1 John 3:2).

St. John is telling us that if we are now living in Christ we are actually moving on our way toward a wonderful eternal destiny, far beyond our present imagining. We know that in the end we shall be entirely like Christ, not at all as we are now—just a bit like him now and then in our rare best moments. The difference between us as we now are and us as we shall be is, as I said, beyond our present imagining, even perhaps our present desiring. Yet you will be you and nobody else, and I shall be me and nobody else. I believe that when we meet for the first time in heaven we shall exchange such greetings as this: "I'd know you anywhere, and you look wonderful: But merciful heaven, how you've changed!" Our change will have been the change of growth and maturation. You and I shall be our real, complete selves for the first time ever. We think of ourselves now as human beings. We really aren't that—not yet. We are human becomings. The fetus conceived only yesterday is a human becoming. The person who celebrates his or her hundredth birthday today is still a human becoming. If you are living in Christ, believing in him and trying to follow and obey him as the Master of your life, you are by his grace becoming ever more and more like him. When that becoming has ceased to be becoming and has changed into full being you will be a human being for the first time ever—and it will be forever.

Carroll E. Simcox was editor of *The Living Church* from 1964 through 1977. He served the Episcopal church as a parish priest for over forty years in Minnesota, Vermont, New York, and Florida. Simcox is the author of many books, including *Three Thousand Quotations on Christian Themes, They Met at Philippi,* and *The Eternal You.* He is now affiliated with the American Episcopal Church and lives in Hendersonville, North Carolina.

Such was the belief of the early Christian we know as St. John the Divine—that title meaning not that he was divine but that he was a teacher, a doctor, of divine truth. And it is also my belief, and it makes my age more gratifying and even exciting in the sense of anticipation, assuring me that today I am closer to becoming my complete self, the finished product labeled Carroll Eugene Simcox, than I was a year ago or even yesterday. I see no reason why any Christian should not experience age in this same way, as a follower and disciple and brother or sister of Jesus Christ in the eternal family of God.

The spirit of St. John is very upbeat. This comes across most positively in his letters. I pray that this spirit possesses you more and more as it possesses me. It gives us a strong and jubilant sense that we are *growing:* growing in Christ, growing in eternal life. There need be no spiritual complacency in this. Like St. Paul and St. John and all the blessed saints we know our lingering weaknesses and the sins that still so easily beset us. But we know also that our most loving and most mighty Lord is continuously working with us and doing the humanly impossible with us—changing our very nature into his own likeness. We read his Sermon on the Mount and we say, "How hard it is for me even to begin to be anything like this!" But all the while he is changing us invisibly and quietly but invincibly toward our own complete selves in which we shall be and do all these presently impossible things as a matter of course, as though we couldn't be or do otherwise if we tried.

Now I want to quote something from Gertrude Stein. She was, as we all know, a very eccentric person, but we must never let that put us off about anybody. Some wise wit has given us this new beatitude: "Blessed are the cracked; for they shall let in light!" I love it; and in so many cases it's so wonderfully true! Stein wrote in her autobiography: "I murmured to Picasso that I liked his portrait of Gertrude Stein. Yes, he said, somebody said that she does not look like it but that doesn't make any difference, she will."

Picasso's remark has the amusing audacity of a human artist who thinks very well of his own work. He reminds me of another audacious artist, much younger than he, a boy of five or six. One day he was drawing a picture at his little desk. His mother looked at his effort and asked what he was drawing. "A picture of God," he replied. "But how can you do that?" she asked. "Nobody knows what God looks like." The artist explained patiently: "They will when I finish this picture!"

Enough now of Stein and Picasso and the young artist who brings God to us in living color, and back to our text: Even now we are sons and daughters of God, but we can't imagine what we'll be like when Christ comes to us after he has put his final touches on us. We know only that we shall look like him. Then we shall see him as he eternally is and we shall see ourselves as we eternally shall be. Picasso fondly supposed that he had painted the *real* and *ultimate* Gertrude Stein so perfectly that all she had to do was to grow up to it. Nothing could be crazier in any human artist than to suppose that he can picture you not only as you presently are, warts and all, but as you are going to be one day in your full and final actuality. But that in truth is what the divine Artist does with each one of us. He sees you exactly and perfectly as you now are: He sees every promising potentiality in you just as he sees every imperfection, every incompleteness. He sees all these things in us that we cannot even begin to see. But he has also in his view the perfected and completed you—the person who is now only becoming, only in the making; and seeing you as you shall be in the end he continues his working with you.

It seems to me as it has seemed to countless other Christians that God is sculpting us, that we are living, sentient clay in his hands. The sculptor does his work by chipping and chiseling at his material until he has worked it into exactly the form and shape he wants. This chipping and chiseling can be painful to the human raw material. You are the one who does the feeling. You are alive and sentient and it hurts. We can squirm under God's chiseling and we can complain and rebel and slip away from his hand. But as long as we live by our faith in Christ we cannot escape from the divine Artist, and when we come to our senses we find that we don't want to escape from him. We want him to have his way with us, no matter how much it hurts. All the way through he keeps giving us all sorts of surprising and cheering hints that we shall never have any regrets, that we shall have infinite cause for infinite gladness that we let him have his way with us as he was sculpting us, working us up toward that picture of us he had in his mind.

As I think about this George Herbert comes to mind, a man who has to be a favorite character to most people who know anything about him. He was a priest of the Church of England in the seventeenth century and also a saint and also a poet and also a musician. He loved to meet with some friends for an evening of making music together. One late afternoon he set out on foot, carrying his violin, toward a friend's house for such a musical evening. But on the road he came upon a poor man whose pony cart had broken down and needed very considerable repair. Mr. Herbert went to work helping the man to fix it, and he spent so much time at this that when he reached his destination his friends had gone ahead with the musicale without him. One of them said, "You missed all the music." Herbert smiled and replied, "I shall have songs at midnight!" And we may be sure that he did—in a joyous duet with God. It was one of those hints that God gives to all souls who are alive enough to him to receive his hints and know them for what they are. They are signs of the pleasure God is having in getting on so well with the making of a person who one day will perfectly fit God's picture of him.

Understand this, and post it on your mental billboard where you can never miss seeing it: *You are one of God's unfinished pictures.*

The picture of you, the finished and complete and eternal you whom God has in his mind, is a very *precise* picture—inconceivably precise to our present way of thinking because God has arranged every detail to his own satisfaction. Remember, always remember, your picture isn't finished yet, meaning that it's still being crafted by the divine Artist. When you look at your present self you don't get a very clear idea of what you'll look like when finished. The pictures of the four presidents on Mt. Rushmore didn't look very much like them at an early stage or even a quite late stage of their construction. We must keep in mind that you and I are presently in a very early stage of our own construction, and that's true no matter how old we are in mortal years. There must be some kind of eternal years of which we can form no conception now, but they are the years that will count in the end.

In one of his apt analogies C. S. Lewis wrote: "Your place in heaven will seem to be made for you and you alone, because you were made for it—made for it stitch by stitch as a glove is made for a hand." Remember the promise of Jesus: "In my Father's house are many mansions. . . . I go to prepare a place for you." As in heaven he prepares that particular place for you and that particular place for me, he also comes to each of us to prepare *us* for that particular place for you, for me, for each one. Our Lord's work with us now is to lead us and keep us in a direction, a pattern toward the picture of us that God has had in his mind and purpose for us from the very foundation of the world.

One more point. We must recognize that not only are we ourselves very much still in the making, so is everybody else in the world. Therefore it is most presumptuous on our part to pass any kind of condemnatory judgment upon anybody else. When we do, it is a case of our incomplete pot calling an incomplete kettle black. In one of Henry James's novels somebody is characterized as "eminently incomplete." That phrase perfectly fits us all: eminently incomplete in our present stage of becoming. I can think of few of our Lord's counsels that are more generally disregarded by Christians than his command to judge not, lest we ourselves be judged. The only thing a Christian may permissibly say about the worst-seeming of people must be something like this: "I'm glad that I don't have the Lord's job of trying to make something great or good or even decent out of him. But then I don't have that job. And just maybe the Lord finds *him* better clay to work with than he finds *me!*" This may be literally true. We must listen to Jesus as he tells the self-righteous of every age that the publicans and the prostitutes go into the kingdom of heaven before them.

What matters most is that we place our whole trust in the Lord and give him full control of our lives. We can do this with the assurance that he will make of us eternal beings of such beauty and strength and joy that the difference between our present selves and our ultimate selves will be something like the difference between the worm in the cocoon and the same creature after it has been hatched and has taken its wings. I saw a cartoon many years ago that was a superb expression of the truth—an analogy of the difference between those who choose to let the Lord prepare them for a glorious eternal destiny and those who refuse his invitation and want to stay just where they are. In it were pictured two stolid looking worms in their cocoons gazing at a lovely butterfly as it flew past them, and one of them said to the other: "I'll tell you one thing. They'll never get *me* up in one of them contraptions!" Let us take heed that we refuse not the Lord of life as he offers us his grand invitation to leave our cocoons and accept the exalted and eternal destiny for which we are created.

Eye has not seen, nor ear heard, nor have entered into the heart of man the things God has prepared for those who love him and respond to his call to come up higher.

38. The Sound of the Sublime
Scott Dalgarno

Ezra 3:10–13

> The people could not distinguish the sound of the joyful shout
> from the sound of the people's weeping.

It was a day of celebration; the culmination of much hard work
and decades of hoping against hope. It was a day of trumpets,
cymbals, and fancy dress; a day given over to praising the Lord.
The holy temple, the house of God that had been destroyed by the
Babylonians would soon be standing again. Cyrus of Persia had
liberated God's people and, being a most progressive leader, had
shown himself willing to aid in the temple's rebuilding. And so, the
people of the new Israel were gathered on Mount Zion to dedicate
its foundation. The moment was incomparable. Shouts of joy filled
the air, and yet, in the midst of the sound of praise and singing was
heard another sound; a competing sound, the curious sound of
weeping. Some among the men who were old enough to have actually seen the former temple were dissolved in tears at the sight
of the new beginning. Were these merely the tears of a few odd
ones? No. Ezra tells us that such was the intensity of the sound of
this wail that "the people could not distinguish the sound of the
joyful shout from the sound of the people's weeping" (Ezra 3:13).

So, let me ask, what is the nature of this weeping? Are these
simply tears of joy—joy that the Lord's holy habitation is finally
being restored after lying in ashes for the best part of a century?
Are they tears that come from ancient eyes, happy to have been

---

W. Scott Dalgarno is Pastor of Grace Presbyterian Church in
Portland, Oregon. A graduate of the University of Oregon, he
received his Master of Divinity from San Francisco Theological
Seminary.

preserved long enough to behold such a wonderful sight; something, perhaps, they had not even dared hope for? Or could they be weeping purely for sorrow's sake? Having known the glories of Solomon's golden temple could it be that the plans for the new temple seemed shabby to them by comparison—not fitting for the Lord of Israel? Ezra does not tell us. Perhaps he expects we ought to know without being told. Or, may I suggest, perhaps Ezra knew that the human heart is so complex that it at times harbors, entertains, and expresses several emotions, even contrary emotions, at a given moment: joy and sorrow, regret and holy wonder.

What kind of moment, what quality of experience could inspire both intense sadness and joy, both weeping and cheers? How are we to describe this curious sound? What name might we give it? In a recent television series, "The Power of Myth," Bill Moyers told of a discussion he had once had with an American survivor of World War II's Battle of the Bulge. Having at first been trapped by midwinter snows and a desperate German division this veteran's regiment had been heroically liberated by American forces under the command of General George Patton. One day they faced almost certain death, the next day they found themselves victors. This man's experience was more than merely memorable. It was something he would carry with him forever. Searching for a word to express his feelings about these cataclysmic events the old soldier said that the only word approaching description of such a mixture of terror and supreme elation was "sublime."

The spiritual philosopher, Rudolph Otto, has said that the word *sublime* is not merely an adjective, but is actually an experience. He describes it as an encounter in which he says we "come upon something quite beyond the sphere of the intelligible and the familiar before which we . . . recoil in a wonder that strikes us chill and numb."[1]

"Chill and numb"? Such an experience brings to mind another Old Testament figure: Isaiah of Jerusalem. Isaiah certainly knew the shock and the wonder of the sublime. His life as a priest of the temple under the stable king Uzziah surely must have been comfortable, even predictable. But with the king's death everything in the kingdom was thrown into upheaval. For Isaiah, the future now seemed vague. It had become something, perhaps, to be feared. And within the vacuum of loss and fear of unknown tomorrows, Isaiah experienced an encounter with the holy. "Chill and numb" may best describe Isaiah's initial reaction to his vision of the Lord sitting "high and lifted up" upon the throne of the universe. Isaiah's priestly liturgy had become ashes in his mouth. "I am a man of unclean lips," he confessed (Isa. 6:5). But through the grace of God, Isaiah found cleansing, renewal, and a new calling in the midst of his holy encounter. Life would never be the same for him again.

I think you'll agree with me that the most illustrious member of our Portland neighborhood, until his recent transfer, was Father Lawrence Jenco. As you know, several years ago Father Jenco was held hostage in Lebanon for many months. For Father Jenco the ordeal consisted of deep loneliness, blindfolds, dark rooms, and stark terror. I had the opportunity to talk with him briefly some days ago, and he related to me the story of one very special night of his captivity—a night in which he was led up to the roof of the building where he was being held. There his captors sat him down and began unwinding his blindfold. Father Jenco had been told many times that if the blindfold were ever removed in the presence of his captors it could mean only one thing: immediate execution. And yet what met his wondering eyes was not the sight of a gun, but the most startlingly beautiful vision he had ever seen. His captors had led him to the rooftop to see the full moon spread out over the city. It was something he had not laid eyes on in over a year, something he wondered if he might ever see again. One moment he had felt so close to death, the next he had never felt so alive. "Yes," he thought to himself, "there is beauty in the world, after all"; even his captors could be kind. A remarkable moment; surely a sublime moment. To think that such an awesome vision could exist amidst such a dark night. He could never look upon a full moon with the same eyes again.

Now, one is tempted to say that such experiences of the sublime as that of Father Jenco or Isaiah, or even the veteran of the Battle of the Bulge are extremely rare, and are reserved for only a few special individuals. Well, of course they are, and yet, are there not experiences that, if not of the everyday variety, are at least common to most individuals, experiences that are every bit as life changing?

I have never been a hostage, nor have I had a vision of the Lord of hosts, nor have I ever been in combat, but, as most of you know, I recently became a parent for the first time. It is a most common human experience, and yet I found it to be, at bottom, an extraordinary mixture of wonder and terror. I had read the pre-parenthood books, heard all the "new father" stories, and still the initial experience of the birth of our Meg was one of supreme shock. Nothing could have prepared me for those first intense feelings. I knew in my bones that life for me had changed unalterably, and forever. God had dictated that this little one must increase and from now on I must decrease. And then something else equally unexplainable happened—something truly wonderful: Almost overnight I fell head-over-heels in love with this lovely little girl. Yes, life for me had changed, and yes, I had taken second place to another, but I would have it no other way. Jesus once put the experience of birth this way: "When a woman is in travail she has sorrow, because her hour has come; but when she is delivered of the child, she no longer remembers the anguish, for joy that a child is born into the world" (John 16:21). Joy and sorrow; wonder and tears.

There is a lovely gospel song in our hymnal that celebrates God's gift of new life: *Because He Lives*. Its second verse begins: "How sweet to hold a newborn baby." Yes, "sweet" is a good description, unless the baby is your own. If it is your baby only a word like "sublime" will do.

So, you may never, in this life, behold a vision of the Lord God "sitting high and lifted up" on his holy throne, but there are those moments that the poet T. S. Eliot speaks of, when life will "drop a question on your plate"[2]: When you're holding your newborn, or sitting with a dying parent, and the Holy Spirit seems to enter the room, and life takes on a dimension you never imagined before. At such times you find past assumptions about yourself challenged mightily; "truths" you had taken for granted dissolve, and you are compelled to acknowledge that the waters of your life run deeper than you had ever thought.

These moments full of contrary emotions we have trouble making sense of can be terrible ordeals, but they can also witness to the undeniable action of God in our lives. Perhaps we are on a quest for peace with a troubled family member, and to our dismay, things get out of control; we find out things about ourselves and our loved ones we never knew before. At first we may feel devastated, but then, if we are blessed, we may find life and hope begin to open up for us and our family once again. God has touched us. We have prayed for peace, and the peace the Lord has given us, we find, truly "passes all understanding" just as the apostle promised in his Letter to the Philippians. We had set our sights on one outcome for our problem, and nothing had prepared us for God's mysterious providential working. And what had Paul, the apostle to say about our puny expectations? Simply this: "No eye has seen, nor ear heard, nor the heart of man conceived, what God has prepared for those who love him" (1 Cor. 2:9).

Can we let God be God? Can we see that regardless of our hopes and expectations God will work out God's will for us? Might we consider that such an outcome could be much more profound than anything we might dream up on our own? Perhaps spiritual growth amounts to coming to terms with just this holy truth. Our God will be sovereign over our lives and the effect of that sovereignty can at times be both disturbing and incomparably wonderful.

Consider, finally, the experience of a most remarkable man, the explorer Balboa.[3] Seeking new trade routes, he landed in Panama in 1513. What could he and a party of his men have expected to see when climbing a shallow opening in Panama's Darien coastal mountain range? Certainly not what they found. Before reaching the low passage, Balboa and his men must have heard what surely would have been an awesome sound: the sound of a muffled kind of roar. Then came the sight—not the hoped-for river, but something way beyond their wildest hopes. What they saw was a European's first glimpse of the mighty Pacific Ocean in all its glory and vastness. It was a vision beyond comprehension, something infinitely wide with possibility. And the sound of that ocean? Let me suggest that the sound must have been nothing less than the kind of sound heard by those present for the dedication of Ezra's temple: the incomparable sound of the sublime.

NOTES

1. Mircea Eliade, ed., *Encyclopedia of Religion*, vol. 11 (New York: Macmillan, 1987), 139.

2. T. S. Eliot, "The Love Song of J. Alfred Prufrock" in *T. S. Eliot: The Complete Poems and Plays 1909–1950* (New York: Harcourt, Brace, and World, 1952), 4.

3. Suggested by John Keats's poem, "On First Looking into Chapman's Homer" in *The Norton Anthology of English Literature Vol. 2*, 347. (Note: Keats mistakenly cites Cortez as the explorer in question.)

39. Getting Your Priorities Right

John M. Buchanan

Luke 16:10–13

In his memoir, *The Good Times,* Russell Baker, *New York Times* correspondent and columnist, begins with an amusing observation about his mother who died years ago, but still roams free in his mind, and wakes him some mornings before daybreak. He hears her saying . . .

> "If there's one thing I can't stand, it's a quitter." I have heard her say that all my life. Now, lying in bed, coming awake in the dark, I feel the fury of her energy fighting the good-for-nothing idler within me who wants to go back to sleep instead of tackling the brave new day.
> Silently I protest: I am not a child anymore. I have made something of myself. I am entitled to sleep late.
> "Russell, you've got no more gumption than a bump on a log. Don't you want to amount to something?"
> She has hounded me with these same battle cries since I was a boy in short pants back in the Depression.

John M. Buchanan is Pastor of Fourth Presbyterian Church in Chicago, Illinois. He received his Master of Divinity from the Divinity School of the University of Chicago and Chicago Theological Seminary. He was previously pastor of Broad Street Presbyterian Church in Columbus, Ohio, and of churches in Indiana and has been the subject of articles in the *Chicago Tribune* and *U.S. News and World Report.*

"Amount to something!"
"Make something of yourself!"
"Don't be a quitter!"[1]

The book strikes a familiar chord with people whose values, hopes, dreams, and expectations have been shaped by the American experience in the middle of the twentieth century, which means most of us. We either lived through the Great Depression, or were raised by parents who did, or at least by parents whose values were very much shaped by that economic trauma. Those values are frugality, responsibility, a suspicion of credit, and an aversion to indebtedness, most of all a sense that survival means hard work, the willingness to delay gratification and to work very, very hard. Russell Baker's mother's litany—"make something of yourself, work hard, don't quit, get ahead"—is familiar to all of us, I suspect, and still drives many of us.

It may, in fact, define us more accurately than we suspect, or even want to know about.

Each of us has a *center* of value, on the basis of which our lesser values gain their meaning. That center of value, said the late H. Richard Niebuhr, is essentially theological, whether or not we are traditionally religious. It is our god. Russell Baker is candid enough to identify his mother's litanies as his center in a way that helps us identify our own. The point is that each of us has one—a center of value that forms our other values, that shapes our hopes and dreams and expectations for the future, even our ultimate future. That is to say, each of us has a god.

And that is the point of what is arguably the most troublesome story Jesus ever told: certainly one of the most intriguing. If the "charming rascal" is one of your favorite literary character types, you're going to love the man in this story. He's a steward, an estate manager actually, in the employ of a wealthy land owner. The land owner leases his property to tenant farmers whose rent is a percentage of the produce they harvest from the land. The steward's job is to manage the systems for the owner: negotiate the percentages, keep the books, collect the produce at harvest time. It is an important job. The owner depends on his steward's effectiveness and most of all, honesty.

This particular steward, said Jesus, was charged with wasting his master's goods. The owner called him in, gave him notice, told him to bring the books up to date, clear out his desk, move on. He was fired.

The man does not argue, explain, or plead his case. Instead, without wasting a moment, he goes to his office, summons the tenants one by one, who do not know apparently that he has been fired, and announces that the percent they owe has been reduced, and the landlord has lowered the rent. The implication is that he, the steward, has been instrumental in arranging this happy surprise. The farmers are delighted. Nothing like this has ever happened before.

When the land owner discovers what has happened he has only two options. He can jail the dishonest steward and reverse the damage done—but there's already a celebration going on in the town square. His tenant farmers are, at the moment, perhaps at the pub, lifting their glasses to toast his generosity and his steward's kindness. He decides not to tell them it is a mistake and that their good friend is under arrest.

The other option is to absorb the loss, essentially to pay the price himself for his steward's salvation. That is what he does. He shows unusual mercy—amazing grace—and then he commends the steward for his shrewdness, his sense of priority.

It is a subtle point. . . . God's amazing and dependable graciousness, God's unexpected and always surprising willingness to love us and accept us. This man is not a moral model for anyone. But, to his everlasting credit, he does know what the most important issue in life is and where to take it. He knows somehow that he can depend utterly and ultimately on the generosity and grace of his master.[2]

And then, in case we miss the point, Luke reports an intriguing saying of Jesus: "No servant can serve two masters, you cannot serve God and mammon."

Mammon—what a great biblical word. It's money, but it's more than money. It's the mystique of money, the essence of wealth. It's money in capital letters. It's the gorgeous ads in the Sunday paper supplement. . . . It's trudging across an acre of lush Kentucky bluegrass to borrow a cup of Johnny Walker Black Label from your neighbor. It's a car you never quite get to see because its name is Infiniti. It's a culture that invests its most creative architecture no longer in cathedrals but in vertical shopping malls. Mammon is whatever shapes your dreams. It is your center of value. It is whatever you worship. It is whatever you expect to save you.

Mammon is defined by Russell Baker and children of the depression as accomplishment, success, security. Comedian George Carlin, who would probably be surprised to be used as a sermon illustration, defines it as "stuff"—the accumulation of things for which we must provide space: shelves and drawers and garages and walls and cabinets and boxes and trunks. Mammon is defined for many of us, at least partially, by the word comfort. Being comfortable is more important than we realize, therefore more powerful in actually determining our values and our behavior.

Another contemporary variation on the old theme of mammon might be called "self-fulfillment." "Pollster Daniel Yankelovich estimates that as much as 80 percent of us are in some way involved in the quest for fulfillment. 17 percent . . . spend much of their time assessing and reassessing their personal lives, their jobs, and friends, and mates, from the perspective of the needs and wants of the self. . . . They are the ones most preoccupied with finding spiritual, mental, and physical wholeness through diet, exercise, meditation, psychotherapy . . . and many have stumbled into . . . the 'fulfillment trap,' wanting more than they can have and putting self ahead of social relationships."[3]

Jesus would put it this way—"You cannot serve two masters." Theologically, you can't serve God and mammon. It's not that mammon is bad. Jesus has been consistently misunderstood on that point. He did not condemn wealth in and of itself. He did not condemn ambition or hard work. He told one wealthy young man to sell all he had and give to the poor, but that was a particular prescription, not a universal model. What he said here is that wealth, or any form of mammon, doesn't work if we look to it for our salvation. It's that simple. It doesn't work. And there is a sense that people who have it know it best.

Harvard professor Harvey Cox observes that there is a revival of Eastern spirituality in Western culture precisely because materialism doesn't work as a source of ultimate meaning or salvation. Professor Cox notes that Young Urban Professionals are "victims of a painful overload of contradiction" between the stated value systems of our society and the actual values that operate in the marketplace. "They are pulled apart. In family and religious life they have been taught to share and cooperate and even to love, but the world of classroom and market requires them to connive and compete if they wish to succeed."

Cox says one of the appealing resolutions for many thoughtful young adults is a vigorous, disciplined, cult-type religiosity that provides "a chance to test and stretch themselves as opposed to the debilitating pursuit of comfort that is the chief characteristic of consumer culture."[4]

Mammon doesn't work. The first rule of economics, someone said, is that "you can't have everything." You have to choose. Individuals and nations. Priorities must be established. In theological terms, a god must be chosen and served.

Saying yes to God, that is, means saying no to other gods. It is a matter of very basic theology.

The trouble with us, the Bible concludes, is that we are always getting our priorities confused. We are looking for the meaning of our lives in the wrong places. In the biblical idiom the trouble with mammon is not that it is evil. The trouble is that it doesn't work. In fact, all that mammon is good for is producing worry and anxiety. If your job is the most important thing in the world to you, you're going to worry a lot about it. If it's your house, your automobile, your position in the community, your sex life, your children, you're probably worrying a lot.

One of the basic insights of our faith is this: If you try to squeeze something infinite out of something finite, you will not only be unsuccessful and frustrated, you will very likely squeeze the life out as well. One of the lessons in life that parents must learn is that if children are expected to provide peace, happiness, contentment, the load will be too heavy for the relationship to bear. If your ego, your sense of self-worth, is dependent on your child's accomplishments, athletically, academically, economically, or socially, the child involved is being asked to carry a very heavy load. In fact, it won't work. Or if your happiness is dependent on your apartment or automobile, you're in trouble spiritually. And the ultimate irony is that if you look to mammon, the mystique of wealth, prosperity, and security to provide happiness, peace, and salvation, you probably will not ever enjoy very much of what you already have.

The truth of the matter is that you and I only deeply enjoy what we don't ultimately need. The truth is that it is not possible to enjoy that which you depend on. Psychologists know that obsessive need—dependence—is not a strong basis for a healthy re-lationship. The truth is that children are far better off when par-ents do not need them for ego fulfillment. And they are far more enjoyable—which may be one of the reasons grandparents so ab-solutely enjoy their grandchildren.

The truth is that you cannot enjoy anything if you load it up with expectations and demands and insist that it reward you with happiness, peace, and contentment. You can't enjoy anything that exerts that kind of power over you. You can't enjoy your sexuality if you look to it to demonstrate your masculinity or femininity or attractiveness or youth. You won't enjoy romance or friendship or family affection if you need it to provide something to yourself. And mammon as money . . . Frederick Buechner quips that "there are people who use up their entire lives making money so they can enjoy the lives they have entirely used up."[5]

Jesus told a story about a man who was as flawed as anyone in the Bible and as human as anyone I know, but a man who knew at least where his salvation would be found. He concluded it by teach-ing us that it is a matter of very great importance that we get our priorities straight.

If we give our hearts to mammon, whatever that might be for us, we will not be happy and, in the process, we will miss the saving miracle of God's unusual generosity, God's amazing grace, God's unconditional love for us which is, he taught, the only source of our salvation.

The radical word of Christian faith, to would-be disciples in first-century Galilee and would-be disciples in the twentieth cen-tury is that in order to experience salvation we must say "no" to all the other gods who clamor for our love and hope and faith and enthusiasm and passion, and say "yes" to the God who has loved us into being and came to be among us and to teach us and to live and die with us and to rise again for us in Jesus Christ.

We are God's top priority it would seem. God has decided to love us, to give us life and the capacity for love and joy and peace. God has decided to give us life eternal, life in all its fullness, life blessed by beauty, life with all its potential for creativity and ac-complishment, life with its wonderful capacity for love and passion and intimacy and ecstasy, life—which in Jesus Christ is diminished by nothing, limited and hemmed in ultimately by no thing, not even death. That's what God has decided about us, we believe. And after all the deciding, God made one more decision, namely to allow you the final one, the big one, the only one actually. *Who will you serve? . . . Who will be your God?*

NOTES

1. Russell Baker, *The Good Times* (New York: William Morrow and Co., 1989), 7.

2. Kenneth E. Bailey, *Poet & Peasant and Through Peasant Eyes* (Grand Rapids, MI: Eerdmans Publishing Co., 1983), 86ff.

3. Wade Clark Roof and William McKinney, *American Mainline Religion* (New Brunswick: Rutgers University Press, 1987), 47.

4. Harvey Cox, *Many Mansions* (Boston: Beacon Press), 189.

5. Frederick Buechner, *Whistling in the Dark* (San Francisco: Harper & Row, 1988), 80.

40. Wayside Sacraments
Robert P. Mills

Philippians 4:8–9 RSV

Ralph Waldo Emerson once wrote, "Never lose an opportunity of seeing anything that is beautiful; for beauty is God's handwriting—a wayside sacrament. Welcome it in every fair face, in every fair sky, in every fair flower, and thank God for it as a cup of blessing."

Until I read these lines, I don't believe I'd thought of beauty as a sacrament. A sacrament is literally a holy thing. To be holy is to be set apart. Emerson may or may not have shared our Christian understanding of holiness as being set apart by God for God's service, but he recognized in the beautiful face, sky, or flower something clearly set apart from its surroundings by its beauty. In that sense, a thing of beauty is a holy thing, a sacrament.

The wayside can be anywhere we happen to be journeying: along the interstate as we vacation; along the edge of the field as we plow; along the path we take as we walk to the mailbox. Familiar though the route may be, any given journey can bring us into unexpected contact with a wayside sacrament.

Of course, before we can recognize something as a wayside sacrament we need to know just what it is we're looking for. Then, once we've recognized a thing as holy, whenever we pause to think about it, our thoughts gradually lead us to the God who created

---

Robert P. Mills is Pastor of Big Creek Presbyterian Church in Hannibal, Missouri. He received his Master of Divinity from Princeton Theological Seminary. Named an Outstanding Young Man of America, Mills has also been an instructor of piano theory and composition.

that which we admire. But before we can meditate upon such wayside sacraments we must first learn to identify them. That's what our Scripture lesson for this morning helps us to do.

When the Apostle Paul wrote to the church at Philippi it was from a Roman jail. The Philippian church was the first he had founded in Asia. Throughout his ministry the Philippian Christians had been particularly supportive of Paul and had remained especially dear to him. Philippians was probably Paul's last letter, written shortly before he was executed for his faith. Evidently sensing his death to be imminent, Paul writes to beloved brothers and sisters in the faith one final time, that they might continue to find peace and joy in their relationship with God, even after their relationship with Paul has been severed.

As he nears the end of his letter, Paul lists eight things for the Philippians to "think about." His list is more suggestive than comprehensive. And it doesn't include what we have come to think of as characteristically Christian attributes; love, joy, peace, patience, gentleness, self-control. Instead, it sounds almost as if Paul lifted his list straight out of a secular Greek textbook on ethics or philosophy.

The things Paul says to dwell on are ordinary, if uncommon. It doesn't take the training of a theologian or the intellect of a philosopher to recognize and think about the qualities of being honorable or gracious. Any Christian can pause to consider the causes and effects of honor and graciousness. Every Christian should.

But none of us sees such traits as often as we'd like. It is in part because of this uncommon ordinariness that, even though Paul didn't use the term, we can label such qualities "wayside sacraments." As we briefly touch on each of these eight items, may we come to feel more deeply the peace that fills us as we think about these things.

The first wayside sacrament Paul says to meditate upon is "whatever is true."

Truth is indeed a precious commodity. Mark Twain said that for that reason it should be used only sparingly. Our society seems to have canonized Twain's witticism. Today many find acceptable, even admirable, the ability to bend the truth, to fudge the truth, to tell less than the whole truth, or to phrase the truth in such a way that it remains obscure. If you can do these things well enough, you may get elected to public office or even be asked to head a savings and loan.

Moreover, there's serious debate about the very existence of such a thing as "truth." Philosophers write learned discourses questioning the philosophical foundation of the notion of the absolute. Ethicists declare relatively good or relatively bad such acts as incest, adultery, and the taking of human life. Ostensibly Christian theologians excoriate the misplaced arrogance of those unsophisticated Christians who actually believe that Jesus Christ is *the* way.

Yet, in spite of philosophers, ethicists, and theologians, truth does exist. Occasionally we stumble upon it. Truth may come to us as words out of the mouths of babes; it may come as a single sentence in a book or magazine; it may be a thought that appears unbidden in our minds. But every now and then something strikes a chord so deep within us that all we can do is to respond by saying, "Yes. Of course. Now I see. It couldn't possibly be otherwise."

At such moments, truth becomes a sacrament, a holy thing, set apart by God for the purpose of leading us to God. When God grants such moments, savor them. Truth is a wayside sacrament.

The second sacrament Paul lists is, "whatever is honorable."

The Greek word here translated "honorable" originally had religious overtones; it might be translated "worthy of reverence." Just as we nowadays question whether or not anything is true, so we question whether anyone or anything is worthy of our reverence. Or, to ask that question in the vernacular, Why don't we have heroes anymore?

In a single week Pete Rose was sentenced to jail, a senator and a congressman respectively were denounced and reprimanded, and the press reported that some rock stars lip sync supposedly live concerts. Nor has the Church escaped such demythologizing scrutiny: Recently nationally and even internationally prominent preachers have been involved in well-publicized sexual scandals. Once we rule out sports, politics, entertainment, and the Church, where are we to look for heroes, for those worthy of reverence, for whatever things are honorable?

Perhaps we need to look a little closer to home. Perhaps we only need to look as far as the child who has the opportunity to tell a lie but tells the truth instead and takes the consequences. Perhaps we only need to look as far as the person handing money back to a cashier who returned the wrong amount of change. Perhaps we only need to look at those who quietly help meet the needs of others without seeking publicity or reward.

Think about whatever is honorable. For honor is a wayside sacrament.

Third on Paul's list, "whatever is just." *Justice* is a term that today finds itself at the center of innumerable discussions.

Unfortunately, there's little agreement about the definition of the term. Some consider it an act of justice when a murderer is executed for his crime. Others consider it justice when capital punishment is outlawed.

How are we to think about whatever is just, with so many definitions of justice competing for our attention? We can start by looking at the word Paul used, which has the same Greek root as our word *righteous,* a characteristic ultimately ascribed to God alone. When we think about that which is just or righteous, God and God's recorded acts should be our only standard.

Whenever we see an act that unquestionably reflects the righteousness of God, we have encountered something just. We should pause and reflect on whatever is just, for justice is a wayside sacrament.

Paul's fourth wayside sacrament is "whatever is pure." To speak of something pure is to speak of something unalloyed, unmixed, uncontaminated.

When we speak of pure gold we are talking about that metal that has had all traces of other materials removed from it. Gold that remains mixed with base metals is of considerably less value than gold that is pure. When we hear of a person having pure motives, we understand that he or she is acting from only one purpose, with only one goal in mind. When we think about pure water, we think of water that has had nothing added to it, neither chlorine, nor benzine, nor atrazine.

But when we think and speak of such a physical and moral condition, at best we're using the word *pure* as an approximation. It's almost impossible to remove every trace of every other element from gold or water. It's extremely rare for a person to take any action out of one single motive. So when we think of purity in its absolute sense, we're inevitably led to think of God.

God alone is absolutely pure. That's why Paul said to think about whatever is pure; for such thoughts encourage us to think of God.

Paul next says to think about "whatever is lovely." This was what originally led me to connect these verses with Emerson's observation, "beauty is God's handwriting—a wayside sacrament."

As I looked at this text more closely, I discovered that the word Paul used doesn't have as its principal meaning physical beauty, although it certainly includes the concept. The Greek word literally means, "whatever is worthy of love."

What, in your mind, is worthy of love? Your spouse, your parent, your child? Other relatives or friends? A pet, a rosebush, a family heirloom, a new car? What is it that makes those particular people or things worthy of being loved?

Whoever, whatever, and however you answer, once you start thinking about things that are worthy of love, you'll eventually find that which is most worthy of love to be God. For God is not only worthy of love, but God is the source of all that is worthy of love. When we think of the love shown to us by our parents, children, relatives, and friends, we realize that their love is but a pale reflection of the love God has for us. When we think of loving others, we have those thoughts only because we're enabled to love by the God who first loved us.

Think about whatever is lovely, whatever is worthy of love, and, at least to some degree, you're thinking about God.

Paul next says that we should think about whatever is gracious. Other translations read, "of good report," or "well spoken of."

Paul's main idea here seems to be that what has been deemed to be of honor by all people at all times is worthy of being honored by Christians. When you recall Paul's missionary career, you'll remember that he wasn't afraid to make use of the best that the society around him had to offer. When he spoke to the crowd at the Areopagus at Athens he announced, "I perceive that in every way you are very religious. For as I passed along, and observed the objects of your worship, I found also an altar with this inscription, 'To an unknown god.' What therefore you worship as unknown, this I proclaim to you." He then proceeded to preach the gospel.

Rather than being frightened by the culture that surrounded him, Paul walked around in it, studying and learning from it. Rather than belittling the customs, practices, and beliefs of the Athenians, Paul took from them what was best, what was well spoken of, what was of good report, and used that which was honored by the people to bring honor and glory to God.

We can do as Paul did. Instead of petulantly ranting against our materialistic society we can say, "I see that you are interested in acquiring wealth. Let me tell you about something of incomparable value." We don't need to be afraid of dialogue with those whose concept of faith doesn't exactly match up with our own. We can, without fear, talk of ecumenical cooperation with Methodists, Episcopalians, and Roman Catholics. We can equally speak with confidence to those who practice so-called New Age beliefs (so-called because Paul would have been very familiar with these exact same beliefs and practices), and, like Paul, we can begin by saying, "I perceive that in every way you are very religious." Or, to put it into Campus Crusade terminology, "I see that you are interested in spiritual things."

That which is gracious, of good report, well spoken of, can lead not only us, but others to think about God. These things are wayside sacraments we shouldn't overlook.

The next to the last item on Paul's list is "if there is any excellence," another translation of which would be "virtue."

This is the only time in all of his writings that Paul uses this particular Greek word. What makes its use here especially interesting is that it's a technical term, the most comprehensive term in Stoic philosophy for moral excellence, which is the central theme of their entire ethical system. To the Stoic, this virtue was the highest good, the end to which every human being should devote his or her life.

Why would Paul tell Christians to think about the central tenet of the reigning secular philosophy of his day? Why would he accord the status of a wayside sacrament to a belief not distinctive to the Christian faith? In answering those questions we learn an important lesson about the ways of God.

God is the Creator of every human being, Christian and non-Christian alike. Because we were created by God to be in fellowship with God there is, in Pascal's phrase, a God-shaped void in every human being. The Christian has filled that void by accepting Christ's saving work of life and death and resurrection. The non-Christian is still seeking. And sometimes the attempts are admirable.

I've said before that if I weren't a Christian I'd be a Stoic. I find much to admire in their philosophy of dealing equally with whatever life hands out, be it fame or obscurity, poverty or wealth, health or lingering illness. And I admire their striving after virtue, their single-minded desire to live according to the highest standards of conduct in thought, word, and deed. That a person has not yet accepted God doesn't mean that God hasn't already taught him or her a great deal.

Stoicism has much in common with Christianity, and in the earliest church, Stoic language and categories of thought proved excellent vehicles for Christians to communicate their newfound faith to the world in which they lived in language which that world could understand.

Virtue was one such category. Christian and Stoic alike could share an appreciation for a life lived in pursuit of the highest good. Paul understood that when he told the Philippians to think about anything of virtue.

The final item on Paul's list is "if there is anything worthy of praise."

Here Paul provides both a summary and an open-ended expansion of the seven sacraments he's already listed. Anything worthy of praise includes everything that Paul hasn't yet mentioned. It allows you and me to be open to those things that are consistent with Paul's intent yet that didn't make his list.

Anything that is worthy of praise has the potential to become wayside sacrament.

After Paul has finished his list he tells the Philippians to "think about these things." The word translated "think about" is crucial to our understanding of this verse, for it suggests much more than merely abstract contemplation, more than simply sitting on the couch and letting pleasant thoughts float within an idle mind.

The word Paul uses here is the root of our English word *logic*. It means not merely "think about then let the thought pass on through," but "think about then act in accordance with what you have learned from the effort." This is the same word a workman would use in taking measurements before beginning a construction project. It could equally well be translated "weigh, consider, calculate."

Paul's instruction to the church at Philippi wasn't that they merely sit around and indulge in idle speculation about things that were worthy of praise. No, Paul knew all too well that just sitting around and thinking inevitably turns the mind as soft as the body.

As we have heard from James over the last three weeks, faith and works are essential components of one another.

Paul's instruction to the Philippian Christians, and to us, is that we think about such things, consider, weigh, and calculate their effects, so that we might have the peace that God intends for us. The verse we've been considering is bracketed by the concept of God's peace. In verse 7 Paul spoke about the peace which passes all understanding. In verse 9 it's, "What you have learned and received and heard and seen in me, do; and the God of peace will be with you."

Norman Vincent Peale wasn't the first to discover the value and the power of positive thinking. Paul was way ahead of him. We focus a lot of attention on the things that are wrong with our world. That's understandable. There's plenty of it.

But what Paul knew, and what Peale rediscovered, is that our peace of mind and our power for living the Christian life comes not from focusing exclusively on the negative but from thinking about whatever is true, honorable, just, pure, lovely, gracious, excellent, and worthy of praise.

Paul never meant for us to ignore evils and the horrors that surround us; he'd been through too much in his own life to pretend that bad things wouldn't happen to good people. But he also knew that we shouldn't morbidly dwell on evil to the exclusion of the good that God gives. He knew that the peace of God doesn't come from trying to avoid the bad, but from diligently seeking after the good. He knew the many ways in which God's goodness manifests itself to us—prominently through the sacraments of baptism and the Lord's Supper, but also in quiet subtle ways that might be considered wayside sacraments.

That's why, at the end of his life and ministry, as almost the very last words he would say to his beloved brothers and sisters in Christ, Paul wrote, "Finally, brethren, whatever is true, whatever is honorable, whatever is just, whatever is pure, whatever is lovely, whatever is gracious, if there is any excellence, if there is anything worthy of praise, think about these things . . . and the God of peace will be with you."

Amen.

Index of Contributors

Index of Sermon Titles

Index of Scriptural Texts